Fred R.
Goldstein

New York • Don Mills, Ontario • Wokingham, England
Amsterdam • Bonn • Sydney • Singapore • Tokyo
Madrid • San Juan • Milan • Paris

This book is in the Addison-Wesley Series in **Electrical and Computer Engineering: Telecommunications**

Many of the designations used by manufacturers and sellers to distinguish their products are claimed as trademarks. Where those designations appear in this book, and Addison-Wesley was aware of a trademark claim, the designations have been printed in initial caps or all caps.

Library of Congress Cataloging-in-Publication Data

Goldstein, Fred R.
    ISDN in perspective / Fred R. Goldstein.
      p.   cm.
    Includes index
    ISBN 0-201-50016-7
    1. Integrated services digital networks.   I. Title.
TK5103.7.G744 1992
621.382—dc20   91-27923
                                                    CIP

1 2 3 4 5 6 7 8 9 10-DO-9594939291

To Judy

Preface

The subject of Integrated Services Digital Networks (ISDN) has seen no shortage of interest within the past decade. Practically the entire worldwide telecommunications industry has been actively participating in developing ISDN, with both network and equipment suppliers investing heavily. And there has been no shortage of books and articles on the subject. So why *ISDN In Perspective?*

Most of what has been written about ISDN to date comes from one of a narrow range of perspectives. In may be an academic treatise about the underlying technology or a dispassionate description of the detailed architecture and protocols. These are very useful to developers and implementors, but for a technology to be successful it must draw the interest from beyond the narrow implementors' and suppliers' community. It must draw the interest of *users.*

And while much of what has been written about ISDN has addressed the ways in which it can be used, too much has addressed the applications to which its developers and suppliers would like to apply it, not the applications that its potential customers are most likely to find useful. This discord has crippled ISDN's acceptance. *ISDN In Perspective* attempts to incorporate a user-centered view of ISDN, as well as a discussion of the technology.

 The author makes no claims of impersonal objectivity. Some paragraphs, like this one, are marked with an eyeglass symbol. These are the author's perspectives, freely mixing opinion with fact. The remaining sections of the text are intended to be somewhat more objective.

This book is not intended to provide a complete description of ISDN or a comprehensive discussion of its details. Readers who need additional information, such as developers and classroom users, are advised to consult the relevant standards or an additional text such as Hermann J. Helgert's

Integrated Services Digital Networks: Architectures, Protocols, Standards (Reading, Massachusetts, 1991: Addison-Wesley Publishing Co., Inc.).

Organization of the Chapters

The order of chapters is based upon the ten-week course taught by the author in the State-of-the-Art Program at Northeastern University. Chapter 1, *The Invisible Elephant,* introduces ISDN in its historical context. This is general background information to provide the broadest perspective on the material to follow.

ISDN combines digital switching and digital transmission. These concepts predate ISDN and are the subject of the next two chapters. They take a digression common to most ISDN books and courses: Rather than address ISDN per se, they describe the technologies that have come together to create ISDN.

Chapter 2, *Messages, Circuits, and Packets,* provides introductory material on the three principal switching disciplines within telecommunications. ISDN addresses them all. Many readers are familiar with one or another, but most are not equally familiar with each of them, so all are discussed as a background for the ISDN-specific discussion to follow. Individual readers may choose to skip these sections as they see fit. Chapter 3, *Transmission Systems: The Digitization of the Network,* describes the movement from analog to digital transmission systems, which has had a crucial role in making ISDN a practical necessity for the long-term future of telecommunications.

Chapter 4, *The Integrated Services,* describes the various services that an ISDN can offer to its subscribers. Chapter 5, *ISDN Architecture and Reference Model,* addresses the organization of the network and the ISDN-specific jargon that surrounds it. The order of these two chapters is not important: Both topics in some way depend upon one another, so their ordering here is a bit arbitrary.

The next two chapters address ISDN-specific protocols. Chapter 6, *The ISDN Hop-by-Hop Protocols: Layers 1 and 2,* addresses the lower-layer protocols that operate between the subscriber and the network and support the user services and higher-layer protocols. Chapter 7, *The ISDN Call Control Signaling Protocols,* examines the way in which ISDN's native call control protocol, DSS1, operates, both for basic call control and for supplementary service control. The chapter then provides an outline of Signaling System No. 7, which is used within public networks to provide corresponding services.

Chapter 8, *Broadband ISDN,* takes a glimpse at the futuristic world of a high-speed network designed around fiber optic transmission and a novel new switching technique that attempts to combine circuit and packet switching into one. While conventional "Narrowband" ISDN is already here, Broadband ISDN is still in the early stages of development. Its predecessors, based upon the Metropolitan Area Network, are also summarized.

Finally, we wrap up with Chapter 9, *ISDN in Practice*, which describes the state of ISDN development as of this writing. It addresses the reasons why ISDN has been successful in some cases and a disappointment in many others, and it gives the reader ideas about how and when to make use of the technology.

Acknowledgments

This work is not entirely my own: ISDN is the fruit of thousands of people's labor, and a mere work of reportage such as this one cannot help but owe these developers a debt of gratitude for their efforts. I would especially like to acknowledge the help of my colleagues on ANSI-accredited Technical Subcommittee T1S1 and its predecessor T1D1, who have been most helpful in teaching me about ISDN and its lore. I would also like to thank my co-workers at Digital Equipment Corporation, who have given me the opportunity to learn about and participate in the development of this new technology. Special thanks also go to my wife, Judy Hyatt, for indulging me during its writing.

Particular credit should go to this book's referees, without whom it would not be nearly as fair or accurate. Special credit is due to Dan Grossman of Motorola-Codex Corp. as well as to Steve Silverman of Mitre Corp., Nick Lippis of Strategic Networks Consulting, and Alan Kotok and Pierre Jardin of Digital Equipment Corporation. And much credit is due to the editors, Tom Robbins and Abby Reip of Addison-Wesley, for their efforts. These are only some of the people who have helped this book become what it is; all deserve credit.

Arlington, Massachusetts   Fred Goldstein

Contents

The Invisible Elephant

What is ISDN?

The hardest part of understanding Integrated Services Digital Networks
(ISDN) may be just figuring out what ISDN is. Some of the marketing that
has accompanied its introduction would have us believe that ISDN will be
the solution to all of our telecom problems, from voice to data and on to
image and even maybe video. But according to other observers, ISDN is just
another welfare project for telephone companies and their engineers and
will have little effect on the way most of us live and work.

   The truth lies somewhere in between these extremes. Those who sell
ISDN are often a bit out of step with those who build it, and both are a bit
out of step with those who will use it. But that's not surprising, given the
climate that ISDN grew up in. The worldwide telecommunications industry
has had to shift from being a slow-moving wing of the utility or postal monopoly to becoming a fast changing and competitive high-tech business.
And the vehicle that much of the industry has chosen to ride along the

forefront of that change is called ISDN. Its successes and its failures will both dictate the shape of telecommunications for years to come.

But what is ISDN anyway? The name tells us a little, but it's really just a label, invented, as it were, before the product. ISDN obviously involves telecommunications *networks*. These networks are obviously *digital*, but it's not so readily obvious what that means to their actual users. And what are *"Integrated Services"*? This term apparently means that the network provides both voice and data services and possibly others, but how tightly are they integrated and what does that mean to users?

Describing ISDN brings to mind the parable of the blind men and the elephant. To the one who found the tail, the elephant was like a rope. To the one who found the trunk, the elephant was like a hose. To the one who found the elephant's side, it was like a wall; the one who found the leg thought that the elephant was like a tree. None of them had a vision of the elephant in its entirety. ISDN is a lot like that elephant, but with a twist: No one really has a complete vision of the elephant because the elephant itself is invisible! Everyone who has been involved with the original development, promotion, or deployment of ISDN has a particular view of what ISDN is, and these views are quite diverse.

But like those of an elephant, the many parts of ISDN do eventually come together to form a whole. ISDN, like the elephant, has evolved from more primitive ancestors, and some of its characteristics are there for historical reasons. Some of ISDN's features might seem as odd as the elephant's trunk or floppy ears, but others could prove as rugged as an elephant's hide or as precious as its ivory.

The Evolution of ISDN

Where does ISDN come from? A useful perspective of ISDN can be gained by examining its ancestry. ISDN is in many ways simply a name applied to the logical next stage in the evolution of telecommunications and of the public telephone network in particular.

A network contains two fundamental elements: *transmission* and *switching*. Transmission facilities carry the signal between locations, while switching facilities tie transmission facilities together into a coherent, interconnected whole. Both the transmission and switching fields have gone through a lengthy evolution, and both have made the move from analog to digital technology. But those moves were made rather independently of one another, with digital switching and digital transmission both fitting into an analog world. ISDN, in effect, is the blueprint for recasting the network in the digital mold, the last few digital pieces in the puzzle. It's the digitization of the last mile.

So what, specifically, does ISDN refer to? Here, one can benefit from observing the historic mission of the telephone companies, as they have seen it. Telephone companies don't provide *things*, they provide *services*. ISDN refers to a specific set of services provided by means of a limited, standardized set of interfaces. It's defined at the interface between the telephone company's subscriber and the network. What goes on inside the network is not necessarily defined by ISDN, provided that it's capable of providing the services. But the services are in large part defined by the inherent capabilities of the network, not by any abstract set of user requirements.

Digital Came First

The evolutionary path leading to ISDN goes back at least as far as the middle of the nineteenth century, when Sam Morse was stringing the first telegraph wires. The telegraph, of course, was a digital device, with two states: key up and key down. Figure 1.1 shows a simple diagram of a telegraph network and a voltage diagram of telegraph signals. The telegraph provided an early form of data communications, and, in so doing, changed the face of civilization. Suddenly, messages could be sent long distances within minutes, faster than people could deliver them in person.

The telegraph industry was very profitable and growing rapidly when an acoustician and teacher of the deaf, a certain Mr. A. G. Bell, ostensibly set out to create a "harmonic telegraph." Today we would call that a frequency division multiplexor. But Bell got a little bit off track, and — if you believe the official story — he accidentally stumbled upon the telephone. He filed his patent in 1876, and within a few years the telegraph industry was old news.

Figure 1.1 *(a) Simple telegraph network. (b) Telegraph signals as viewed over time, with voltage either on or off.*

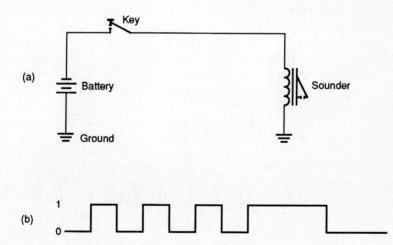

The Early Years of Telephony

The Bell telephone was an analog device. It carried voice by modulating an electrical current with a waveform that was analogous to the acoustical waveform that the ear could hear. Unlike the simple binary (up-down, on-off) nature of a telegraph wire, a telephone wire carried a continuum of electrical current, as shown in Fig. 1.2.

Once the telephone caught on, development of telegraphy lagged; the biggest change was the replacement of the manual key by the teletype machine during the first half of the twentieth century.

For the duration of Bell's 1876 patent, telephones were all manually interconnected. Calls could be placed only with the assistance of the manual switchboard at "central." The dial was invented by Almon Strowger, a Kansas City undertaker, in the 1890s, but Bell telephone companies remained all-manual until the 1920s, as they had no intention of paying royalties for Strowger's patents!

Early telephones were powered by batteries and had a limited range, crosstown calls being about the limit. In the 1890s, just as its patents were running out and competition was beginning, AT&T (then, of course, owner of the "Bell System") purchased the patent on a new device, the loading coil. This greatly increased the volume on long-distance telephone calls and allowed subscribers to be located farther from the central office. (This invention came back to haunt us later. Loading coils and ISDN do not get along!) Bell phones could thus call between nearby cities, while its competitors' phones could not. The invention of the vacuum tube amplifier made long-distance calls possible.

Figure 1.2 *(a) Simple telephone circuit. (b) Analog signals as viewed over time, with voltage mirroring the acoustical waveform.*

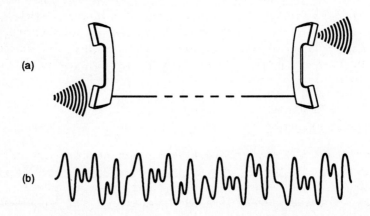

Analog Carrier Systems Made Long Distance Possible. Analog long-distance transmission technology was the focus of much development effort between 1900 and 1980. During the 1920s, Bell Laboratories developed a way to put many different conversations on the same piece of wire, in effect superimposing on it a radio spectrum with many channels. This *analog carrier* technology continued to be improved until by the 1970s, several thousand conversations could be carried over a single coaxial cable or over a microwave radio transmitter. Each channel was assigned its own channel, 4 kilohertz (kHz) wide.

Analog transmission systems like these helped to make long-distance telephony affordable and popular. But they have certain disadvantages that led to their eventual replacement with digital media. Analog systems, by their very nature, tend to get noisier with distance. Practically every component between mouthpiece and distant earpiece is capable of adding a little bit of noise into the link, so by the time a call covers transcontinental distances, it has a rather distinctive sound to it: noisy, with perhaps a sprinkling of cross-talk from other connections.

Digital Transmission Has Proven Advantageous. Digital transmission systems were introduced in the 1960s, beginning with the T1 carrier system. This system sent an impressive 1,544,000 bits per second (bps) down a twisted pair of copper wires. T1 carrier systems were terminated by channel banks (specialized analog-to-digital converters) that converted each side of a voice connection into a 64,000 bps stream. Thus a T1 carrier system could carry 24 simultaneous voice calls. T1 systems initially became popular for short-haul applications, such as linking together nearby central offices, later providing local service to customers that were far enough from the central office that it was cheaper to put in a pedestal with T1 multiplexing equipment than to string more outside wire.

These early applications of digital technology were invented by the telephone industry for its own benefit. The fact that they were digital was neither obvious nor important to customers. The telephone companies did care, however, that digital systems were easier to maintain than analog ones and eventually cheaper, too. By the late 1970s the digital transmission trend was clear. The development of practical long-haul optical fiber carrier systems, all digital, finally made analog transmission systems obsolete once and for all.

Digital Switching Systems

The earliest telephone switches had very powerful processors attached to them and were capable of performing complex feats and providing many useful features. But these controllers — human operators — had certain limitations, especially as telephone traffic increased, and so the automated dial telephone became dominant. Like the transmission systems of the day, early automatic switching systems were based on analog electrical technology.

Mr. Strowger's first automatic telephone exchange required several wires to go to each instrument. In addition to the two wires of the talk path (*tip* and *ring*), each of the three digits in the telephone's number required a separate wire and a separate telegraph key–like button on the instrument. This was obviously impractical, and by the time the device was commercially available, the signaling functions had been folded onto tip and ring. Today we call this *inband signaling.* You can't dial while talking or talk while the phone is ringing. This is rarely a problem, except perhaps when trying to use a modem and call waiting. And to be sure, inband signaling isn't really as universal as it seems: Multiline telephones in the analog world require many separate wires going to their control units; only the simplest telephones actually use only one pair.

While the Strowger step-by-step exchange remains in widespread use today, especially in rural areas and underdeveloped countries, computer-controlled switches have been replacing them since the 1960s. (One can even make a case that AT&T's crossbar exchanges, introduced in the 1930s, used a form of computer control, albeit with the computer built out of relays.) The crossbar exchange and the early computer-controlled models still used electromechanical switch contacts, providing a simple electrical path between the incoming and outgoing sides of a connection.

Indeed, all telephone switches remained analog until the 1970s, when manufacturers first introduced switches that converted voice to digital bit streams for internal switching purposes. These digital private branch exchanges (PBXs) were followed by digital central offices. For the most part these switches used conventional analog interfaces; the earliest digital interfaces were T1 carrier trunk connections. And for most users, the fact that the switch was digital was irrelevant.

So why did digital switching completely overtake analog? In the early days, some digital PBX vendors stressed the idea that since voice was being carried in digital form, a digital PBX could be useful for switching data as well as voice. And by 1980, most major PBX manufacturers had announced some kind of data-switching capability. A new buzzword burst upon the scene: *integrated voice and data* (IVD). Plain old telephone service wasn't good enough, vendors claimed; systems had to be integrated.

Had integrated voice and data switching actually caught on, then the need for ISDN would have become obvious: It's a way for the public network to provide a standardized integrated voice and data-switched service. That's one perspective on ISDN. But it's not a very accurate one!

 Digital switches didn't replace analog ones because customers needed to integrated voice and data. In fact, the IVD fad didn't last very long. Hardly anyone today uses the telephone switch for their primary local area data connectivity. No, the reason that digital switches have caught on is more fundamental than that: They're cheaper! Digital switches are nowadays cheaper to build, cheaper to install, and cheaper to maintain than their analog predecessors.

A Pot of Glue

It makes sense, then, that a digital transmission system and a digital switching system should be able to talk to each other digitally. But that isn't always how it's done. Even if a T1 carrier from the digital central office is directly terminated on a digital PBX, the signaling that is used to set up and tear down calls is often based upon analog norms (see Fig. 1.3). Dialing, for example, is still often accomplished by sending digitized bit patterns representing Touch-Tone digits down a 64,000 bps channel at only ten digits per second! Or worse yet, it is done by sending dial pulses at only ten pulses per second—the speed of a manual dial!

That, then, is what ISDN brings to the equation. It is the worldwide telecommunications industry's design for an end-to-end digital network, in which all of the components are recognized to be digital and are connected to each other accordingly. The old analog protocols are set aside in favor of new ones. ISDN is the pot of digital glue that the telecommunications industry is using to make its digital transmission and digital switching systems work together to achieve their maximum potential.

Figure 1.3 *Before ISDN, digital transmission and digital switching were often tied together via analog means.*

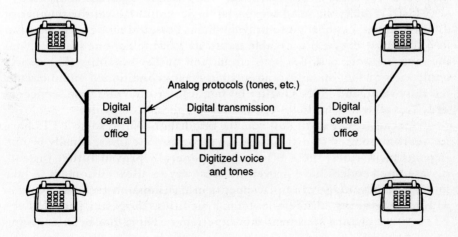

Benefits of ISDN

The invention of a new and stronger adhesive should not be discounted as trivial. While ISDN is in some respects just a new way to make telecommunications network components work together, it is a stronger bond than the old analog model could support. Both telephone companies and their customers will benefit from it, but only if they apply it wisely. ISDN for its own sake, on the other hand, is just a big sticky mess!

The telephone companies have the biggest stake in ISDN, of course. The ISDN development process began at the International Telephone and Telegraph Consultative Committee (CCITT), an arm of the International Telecommunications Union (ITU), the United Nations agency that coordinates international telecom. While representation at the CCIT is nominally held by member nations, it is their telecommunications authorities — in most countries the Post, Telephone and Telegraph (PTT) agencies — that dominate most of its deliberations. They view ISDN as a way to modernize their telephone networks, reduce costs, provide additional services, and increase their income.

Reducing Special Services Expenses

In an analog world a telephone company has to provide many different services. In addition to bread-and-butter POTS (plain old telephone service) and long distance, data users require low- and high-speed private lines as well as packet-switched services. Corporate voice users require tie lines, and radio broadcasters require high-fidelity audio lines. Alarm companies require low-speed telemetry lines, and telegraph (Telex) users require switched low-speed digital services. Each of these services has its own requirements for provisioning. Between the technical and administrative ends, these "special services" have been very costly to provide, yet are increasingly important to users.

ISDN reduces the need for special services and reduces the number of different interfaces needed to provide them. Low- and moderate-speed (up to 64,000 bps) data users are able to use standard telephone facilities, and the same network provides both circuit and packet switching. The consistently high quality of audio transmission makes conditioned audio circuits less important, and ISDN's higher bit rates can provide premium services as well. This all translates to lower costs for telephone companies.

Special services will still remain important. While some PTTs have for years attempted to discourage the use of private lines, usually by outrageous tariff rates, these efforts have generally proven futile. Instead, private line services have proven the best way to allow customers to take immediate advantage of improvements in transmission technology, even without upgrading obsolete switching facilities. ISDN has provided the PTTs with a chance to repeat this experience: There has been considerable talk about ISDN's making private lines obsolete; instead, it will probably complement them.

It is possible, however, for some private line services to be delivered by using ISDN technology. A private line data channel might, for instance, be created by "nailing" a path through an ISDN switch. Even if that is not done, ISDN has made available, at mass production prices, local transmission technology that simplifies the provision of medium-speed (64 kbps to 2 Mbps) digital channels. That is the fastest-growing portion of the private line business, so ISDN provides some benefits to users of these services, even though the users are not formally part of ISDN!

One Network Instead of Several

Another way in which telephone companies benefit from ISDN is by having one network that takes the place of several pre-ISDN networks. While the POTS (voice) network is certainly the bread and butter of the telecommunications industry, most major carriers also offer packet-switched data services, and many offer circuit-switched data services as well. Some carriers also provide wider-bandwidth switched networks for video conferencing, and most telephone companies (outside of North America) also provide telegraph (Telex) service.

All of these services can be provided by ISDN. By providing different *bearer services* on a dial-up or subscription basis, ISDN simplifies the development of public networks. Economy of scale can make the lower-volume services (especially data) more affordable, while higher-volume services (like POTS) are essentially unaffected.

So *that* is what "integrated services" is all about! It doesn't mean that the customer buys one device that provides the full range of voice, data, and image services. (That's possible, of course, but generally pointless!) "Integrated services" means that one *digital network* can provide many different services to many different users. The main question that remains, then, is whether by being a jack of all trades, ISDN is master of none. As we shall see, while ISDN is not the master of all trades, it still has much to offer.

Customers Win Too

ISDN benefits customers for the simple reason that no matter how hard they try, telephone companies can't hold off market forces forever. Simple economics dictates that in a competitive marketplace, *price* (to the customer) tends to approximate *cost* (to the provider). Telephone companies, of course, are used to being a monopoly. Regulation is justified as the alternative to market forces, to prevent monopolies from taking unfair advantage of their position. This has worked marginally well in the United States but much less successfully in many other countries where the PTT regulated itself, subject only to (weak) political forces. But the trend toward "deregulation," by allowing increased (if still limited) competition and fewer restrictions on how customers make use of carrier services, has also made it harder for carriers to price services without regard to cost. So when ISDN results in lower costs to the carrier, it eventually trickles down to the user in the form of lower rates.

Three Ways to Use ISDN

Since ISDN is so flexible, it can be applied to perform quite a wide range of functions. Most applications fall into one of three categories. The first is **voice telephony**. Here, the simple fact is that most telephone users wouldn't know the difference between ISDN and analog POTS! Both are capable of providing a high-quality switched voice service.

ISDN's main strengths here are twofold. One is in offering a *standard* for attaching feature-rich digital instruments to the public network, whereas pre-ISDN installations relied upon either proprietary electronic instruments or complex electromechanical arrangements. The second advantage of ISDN is most evident in those features for which the analog "standards" just aren't very good. These include PBX trunks, especially with *Direct Dialing In, Call Waiting* service, and *Calling Line Identification.* These services have been grafted onto analog telephony in the best manner available while using analog technology, but that still leaves a lot to be desired. ISDN was designed from the beginning to accommodate these along with many other services, some of which haven't even been invented yet.

The second major application for ISDN is **wide area data communications**. Wide area basically includes everything beyond the building or campus area, beyond the scope of the PBX or Local Area Network (LAN). Before ISDN this was the scope of modems and costly private lines (special services). Even the best dial-up modem can achieve speeds of only perhaps 14,400 bps on an analog telephone line, while ISDN provides 64,000 bps for essentially the same cost (if not necessarily the same price, since telephone companies are known for rather arbitrary pricing). ISDN will generally provide lower error rates than modems too. So for wide area data users, ISDN is a huge "win."

The third major application for ISDN is **local area data communications**. Here, ISDN is used in place of the integrated voice and data PBX, linking together computers and terminals within a facility. Alas, while ISDN was conceived during the years when "IVD" was all the rage in PBX marketing, it is coming to market long after high-speed data-only LANs have become established. Compared to using modems on the wide area network, ISDN is better, faster, and cheaper (pick three). But compared to a LAN, for most local area data communications, ISDN is slower and more costly. That some telephone companies still attempt to sell ISDN into this market is evidence that monopolies are slow learners! As the song says, two out of three ain't bad.

ISDN Is Defined by Standards

Most people think they know what a telephone looks like and assume that all telephones, or at least the simple analog ones, work in pretty much the same way. To some extent that's true, but there are substantial differences and even incompatibilities between the different telephone systems around the world.

Telephone service has almost always been offered by monopolies. In most countries these monopolies were controlled by the government, so they did not simply operate for a profit motive. Quite often, the telephone administration (PTT) had a secondary agenda: to promote that country's own telecommunications industry and captive manufacturers. In some cases the PTT simply prohibited its customers from attaching their own choice of equipment to telephone lines and instead rented equipment that it purchased from a national vendor. In many cases, though, the PTT established "standards" for its national vendor that ensured enough incompatibility with the rest of the world to discourage foreign suppliers from trying to compete.

So if you buy a telephone in England and take it to Germany, it might work, but it probably won't ring unless you remember to bring along a British "master plug." And if you try to use a Danish rotary dial telephone practically anywhere else, you might get a wrong number because the dialed digits are laid out differently. This sort of technical protectionism was a petty annoyance in the past, but it has become intolerable with advancing technology. One of the goals of ISDN, then, is to have a new set of worldwide standards that encourage *terminal portability* — the ability to use the same equipment in many different countries. This not only promotes the goal of a "single market" for Europe, but also allows the PTTs to seek competitive sources of equipment beyond their usual captive suppliers.

Proactive Standards

While the benefits of standards are clear, they are actually created by more than one process. Many popular "standards" are created de facto, with no official backing. For example, the popular "clone" personal computers all conform to a standard that was created by IBM Corp., when it released its popular Personal Computer (PC). IBM did not intend to create a widely imitated standard, and there is no official document that describes just what makes a computer a clone, but the PC is a standard nonetheless.

Telephones similarly used to be subject only to de facto standards, with hardly any opportunity for a consensus process. In the United States, AT&T acted as its own standards body; the ordinary analog telephone instrument that everyone uses was defined by AT&T. Indeed, most of the North American telephone network was simply designed by AT&T without regard to formal standards. T1 carrier, for instance, was simply invented and placed in service; only later did an international standards document come to recognize what had already become widely accepted.

A somewhat different standardization process, in which formal standards are created shortly after a design has been field-verified, has been applied in many other instances. For example, the popular Ethernet Local Area Network was invented in the 1970s by Xerox Corp. While Xerox created a few working implementations, Ethernet saw little other use until Digital Equipment Corp. and Intel Corp. joined Xerox in a three-way partnership to create a "standard" Ethernet. The original Xerox-Digital-Intel standard was then published and implemented in specialized integrated circuits. While that was happening, the Institute of Electrical and Electronic Engineers (IEEE) convened a standards committee (IEEE 802) to study Local Area Networks. This led to a formal industry standard, IEEE 802.3, for LANs based on Ethernet technology. There are significant differences between the original three-company Ethernet and IEEE 802.3, enough to make the two incompatible, but Ethernet's fundamental operation was unchanged.

What the de facto IBM PC standard and the formal (de jure) IEEE 802.3 standard have in common is that they were both created *after* the original product was working. ISDN, on the other hand, was not invented in a laboratory or placed in service anywhere before being turned over to a standards body. Instead, it was created by a standards body, which set out to write a standard in advance of deployment.

This *proactive* approach has both advantages and disadvantages. One major advantage is fairness: No manufacturer gets a head start by having its design adopted as standard. An open standards process also promotes consensus and allows widespread review of proposed standards before they become final.

And in the worldwide telecommunications industry, in which a network standard is meaningless until it is widely deployed, it's simply not practical to deploy a major new service and have to substantially retool it later once a standards committee finishes its deliberation. Computers have a typical economic lifespan of about five years. Telephone networks at that age are just getting broken in.

But proactive standards have disadvantages too. Since the standard precedes widespread usage, there is a greater risk of error. As a worst-case scenario, standards can end up reflecting compromises that, when finally put together, just don't work! While much of ISDN has reached the stage at which it is no longer at risk of a total failure, the standards development process is still continuing, with new ISDN service and protocol definitions continuing well into the 1990s. Some errors may creep in, which implementors will have to learn to work around. And since most manufacturers and network providers will not want to invest too much money and effort in prestandard designs that could become obsolete when the standard is complete, deployment of ISDN typically lags behind a slow, laborious standards process.

This leads to another aspect of the definition of ISDN. For a network to be considered truly ISDN it must offer **standard interfaces** and provide, at minimum, a **standard set of services**. A network that offers integrated voice and data or uses digital telephone instruments is not necessarily ISDN. A true ISDN doesn't necessarily offer any novel services, but it offers services in conformance with a standard to ensure compatibility with different vendors' ISDN terminal equipment. For a piece of terminal equipment to be considered truly ISDN, though, it need merely use, in accordance with standards, whichever ISDN services are appropriate to its application.

The CCITT Takes the Lead

Quite a few organizations have taken a role in the development of ISDN standards. At the center is the CCITT, which began the process in the 1970s and in 1980 issued a one-page description of what it hoped ISDN would become.

As a United Nations affiliate, the CCITT gives voting power to countries. Other organizations may attend the meetings, but final decisions are made along national lines. Most countries, in practice, are principally represented at the CCITT by the constituency with the largest stake in its deliberations' outcome: the PTT. Some countries with more competitive telecommunications markets have a greater diversity in their delegations. In the United States, for example, the CCITT delegation is led by the Department of State, which turns for guidance to the American National Standards Institute (ANSI) and other industry and governmental bodies.

The net result is that the CCITT displays some bias in favor of the PTTs and has even been labeled an "international telephone cartel" for its activities that coordinate the (very expensive) international long-distance telephone network. But in its more technical role of defining ISDN, the CCITT has been more concerned about defining a practical and implementable set of standards. Many compromises are made, with manufacturers and users playing an active role. Considerable room is left for companion national standards, which fill in some of the blanks.

Indeed, the CCITT is not totally comfortable issuing "standards"; instead, it issues "Recommendations." These are often viewed as less binding than standards, although they serve the same function. In practice, of course, not all standards are necessarily binding. One can choose to use them or to ignore them. But there are obvious risks in being nonstandard in a world where standards are ever more important, and that certainly describes telecommunications!

The CCITT is organized into Study Groups, each of which has its own mission. Study Group XVIII was created in 1980 for the purpose of defining digital networks; ISDN is by far its biggest activity. But while ISDN architecture and some of the details are defined in Study Group XVIII, the actual production of signaling protocols is in the hands of Study Group XI, which consists of protocol specialists (see Fig. 1.4). And while Study Group XVIII used to create detailed descriptions for proposed new services, that task has now moved to Study Group I.

The different Study Groups meet separately, each a few times a year. So a new standard usually takes several years to be completed. This suits the historically slow-moving pace of the telephone companies and PTTs and helps account for why ISDN standards have been so long in coming.

Once every four years, the CCITT holds a Plenary Assembly at which national delegations officially approve the work of the various Study Groups. The

Figure 1.4 *CCITT Study Groups develop protocols in conjunction with national standards bodies.*

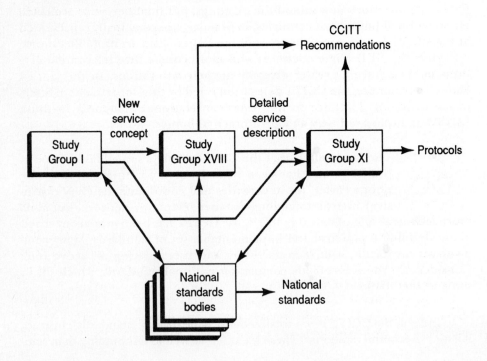

collected set of Recommendations is then republished. A set of Recommendations is known by the color of its cover, which rotates through a 24-year cycle of six colors. In 1984 the Red Book included a rough cut at the ISDN protocols, while the 1988 Blue Book included a more complete and implementable set. If a new standard is ready for publication between cycles, it can be released as a Gray Book. Thus there was a Gray Book in 1986. More recently, additional flexibility has been created to encourage the adoption of Recommendations in advance of the quadrennial editions. Thus some post-1988 ISDN standards have been adopted in advance of the full 1992 White Book. (This will actually be published during 1993; the year shown is the one in which the last Study Group meeting was held.)

At the end of each four-year cycle, all of the Study Groups officially go out of business, but most are immediately restarted by the quadrennial CCITT Plenary Assembly. This gives the CCITT a chance to revise its organization.

National Standards Follow

With the ISDN program firmly in place, much of the CCITT's "grunt work" is performed by other organizations. New ideas and developments are often filtered into CCITT by way of national standards committees. These may have a large and diverse membership, thereby allowing many organizations (including manufacturers and even some users) indirect access to the CCITT and direct input to national standards.

America after the Bell Era. The breakup of the Bell System radically changed the telecommunications standards landscape in the United States. While there was a government-sponsored U.S.-CCITT national committee before 1984, domestic telecommunications standards were usually just dictated by AT&T. But in 1984 a new organization was created for the express purpose of coordinating U.S. telecommunications standards. The Exchange Carriers' Standards Association (ECSA) coordinates the activities of Committee T1, an accredited technical committee operating under the procedures of the American National Standards Institute.

While there are ANSI standards in many areas of commerce and industry, ANSI's role is primarily to publish standards written by accredited technical committee as well as to ensure due process and provide coordination. ANSI assigns committee designations to its various members; ECSA was assigned the name T1 because it alludes to the word Telecommunications.

Committee T1 itself is also just a coordinating entity; the real work is performed by its seven Technical Subcommittees (TSCs). The majority of ISDN development takes place in TSC T1S1, which has responsibility for its architecture, service descriptions, and protocols. The physical layer interfaces are handled by T1E1 for customer equipment and by T1X1 for intercarrier transmission systems. Maintenance and network management are handled by T1M1, and quality of service by T1Q1. Personal wireless commu-

nication is handled by the newest TSC, T1P1, while voice and video digitization are standardized by T1Y1 (whose charter includes a broad range of
"specialized topics" that don't quite fit elsewhere). With hundreds of participants at some of these TSCs, the ISDN standards community in the United
States alone is quite sizable!

Monopolies Are Ending Elsewhere. Other countries have their own national standards bodies. Europe, for instance, never had a single telephone
monopoly quite as strong as the Bell System, but its national monopolies
(PTTs) were loath to share power with customers and manufacturers. In
addition to the CCITT, the PTTs' Council of European Posts and Telecommunications (CEPT) dictated pan-European standards before the antimo-
nopoly European Commission mandated change. Now a more independent
and broadly based European Telecommunications Standards Institute
(ETSI) has that role. The PTTs have maintained considerable influence over
ETSI, but at least there's a semblance of democracy!

Individual countries still have national standards bodies too. Broadly
based national standards bodies, akin to ANSI, exist in many countries.
France has AFNOR, Germany has DIN, and the United Kingdom has BSI, for
instance, but these are relatively unimportant in telecommunications areas.
In Japan, though, the long-standing monopoly of Nippon Telephone and
Telegraph (NTT) has been eroding, and its standards-setting authority has
been transferred to the Telecommunications Technology Committee (TTC),
which is modeled after the United States' ECSA.

Thus we have the environment that has given birth to ISDN. In
a world that has come to see an increasing need for international standards, at a time when digital telecommunications
technology has rendered obsolete the technological model that
built the analog telecommunications network, we have a new network design
being created in large part by means of the standards process. It involves
essentially all of the major players in the telecommunications industry, which
have a mandate to support wide area networking. Perhaps ISDN really did
set out to be all things to all people, but its utility comes about only from
widespread acceptance. And that means that it's a technology created by
committee. It's not perfect, but it's a remarkable piece of work nonetheless.

ISDN Fundamental Principles

A few basic concepts have guided the development of ISDN and form the
basic outline from which it has been developed. Many of these are not the
result of ISDN-specific invention but are themselves evolutionary, drawing
from the experiences of proprietary electronic telephone systems as well as

modern public network practice. These concepts will be explored in much greater detail in subsequent chapters.

ISDN interfaces provide multiple channels for information transfer. Both digitized voice and data can be carried across *bearer* channels, the most common variety of which is called the *B channel*, with a bandwidth of 64 kbps. Higher-capacity bearer channels are called *H channels*; a few varieties have been defined. Every type of ISDN access arrangement supports some number of bearer channels. Out-of-band signaling information, as well as a limited amount of packet-switched data, can be carried across a *D* channel; each ISDN access arrangement is generally controlled by one D channel.

Setting aside the futuristic Broadband ISDN (see Chapter 8) for the moment, ISDN interfaces come in two sizes. The *Basic Rate* is designed to support simple applications like telephone instruments and computer interfaces. It has two B channels and one D channel, hence the nickname "2B + D." The *Primary Rate* is designed for bulk applications like PBX trunks and multiple computer connections. It uses the first multiplexed level of the local transmission hierarchy, which is 1.544 Mbps in North America and Japan and 2.048 Mbps in Europe. Thus it is sometimes called "23B + D" or "30B + D," depending upon location.

The concept of a multiplexed digital telephone interface is not novel to ISDN. Before ISDN was even a page of paper, proprietary PBX telephone sets featured digitized voice with out-of-band signaling. Some featured two B channels, allowing data to be used at the same time as voice. ISDN generalizes the concept by allowing the two B channels to be used independently or even to be shared by more than one device plugged into the same line. It also introduces standard *protocols* for the D channel.

The ISDN process has drawn upon other fundamental principles as well. These include a desire to minimize the number of different interfaces and to make use of existing industry practice when appropriate. The CCITT is not known for its radicalism. On the other hand, the Broadband ISDN project, modeled upon an all-optical network, provides an opportunity for a radical new network concept to be developed.

ISDN draws upon over a hundred years of telecommunications history. Combining different services into a single network has resulted in a rather complex whole. Different observers have had different interpretations of what the whole is about, for it may well be too big for any one person to fully comprehend. Thus we must approach the invisible elephant from many perspectives in hopes that we may come to understand and be better able to take advantage of it.

Messages, Circuits, and Packets

Predecessors of ISDN

ISDN combines several different disciplines within the field of *telecommunications*. Yet for all of its importance, we should remember that telecommunications is itself just a segment of the greater science of *communications*. Humankind has been engaging in many forms of communications ever since we first appeared on the planet, using such diverse means as speech, cave paintings, boat traffic, letter post, and advertising. The development of *tele*communications, communicating over a *distance*, is one of the most important examples of modern technology.

ISDN didn't evolve in a vacuum. It owes its existence to the world's telephone companies, which developed it as a way to reduce the number of separate networks that they had to manage while updating them at the same time. In many countries the telephone company is part of a governmental agency called the *Post, Telephone and Telegraph*, or just the PTT.

Postal service dates back to at least the Middle Ages, when royal messenger services delivered letters around Europe. The Holy Roman Empire (which included parts of modern Germany, Austria, Hungary, Poland, and Czechoslovakia) granted this monopoly in 1544 to the Thurn und Tassis family, whose service eventually grew into a large European postal network. The postal services were later nationalized. The Thurn und Tassis emblem, a post horn, is still used by its successor, the Deutsche Bundespost.[1]

In the United States the most famous period in the history of the Post Office is arguably the Pony Express, whose brave riders delivered mail to the "Wild West." But the Pony Express lasted less than two years, its services rendered obsolete by another development of the 1840s, the telegraph. A swift, young pony could outrun a stagecoach team, but Samuel Finley Breese Morse developed a way to send messages at the speed of light, and the era of telecommunications was born. In a sense, the modern era itself was born.

Message Switching

The classical Morse telegraph was not an easy device to operate. It had three basic components. The sending operator used the *key* to cause a *sounder* at the other end to click; a length of *wire* connected the two. The receiving operator had to listen carefully to the sounder and write down the received message. If the addressee of the message was near the receiving operator, the message could be delivered; otherwise, it would have to be sent on to an operator closer to the destination.

Often a message would have to be relayed several times before a young man in a distinctive cap could deliver it to its recipient. Each message carried its own address, but operators had to route the message along its way. Note that the message as a whole was relayed; until it was all received, the operator couldn't pass it along. Thus the telegraph gave rise to the oldest form of telecommunications switching: *message switching*. A telegram was like a letter, a message, handled as one entity.

Indeed, a telegram was enough like a letter that many of the world's post offices decided that it too fell under their monopolies. To enable telegrams to be sent across national boundaries, the International Telegraph Union (ITU) was formed. Many years later, this body (long since rechristened the International Telecommunications Union) became part of the United Nations. The ITU is in turn the parent body of the CCITT and also of the CCIR (International Radio Consultative Committee (CCIR)), which oversees radio transmissions.

Message switching is still alive and well. While the telegram itself dwindles into obscurity, more modern message-switching services, called *electronic mail*, are a major growth area in telecommunications. In some places, the PTT

---

[1] A rather fanciful account of the historical Thurn und Tassis, surprisingly relevant to ISDN, can be found in Thomas Pynchon's 1965 novel, *The Crying of Lot 49.*

or telephone company offers an "E-mail" service, but attempts to monopolize it are futile: E-mail doesn't require a complex network; it can be passed between two computers connected by a phone line. Thus ISDN does not offer a message switching service per se, but its data-carrying capabilities will be a boon to E-mail users and providers of E-mail services.

Circuit Switching

Mr. Bell had just put together his first two crude telephones in his Boston laboratory when, legend has it, he spilled something corrosive and exclaimed into one of them, "Come quickly, Watson, I need you." Watson heard him through the other telephone and came running. That was the first telephone call. With only two telephones in the lab, there was no question as to where the call was being directed to!

Some of the early telephones were used essentially as wired intercoms, directly connected to one another. But the real utility of the device was magnified when it was connected to a switchboard, which could connect any attached telephone to any other.

The early telephone networks could draw upon the experience of the telegraph for inspiration. Telegraph offices were found in major and minor cities, and some major businesses had their own on-site telegraph connections. The telegraph company maintained ownership of the poles and wires, charging out for its services. So it was quite natural for telephone companies to string their own wires to their customers, maintaining ownership of central switchboards and pretty much everything else required to provide service. And because Bell's company jealously guarded its patent rights, no alternatives could arise until Bell's telephone companies had already had time to become well established.

The first Bell switchboards could interconnect only telephones that were themselves directly wired to the switchboards. A telephone could be a few miles at most from the switchboard, so intercity calls weren't possible. Soon, the largest cities began to have multiple central offices, with lines between the switchboards. These *trunk* [2] lines typically appeared along the upper rows of the switchboards, with subscriber lines beneath.

As transmission technology advanced, it became possible for circuits to become longer and still maintain audible transmission quality. Soon multiple switchboards could become involved in relaying a call over a moderately long distance. But this revealed a major difference between the (digital) telegraph and the (analog) telephone: Every telegraph operator along the way received the message intact and relayed it, unchanged, so the quality of the received

---

[2] The term *trunk* refers to any circuit that connects two switching systems together. Thus a line from a central office to a subscriber's telephone is simply a line, but if the subscriber installs a switching system of its own, the system can be properly called a trunk.

message wasn't degraded by distance. But each telephone operator along the way meant that another trunk line was needed, and the received voice became fainter and noisier with increasing distance.

Manual Call Setup

In the era of manual long-distance service, the number of operators required to complete a call increased with distance. Even after transmission technology advanced to the point at which transcontinental calls were possible, individual trunks only ran part of the way at a time. A caller in Boston trying to reach San Francisco might go through operators in, say, New York, Cleveland, St. Louis, and Denver before reaching the San Francisco operator.

The route followed by such a call, then, was computed by the operators as they went along. If there were no circuits along the usual route, the operator might seek an alternative path in the same general direction. This path might be longer or might not have as good a sound quality, but it allowed the call to be completed.

Early Dial Networks

At first, all telephone calls were placed through operators on manual switchboards. The automatic telephone exchange was invented by Almon Strowger, a Kansas City undertaker who (legend has it) feared that he was losing business to a competitor whose wife happened to be a local switchboard operator. The Automatic Electric Company was organized to market the new technology; the first dial exchange to go in service, in 1896, was in La Porte, Indiana.

Strowger's earliest automatic telephone was an ungainly contraption. With its three telegraph key–like signaling buttons, each tied to a separate wire, it could dial a three-digit telephone number. But such an out-of-band signaling arrangement was impractical, so Strowger went back to work and developed inband signaling, wherein the same two wires carried both the dial pulses and the conversation. This turned out to be a fortuitous decision for many reasons. Not only did the spring-loaded dial make the telephone easy to use, but it allowed telephone numbers to be as long as necessary.

The automatic dial telephone exchange that Strowger invented is often referred to as the *step-by-step* (or "stepper") switch. (In Europe it is more often simply called the Strowger exchange.) While it has gone through several refinements, it was such a success that it remains in service today in many places. Even AT&T, which didn't begin to use steppers until the late 1920s (while waiting for patents to expire), manufactured it until 1969.

The step-by-step exchange is a remarkable example of decentralized design. Its basic building block is a switching unit that looks a bit like a coffee can. A given exchange may consist of hundreds or even thousands of these switches, wired together to fit precise requirements. Each stepping switch operates in two dimensions: First, a rotor arm moves vertically, once for each pulse in a single dialed digit. Then the arm spins around past a bank of contacts.

Each stepping switch except the last is called a *selector.* The first bank of selectors in a step-by-step exchange is associated with a special circuit called a *line finder.* This detects lines that go off-hook and connects them to dial tone when its associated selector is ready to receive digits. A selector accepts one dialed digit at a time, moving its contact arm vertically, and then spins horizontally until it finds a free path out. This allows each first selector to be connected to as many as ten second selectors, each second selector to be connected to ten third selectors, and so on. Each selector decodes exactly one digit.

The last switch in a step-by-step exchange is called a *connector.* It differs from a selector because it can decode two digits. The first digit moves the contact arm vertically, and the second moves it horizontally, selecting one specific contact, which is tied to a specific subscriber line. The connector also applies ringing voltage to the called line. Both selectors and connectors have one input and 100 output connections apiece; they differ primarily in how they're used. Figure 2.1 shows a diagram of a step-by-step exchange.

A four-digit dialing plan requires each call to go through two banks of selectors and one of connectors. (Each block of numbers, or *level,* after the first selector has its own switches.) Mixed-length plans can even be developed

Figure 2.1 *In the Strowger (step-by-step) exchange, control is totally decentralized.*

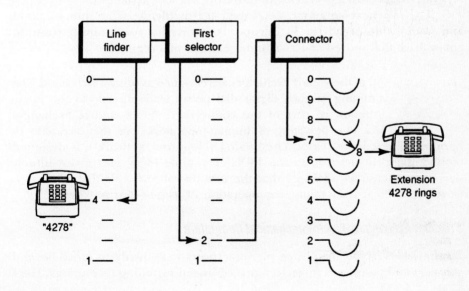

if the switches are wired appropriately. That is not uncommon in Europe, unlike North America, which has fixed-length numbers.

Call routing through a step-by-step exchange is rather deterministic: A call will take the first path that it finds through each dialed level. Even if there is spare capacity at one level, a call that attempts to reach a selector or connector level that is entirely in use will be blocked.

Since there is no centralized intelligence within a step-by-step exchange — each switch is simply wired to the next level as required — it follows that the switches don't all have to be located in the same place in order to work together. Thus a trunk line can be inserted in between the selector banks to provide interexchange calling. The dial pulses (which are simply short bursts of on-hook) need to be regenerated along with the audio, but that's about it. Entire metropolitan areas were automated by using step-by-step exchanges. When AT&T introduced direct distance dialing in the 1950s, even some of the toll centers used step-by-step switches.

A few variants on this theme have been developed. Before Strowger's patents ran out, AT&T pioneered a different type of exchange, called *panel*, which used motors and rollers to accomplish the same effect. Panel exchanges were a bit slow in decoding dialed digits and couldn't be directly connected to steppers, but they were widely used in a few areas. (Los Angeles, for example, was predominantly step-by-step, with no panel. San Francisco had panel but little or no step.) Stromberg-Carlson had a different variant, called XY, usually found in rural areas.

The panel exchange, first deployed in Omaha, Nebraska, in 1921, led with a major innovation whose potential wasn't realized until later. It separated the digit-counting circuit from the assembly that actually made the connection. While digits were counted and switched one by one, its use of a separate *register* was a precursor of more intelligent exchanges.

The *rotary* exchange was developed at roughly the same time as panel and found widespread use in Europe. It featured a continuously running chain drive that moved contacts under control of a register.

All of these early exchanges are classified as using *direct control*. The counting of each digit's dial pulses leads directly to the establishment of part of the connection. Direct control exchanges lack the flexibility of human operators, but they are able to handle quite a lot of calls. The analog telephone network was designed around them. In a sense, so was ISDN! For while ISDN uses many entirely new components, we shall see that the new digital protocols that ISDN uses to set up calls actually mimic the operation of step-by-step switches!

Crossbar Exchanges: Electromechanical Computers

By the 1930s, some telephone manufacturers were ready to move beyond steppers and panel and invent a more advanced switching technology. Here they made a radical break with Strowger's invention: the *crossbar* switch. This was pioneered by Sweden's L. M. Ericsson and by AT&T, as well as ITT (whose version, called Pentaconta, was manufactured until the 1980s in some countries). Crossbar exchanges were divided into two separate functions: The *matrix* carried the actual voice path from source to destination, while a separate *common control* decoded the dialed digits (collected in a register) and figured out the optimal path through the matrix for each call. Once the call was set up, the control circuits could be released to handle another call. This common control could be almost arbitrarily complicated, as it was utilized very efficiently, call after call. It was, in effect, practically a computer, implemented entirely in relays and programmed with wires! Figure 2.2 shows a simplified diagram of a crossbar exchange.

The crossbar exchange translated prefix codes by means of a three-digit analysis. Once the first three digits of the dialed number were collected, a unit in the control circuit (a *marker*) could determine where to route the call, within or without the switch. Then a four-digit selection could point a number at a line. The actual location of the line on the switch didn't have to correspond to its number, though, since the dialed number (DN) was first translated by the marker to a physical terminal number (TN) on the switch on the basis of jumper programming.

While most "advanced" telephone features, such as three-way calling and call transfer, are usually associated with more modern exchanges, they were actually pioneered with crossbars. Very few local exchange service customers were ever offered these features from crossbar exchanges, but many

Figure 2.2 *In a crossbar exchange, a path through the crossbar switching matrices is established under control of the marker, in effect an electromechanical computing device.*

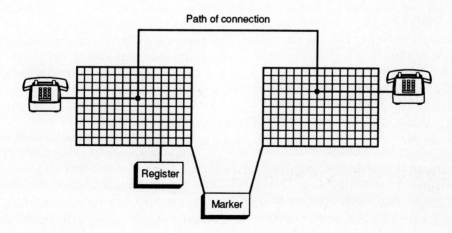

Path of connection

Register

Marker

crossbar PBX systems, and some crossbar public exchanges equipped to provide Centrex service, did. Such flexibility required ever more complex mark-
ers; by the time they were developed, crossbars were well on their way to being
made obsolete by newer technology.

The crossbar exchange was most popular in North America, but some
were found in international markets. Crossbar exchanges were also produced
in Japan; some Nippon Electric (now NEC Corp.) crossbars were even used
by AT&T's affiliated Bell System companies. Crossbars were also widely used
as private branch exchange (PBX) switches, though electronic switches sup-
planted them during the 1970s.

Interexchange Dialing. The crossbar exchange is largely responsible for the
North American numbering plan, in which area codes and prefix codes are
always three digits long and always followed by a four-digit line number. In other
parts of the world, where direct control switches prevailed, mixed-length numbering plans are more common. In a direct control exchange, each digit usually
requires additional hardware. In a crossbar exchange, the first dialed digits are
input to an electromechanical lookup table, and it's easier to build a fixed-
length lookup than a variable-length lookup. So with the adoption of the crossbar exchange, the Bell System standardized on a seven-digit numbering plan.
And when Direct Distance Dialing began to be developed in the late 1940s, what
could have been more natural than to use a common control exchange for
long-distance calling too, with a three-digit area code lookup?

In Europe, where step-by-step technology remained king, toll calls were
often switched through steppers. This led to different numbering plans, with
variable length city codes and local numbers. In some cases, local calls between exchanges required special handling.

In the United Kingdom even today, intercity calls that are too nearby
to incur toll charges aren't dialed by using the standard city code. Instead,
special codes are established in each exchange that directly connect, at the
local rate, to other exchanges. A caller might have to dial "91" plus the local
number to make a call to one nearby town and "92" to another town, even
though those are not the city codes. This makes for a lengthy set of dialing
instructions in a regional telephone directory! But step-by-step exchanges
aren't usually capable of translating dialed numbers, so dialing the city code
might inefficiently route a short-distance call by means of a toll switch some
miles away. This practice is likely to end soon as newer, stored-program control equipment replaces the remaining steppers.

To be sure, not all steppers are equally unintelligent. Some steppers,
particularly in Europe (but also in some U.S. markets, such as Los Angeles),
were equipped with *directors,* which collected a few dialed digits and then
outpulsed something else. This added flexibility to the numbering plan, especially in crowded urban areas and for steppers used as toll switches. More
recently, microprocessor-controlled enhancement devices have been added

to a few steppers that provide modern services like tone dialing, call forwarding, and three-way calling. But their use has been limited, since most telephone companies would rather replace old steppers than pour additional capital into them.

Direct Control Dial Engineering. Nearly a century of direct control switching has left its mark among the people who made it all work. While moving parts might seem primitive in today's computerized world, what could actually be accomplished by using step-by-step and similar technologies was remarkable.

Making a call within a step exchange was straightforward. The selectors and connectors fit together easily enough. But with uniform seven-digit numbering plans being introduced, getting the right number sent to the right place wasn't a minor feat. Assigning the right prefix code to every town was a tricky problem, as the digits had to fit together just right. Any error would require nonstandard dialing or additional switching equipment.

Take, for example, a small town whose three-digit prefix code is 924 and that has 1500 telephones installed (see Fig. 2.3). The town has a step-by-step exchange. To the north is the 858 prefix, to the south 879. To the east the prefix is 492, to the west 385. The 924 exchange's dialing plan requires

Figure 2.3 *In this direct control dialing plan, a call originating on the 924 exchange is routed to a local number if 43xxx or 47xxx is dialed. Other dialing patterns link to other exchanges as soon as enough digits are dialed.*

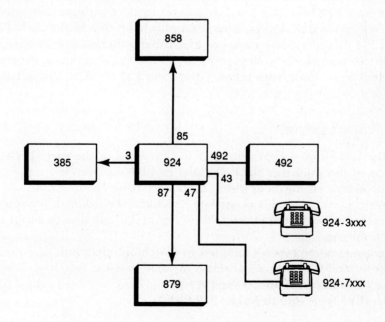

the last five digits of the telephone number to be dialed. (Step-by-step exchanges often didn't require the full seven digits.)

The exchange is set up with *levels* (blocks of 1000 numbers) 3 and 7 operative. Calls can be dialed as 43xxx and 47xxx. Thus the first selector directs 3 and 7 to separate banks of second selectors. If 3 is dialed, it is directed to the 385 prefix to the west. If 8 is dialed, the call must go to a second selector: If the next digit is 5, the call is sent over trunk lines to the 858 exchange to the north, and if that next digit is 7, it goes south to 879.

A further variation on this theme is the *digit-absorbing selector*. This allowed seven-digit dialing without the full-length switch train. For instance, one selector might be used to absorb the initial digit "5" in an exchange whose numbers began "558-2xxx." As a side effect, the caller could dial as many fives as desired; dialing "5555558-2368" would get the same result as simply dialing "8-2368." Some interesting dialing patterns could be developed this way, occasionally leapfrogging an intermediate central office to make a call to a third. Sometimes these patterns weren't even intentional, at least on the part of the telephone companies.

This sort of dial engineering is easy to do for a small town, but what happens when you try to do this in, say, Los Angeles, where each central office may have many prefix codes? Eventually, you run out of workable combinations. That's why Los Angeles' area code 213 was the first one (in 1972) to adopt the use of "interchangeable" prefix codes, such as 605, that could be mistaken for area codes. It hadn't yet exhausted all possible prefix codes, but there were not enough to accommodate the needs of the step-by-step exchanges, at least not without adding costly directors to switches whose days were already numbered.

Not all cities had Los Angeles's problem; many did not use step-by-step at all. If there had been any panel exchanges in place within a metropolitan area served by the Bell System, then it's highly likely that by the early 1970s, most of the central offices were using crossbar switches. But by then, the crossbar was itself obsolete. Beginning in the 1960s, the common control no longer had to be built from relays; computers had come to the telephone world.

Analog Electronic Switches

While the electronic digital computer was invented in the early 1940s, the invention of the transistor (by Bell Labs) in 1948 was even more pivotal in making computer technology widely useful. But while the first transistorized computers became available in the late 1950s and skyrocketed in popularity by the early 1960s, the telephone industry was relatively slow to adopt these new technologies.

Before computers were adapted to switching, electronic components were substituted for mechanical relays in some crossbar switches. The TXE series of British central offices used electronic logic and reed relays; AT&T adapted wired logic into its Model 812 PBX.

Bell Labs developed its first prototype computer-controlled switching system in the early 1960s and deployed its first production model, the No. 1 Electronic Switching System (1ESS), in 1965. The computer in the 1ESS didn't look a lot like the models that companies like Univac and IBM were producing. It stored its programs on a unique ferrite sheet memory, arranged in banks of memory cards. It wasn't blazingly fast either; instead, it was designed for reliability. Its design goal was to be operable for 40 years, with only two hours of downtime. (This specification is still a goal of switch manufacturers, though it is rarely attained. But computers introduced a new element into the equation, *software*, and making software truly reliable is still a dream.)

Space Division Switching. The switching matrix in the 1ESS wasn't electronic: It used reed relays. Other analog electronic central office switches used crossbar relays, while some later models used electronic crosspoints (essentially solid-state relays). Any given connection still involved a discrete path through the exchange, over a conductor assigned to that call alone. Since the calls were separated in space, this technique, in all of its manifestations, was referred to as *space division* switching.

When the 1ESS was being developed, the most practical switch matrix components were electromechanical. The reed relay was an improvement over the metallic crossbar, and its contacts were sealed in a glass tube, but it was still a fairly bulky moving part. During the 1970s, improvements in semiconductor manufacturing led to the introduction of solid-state analog switches, effectively a "crossbar on a chip."

One such popular chip is the Mitel 8804, with a 4 × 8 analog crossbar matrix on a thumbnail-sized chip. A handful of these were combined with a microprocessor to produce the Mitel SX-200, the most popular small PBX of the late 1970s to early 1980s. In the SX-200, each line or trunk *port* has access to each of 32 discrete talk paths on the backplane of the cabinet. It is possible to literally "trace" the path of a call across the switch.

One problem with space division switches is that they get costlier as they get larger. To provide a larger number of ports with access to each other, more switching stages are required. Traffic capacity is also limited: The ability to handle more simultaneous calls requires more crosspoints at each stage. Simple economics, then, led to the use of alternative technologies for larger applications.

Analog Time Division Switching: PAM and PWM. Because any signal can (per Nyquist's theorem) be reproduced by sampling it fast enough, a single physical medium can be used to carry many different signals if enough samples can be interleaved without overlapping. That's the principle behind *time division* switching. A single "highway," or bus, can carry many different conversations at the same time by carrying only short samples at fixed intervals.

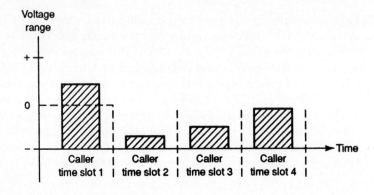

Figure 2.4 *In pulse amplitude modulation the analog signal is sampled frequently enough that the original waveform can be reconstructed from proportionate samples. These may be multiplexed onto a time division highway.*

A simple version of this is called *pulse amplitude modulation* (PAM). In a PAM switch, each time slot on the highway carries a proportional voltage from the sampled voice channel. Each port is told to listen and send on a specified time slot; the rest of the time, the port is gated off (see Fig. 2.4).

The PAM switch is quite inexpensive to build. Voice must be sampled at least 8000 times per second (based upon a desired frequency response of up to 3.4 kHz, plus elbow room for the filters), so there must be that many samples times the number of slots. For example, if there are 100 time slots, then each sample must be 1/800,000 of a second long, minus a "guard band" between slots.

The difficulty with PAM is keeping the slots separate. As long as everything is working right, everyone will remain in perfect synchronization, and time slots will not overlap. But should two time slots become slurred together, perhaps because of improper wiring or a failed component, then crosstalk will result. A 1% overlap would lead to a crosstalk level only 20 dB below full connection volume. This effect limits the capacity of PAM highways. For example, AT&T's Dimension 400 PBX, its first all-electronic model, had a 64-time-slot PAM highway. This allowed only 64 simultaneous connections among its 400 ports. The larger Dimension 2000 used dual highways to increase its traffic capacity.

Another form of analog time division is called *pulse width modulation* (PWM). This begins with a PAM sample, but instead of directly putting its voltage on the highway, it uses that voltage to modulate the width of a fixed-amplitude pulse (see Fig. 2.5). The area under the pulse is a direct representation of the voltage, but the width of the pulse is varied instead of the height. While slightly more costly, PWM is less sensitive to noise and crosstalk and allows pulses to be routed between highways by using digital components that wouldn't be able to carry the analog voltages found in PAM switches.

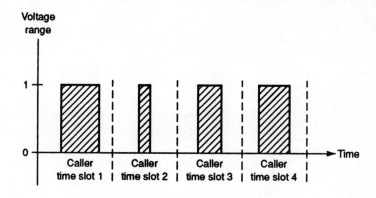

Figure 2.5 *In pulse width modulation the level of each pulse is constant, but its width (on/off ratio) varies in proportion to the amplitude of the original analog signal sample.*

PWM found only limited use but was notably found in the large Danray PBX and tandem switches manufactured in the mid to late 1970s and used in the original MCI dial network. These were *nonblocking* switches: They had as many paths through the switch as there were ports, so every port could be active at once. Nonblocking switching is rarely needed for ordinary local exchange or PBX use but is vital for the trunk switches used for toll calling. (This is because networks are designed to make the fullest possible use of trunk facilities, while most exchange lines are used, on average, only a small fraction of the time.) Note that the Danray switch combined both time division and space division: Each PWM highway was linked to several others, and a call was routed through a solid-state matrix reminiscent of a crossbar. Indeed, it could have been just a solid-state crossbar, but PWM provided improved signal fidelity through cascaded solid-state switches.

Analog time division switching was a transitional phase in the development of telecommunications networks. ISDN uses all-digital representation for its audio services. The simplest and most common form of digitized audio, and the one most often used in ISDN, is called *pulse code modulation* (PCM). The ISDN standard form of PCM uses 8000 samples per second, each transmitted in eight bits (see Fig. 2.6). This was originally invented for use on T carrier transmission systems, which are described in Chapter 3.

Digital Time Division Switching

A higher-capacity time division highway can be built after converting the samples to numeric values, represented in binary (digital) form. Such digital

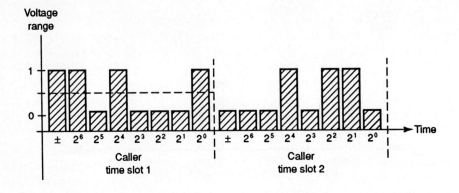

Figure 2.6 *In pulse code modulation, time division highways carry a succession of binary values, each of which numerically represents the amplitude of a sample. The bits in a given sample may be transmitted serially, as shown here, or, within a digital switching system, in parallel along a multiconductor bus.*

techniques, also found in T carrier transmission systems, provide several advantages when applied to switching systems:

- Because the receiver need only distinguish a 1 from a 0, small amounts of crosstalk do not matter.

- Samples can be sent in parallel across a multiconductor bus (e.g., an eight-bit sample can be sent over an eight-bit-wide bus, one bit per sample per time slot on each bus).

- Digital transmission systems can be more easily interfaced when the switch uses the same digitization technique (i.e., PCM).

There is, of course, one disadvantage — or at least there used to be one: Digital switching can be expensive. Since a telephone is an analog device, a *codec*, or coder-decoder, is needed to convert the analog voice signal into a digital bit stream and vice versa.

When the first digital telephone switching systems were being built, in the mid-1970s, codecs were fairly expensive. Various approaches were tried to minimize the expense. The earliest (1980) AT&T No. 5ESS switches used solid-state analog switches to allow up to 120 analog telephones to share 24 codec channels. The (1975) Rolm CBX (a midsized PBX) used a nonstandard PCM format (12,000 samples per second and 12 bits per sample, allowing simpler filters and a linear representation of the sampled value), implemented in 16-channel group coders and decoders. The Harris D1200 PBX used an unusual digitization technique (linear delta modulation, with each bit representing "up" or "down").

All of these approaches, however, have been abandoned over time. Essentially every major digital switching system uses a 64 kbps rate to carry a telephone call. The standard 8000 sample per second, eight-bit per sample PCM codec is now mass-produced on a single chip, often combined with other functions. The question that remains, then, is "Where does the codec go?" It can go into the switch, as is common practice. Or it can go into the telephone set itself, and the switch need never touch analog voice signals. That is the ISDN approach.

In moving the codec into the telephone set, a few new questions arise. How are the bits transmitted over the distance between the telephone and the switch, which may be several miles? How is signaling accomplished? Certainly the old on-hook, off-hook, and power-ring techniques don't work in a digital telephone set. The first digital telephone instruments were introduced as proprietary feature phones, coupled with specific PBX switches, using unique transmission and signaling techniques, and were often very limited in range. (How often does a PBX have to cope with more than a few thousand feet or so of wire to the telephone set?)

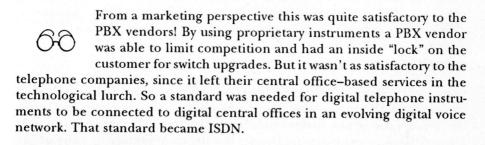 From a marketing perspective this was quite satisfactory to the PBX vendors! By using proprietary instruments a PBX vendor was able to limit competition and had an inside "lock" on the customer for switch upgrades. But it wasn't as satisfactory to the telephone companies, since it left their central office–based services in the technological lurch. So a standard was needed for digital telephone instruments to be connected to digital central offices in an evolving digital voice network. That standard became ISDN.

Digital Switch Architecture

While virtually all digital telephone switches use some kind of highway, there are considerable variations in how this is done. Some of the earlier PBXs featured a single highway that was capable of carrying the needed number of simultaneous one-way talk paths. This *bus* architecture is effective as long as its overall traffic-carrying capacity is adequate; a digital switch carrying PCM over its bus is likely to have substantially more traffic capacity than an analog switch.

The most common example of a bus-oriented switch is the Rolm CBX family, introduced in 1975. The original CBX had a single bus (16 bits wide) with a bandwidth of 74 Mbps, divided into 384 time slots and nominally capable of carrying 150 simultaneous voice calls. Each call required two time slots, one for each direction of transmission. (Some time slots were reserved for special functions such as dial tone and busy tone.) The one-bus CBX could support about 800 telephones. Rolm later introduced the VLCBX, consisting in effect of several separate nodes (each with its own bus) tied together with digital tie lines. Later, the CBX family was replaced by the model 9751, which had a 274-Mbps bus in each node.

Another early digital PBX, the Northern Telecom SL-1, used much smaller highways. Each such "loop" was a serial line (one bit wide) that carried only 32 time slots. All of the loops were interconnected via a central matrix, so the aggregate traffic capacity of the switch could be engineered as required. The SL-1 was thus characterized as a time-space-time (T-S-T) switch. Most digital telephone switches use a similar approach, often with multiple space division stages (e.g., T-S-S-T) or a combination of time and space stages (e.g., T-S-T-S-T).

Both the bus and T-S-T (matrix) approaches have potential advantages. The matrix offers a better growth path; the SL-1, for instance, is expandable beyond 5000 lines yet viable for small (50-line) installations as well. The bus, on the other hand, offers more flexibility in dividing up the time slots. The Rolm CBX could carry several low-speed (i.e., up to 9600 bps) data connections using the same traffic capacity as a single voice conversation.

Note that a digital time slot carries only one side of a conversation, while an analog voice path or PAM time slot may be able to carry both sides of a conversation. That's because it is possible to simply add voltages together in a PAM switch, just as occurs in a two-wire electromechanical matrix.

Circuit-Switched Data Networks

Computers have been using the telephone network since at least the early 1960s. When all of telephony was analog, the only way to carry data across the network was with a *modem* (*modulator-demo*dulator), a device to convert 1's and 0's to sound patterns. During the stringent monopoly years of the 1960s, modems could be obtained only from telephone companies. AT&T's flagship modem was a fairly impressive-sized box, much larger than the telephone set that accompanied it, that used the large discrete (pre-integrated circuit) components of the day. It was called the Model 103 *Dataphone*, and it carried data across dial-up connections at the rate of 300 bps. Faster modems were usable only over specially conditioned leased channels. Typical of these was the Model 202, which could zip along at 1200 bps.

The competitive market of the 1970s spurred tremendous advances in modem technology. By the mid-1970s, private line modems capable of supporting 9600 bps were becoming commonplace, and dial-up modems that could support 1200 bps (at the same time, over the same wires, by splitting the frequency band in half) were also becoming available. But to go 9600 bps over a dial-up circuit required two separate calls, one for each direction, and performance was often marginal.

By the late 1980s, modems were nearing their limits of performance. Just as Nyquist determined the number of samples per second required to carry an analog signal over a digital medium, Claude Shannon (then of Bell Labs) determined in the late 1940s how many bits per second could conceivably be pulled from an analog medium. Given the parameters of the analog telephone network, a theoretical limit of about 26 kbps can be achieved; practical circuits, of course, can only begin to approach that. (A few modern modems, however, take advantage of the superior quality of most connections and run at the fastest speed they can for any given connection. Such techniques are not what the CCITT's dreams are made of, though they do tend to serve as useful line quality testers.) The fastest CCITT-standardized modem speed for use on a dial-up voice-grade circuit is 14,400 bps, using techniques described in Recommendation V.32bis. Modems operating at 19,200 bps are also being standardized by the CCITT, while 24,000-bps modems have also been introduced.

Telex. Circuit-switched digital networks actually predate the computer by quite a few years. Indeed, the predominant form of telegraph service for the past 50 years or more has made use of a circuit-switched digital network called *Telex*. While primitive, Telex is still widely used, especially in parts of the world where other telecommunications facilities are unable to support modern data communications.

The Morse telegraph, with its manual key, became obsolete with the invention of the teleprinter. (Morse code remains in use for shipboard radiotelegraphy but is being phased out there too.) In the 1930s the first Telex networks, essentially dial telephone networks with low-speed modems attached to teleprinters, went into service. The original Telex service made use of the five-level *Baudot* code, traditionally accessed from a three-row keyboard. It ran at 45.5 bps, and later 50 bps, speeds appropriate to the electromechanical printers of the day.

Telex is still an efficient service in many places because it needs so little bandwidth. Just as Mr. Bell's original telephone was ostensibly an outgrowth of an attempt to carry multiple telegraph signals over one wire (something that his contemporary, Emile Baudot, had indeed succeeded in doing), a Telex machine requires far less bandwidth per connection than a telephone call. A single analog voice channel can carry perhaps two dozen Telex connections. While the local connection from the Telex machine to the network is usually not multiplexed, extensive multiplexing is used on long-distance and especially international circuits. And Telex is very heavily used for international traffic.

In the United States, AT&T invented its own variation on Telex, known as TWX (TeletypeWriter eXchange). This made use of an eight-level code, accessed from a more typewriterlike four-row keyboard. The quintessential TWX machine was the Teletype Model 33, capable of pounding out a good ten characters per second with a line transmission rate of 110 bps. TWX originally made use of the dial telephone network and uses ten-digit numbers that look like telephone numbers. AT&T later sold its TWX service to Western Union; in 1990, AT&T bought it back along with the rest of the domestic Telex business.

TWX is more popular than three-row Telex within the United States but has never been deployed outside of North America. Instead, many countries have more recently deployed a 1200 bps *Teletex* service.

These telegraph networks provided a low-speed digital service while still using analog transmission technology (modems). As competition developed during the 1970s, it became possible to build faster circuit-switched networks that used all-digital transmission instead of modems. One such network was Datran, built in the mid-1970s by Wyly Corp. It offered dial-up services at 2400–9600 bps, carried over a dedicated microwave network. Faced with increased pressure from AT&T and other carriers, Datran went bankrupt before becoming well established; its facilities were folded into the growing Sprint network.

In a sense, Datran established the pattern for circuit-switched digital networks. Several more attempts were made, but none was a big success. In several European countries the PTTs established a circuit-switched data network with interfaces based upon CCITT Recommendation X.21 and X.21bis, providing up to 48 kbps service with faster call setup times than the telephone network, but the idea never caught on in many other countries. Alternatives not based upon X.21, such as AT&T's Accunet Switched 56 service, are becoming fairly common, though. In the United States, "Central Office LANs," typically offering 19.2-kbps switching within the area served by a local exchange, have been actively promoted by several Bell Operating Companies, but total sales have been small. Some carriers have chosen to not offer pre-ISDN circuit-switched data services because ISDN will make them obsolete soon enough.

Integrated Voice-Data PBXs. When digital voice switching became popular in the late 1970s, an obvious comparison was made between voice and data switching. After all, data is digital. So it seemed to follow that a telephone switch that is capable of carrying digitized voice should also be capable of carrying data. While public networks were generally unprepared to do so, PBX manufacturers ushered in an era of *integrated voice and data* (IVD) switching.

In the early 1980s, virtually every PBX offered had some kind of modemless data capability. While leading digital PBXs such as the Northern Telecom SL-1 and Rolm CBX had data ports added to them, startups such as InteCom and ZTEL used IVD as their principal selling point. InteCom featured a nonblocking digital switch and proprietary telephone sets with data ports built in; ZTEL and CXC promised to combine the PBX with the emerging technology of Local Area Networks. At least two dozen companies also offered "integrated voice-data workstations," essentially telephones glued together to computer terminals.

During its 1981–1984 Study Period the CCITT was actively writing its preliminary recommendations for ISDN. This was happening at the same time that consultants, magazines, and marketers alike were touting the

Table 2.1 *Typical terminal-to-host data traffic compared with voice telephone traffic.*

	Voice	Data
Average call duration	3–5 min	15–60+ min
Digital transmission rate	64 kbps	9.6 kbps
Percentage intraswitch traffic	20%	80%
Feature use	High	Low
Direction of calls	Both ways	One way per device

wonders of IVD, so it is not surprising that many ISDN advocates were looking to ISDN to become the industry standard for IVD switching.

But a funny thing happened on the way to the bank. The marketplace responded, and not the way IVD's promoters had foreseen. Lower-cost and more functional alternatives were available. *Data switches* operated like PBXs but only for data; they were typically far less costly than data ports on IVD switches. *Local Area Networks* provided far higher speeds, typically at lower cost than IVD. And for some applications, separate *packet switches* were preferable.

Circuit switching is the natural way to handle voice traffic, but it's not necessarily the best way to carry all sorts of data. And the nature of voice and data traffic, even through a circuit switch, varies. Table 2.1 gives a comparison of typical voice versus data traffic. The data traffic is a simple asynchronous terminal connecting to host computers, the way most IVD PBX switches were used.

It can be seen that circuit-switched voice traffic and data traffic are very different, so combining them into one switching system might make about as much sense as combining, say, a passenger car and a truck. A few luxury pickup trucks are made, but they sell into a rather narrow market niche.

ISDN itself may be ideal for integrated voice and data switching, but as a local premise technology, such integration doesn't guarantee it much of a market. While IVD PBXs were aimed at local area (intrapremise) switching, ISDN promises worldwide coverage. ISDN's eventual success will come not from how well it integrates voice and data, but from the strength of its individual capabilities. For many kinds of data transmission and for many voice applications, ISDN is the most appropriate, economical technology.

Packet Switching

The most distinctive characteristic of circuit switching is that it provides a fixed amount of bandwidth, either analog or digital, for the duration of a call. While this is a very natural way to handle voice, most data communication is not characterized by a steady flow of data at a constant rate. Data communication is typified by *bursts* of traffic. For example, an electronic mail user who is reading incoming mail on a multiuser remote computer system typically gets a screenful at a time (sent in the direction from computer to terminal), then pauses to read it, then types a key or two (sent in the direction from terminal to computer) when he or she wants another screenful to be sent. While the user is reading the screen, the line between the computer and the terminal might be idle.

A circuit-switched data connection is not an especially efficient way to allocate bandwidth for this type of user. Either a lot of bandwidth goes to waste or, if less bandwidth is allocated, the user has to wait longer for the data. Wouldn't it be better if costly high-speed transmission facilities could be shared by multiple users, using bandwidth only when necessary? That is the logic behind the newest of the three major switching disciplines, *packet switching*.

To be sure, even voice is not always handled as a steady stream, either. Because each side of a human conversation is marked by silent periods (typically a little more than half the time), it's possible to conserve network bandwidth by packetizing voice, transmitting only packets that go above some threshold of volume. This is called *Time Assignment Speech Interpolation* (TASI) and is widely used on high-cost international circuits. Older analog TASI systems caused substantial degradation of speech quality. Newer all-digital systems perform better, though they are sometimes still noticeable. Some even intermix voice and data. But voice packetization is very, very different from data communication; these systems are not the same as data-oriented packet switches. It's not reasonable to simply carry telephony over a packet-switched data network.

Packet-switching technology is often described by analogy to what preceded it — the mail. A packet is essentially an electronic envelope carrying a finite amount of data across a network. Every packet begins with a *header*, which carries the information that the network needs to route it to its destination. This is followed by the actual *user data*, the contents of the packet. The principle is simple; the implementation might not be. There are any number of different ways to perform packet switching. A few standards have evolved and have become part of ISDN.

The Layered Model

Far more than circuit switching, packet switching depends upon the interaction of *protocols* both between users and the network and between users themselves. Quite a few functions are performed in a packet-switched data network. Some of these functions are left to the users (customers' computers) themselves, and the protocols that accomplish them are thus referred to as *end-to-end* protocols. Some of them operate between users and the network as a whole and require the coordinated actions of the network nodes at both ends of the connection. These are sometimes called *edge-to-edge* protocols. Others operate independently across the individual links within the network or across the links between the users and the network. These are *hop-by-hop* protocols. Just which functions are left to each of these categories can vary from network to network.

The nearly universal approach to describing and implementing packet switched data communication is referred to as *layering*. By assigning functions to separate layers a complex problem can be reduced into relatively simple components. This makes it practical to implement complex protocol suites, with each layer implemented separately. Layering also adds discipline to the design of the network. Each layer delivers a specific *service* to the layer above it and receives a specific service from the layer immediately beneath it. Thus the design of the protocol that works at any given layer can begin with the definition of the service expected from it.

Another feature of layering is *encapsulation*: A higher-layer protocol is encapsulated within the payload of lower-layer protocols (see Fig. 2.7). Thus

Figure 2.7 *A layered protocol architecture encapsulates higher layers inside the payload of lower layers. Each layer can thus be cleanly distinguished from all others.*

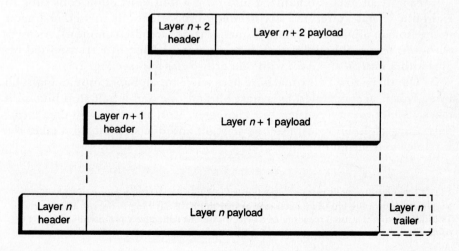

the various headers associated with each layer are arrayed one after the other in front of each packet. Layering also prohibits any protocol from "peeking inside the envelope" at the control information of the higher layers. Each layered protocol operates independently of the others.

X.25 Levels versus OSI Layers. In the early days of public network packet switching, as standardized by CCITT Recommendation X.25, three *levels* were often referred to. While "levels" have largely been replaced by "layers" in modern discussions, today's layers are potentially more complex than the packet-switching levels of old. And there are more of them: The widely-used Open Systems Interconnection Reference Model (OSIRM) describes data communication in terms of seven layers. The first two OSIRM layers correspond to the original levels 1 and 2 used in public network (including ISDN) packet switching, while X.25's level/layer 3 is a subset of OSI Layer 3.

Layer 1, the *Physical* layer, provides bit transport between adjacent devices. Included within this are modems, line codes, connectors, transmission multiplexing, circuit-mode networks, and other parts of the connection that deal in raw bit *transmission*. Packet switching really begins at Layer 2, the *Data Link* layer, which passes variable-length frames between intelligent devices and extends into Layer 3, the *Network* layer, which is responsible for routing packets across the network.

The Hop-by-Hop Layers: Frames. Even before packet switching was invented, there was a need to establish reliable, error-free communications between computers. While Telex machines, like the *asynchronous* computer terminals ("glass teletypes") that followed them, treated every character on its own, many "intelligent" computer terminals operated *synchronously*, in "block mode," sending and receiving a screenful of information at a time.

Almost all data is organized into *bytes*, a unit most often consisting of eight bits.[3] That's often the size needed to represent one written character in the Roman alphabet (although smaller codes are also common). An asynchronous terminal handles each byte separately: Each byte transmitted begins with a *start bit* and ends with one or two *stop bits* (see Fig. 2.8).

The three-row Telex machine uses a five-bit alphabet, not an eight-bit byte. This is accompanied by a start bit and one and a half stop bits, so it takes 7.5 bit times to transmit one character. Most asynchronous data terminals, using eight-bit bytes, use one start bit and one stop bit, so it takes ten bit times to transmit one character.

---

[3] CCITT standards usually refer to *octets* instead of bytes. An octet is a group of eight bits. Within a protocol the bits of an octet may or may not have anything to do with one another. This differs from the usual meaning of a byte, whose bits collectively represent all or part of some value.

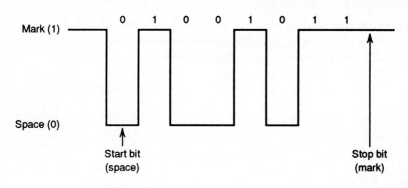

Figure 2.8 *In asynchronous data transmission, each character begins with a start bit and ends with a stop bit.*

In synchronous data communication, devices send variable-length blocks of information, usually many bytes long, on demand. Start bits and stop bits aren't used. Instead, the bytes are run together between some form of bounding patterns that identify the beginning and end of the block. Thus the block is called a *frame.*

A frame typically ends with some form of checksum, to enable transmission errors to be detected, so errored blocks can be retransmitted until they are received correctly. A frame protocol is also likely to contain other information in its header, as required to operate the error-correction protocol. The frame header may contain addressing information, but it needn't contain the ultimate address; it needs an address only if there are multiple devices sharing the same physical layer entity. In the OSI Reference Model, frames live within the Data Link layer, which after all usually operates hop by hop. (In proper OSI terminology they aren't even called frames; they're Data Link Protocol Data Units.) Many synchronous terminals can be attached to multidrop circuits, in which one physical line supports many users. The frame address is needed to identify each user. A Local Area Network is an extension of this; LAN protocols such as Ethernet and Token Ring provide addressed frames. Point-to-point circuits, in contrast, often operate without frame addresses.

Data Link protocols may, however, have some means of identifying what type of higher-layer data is being carried. This could be found via the address of the appropriate higher-level entity, or encoded in a separate field. This enables the receiving entity to process its contents correctly.

Common Frame Protocols. Several Data Link protocols are found in common use today. Probably the oldest one is the *binary synchronous,* or *bisync,* protocol that was used by IBM for most of its terminals until the late 1970s. While bisync is not very popular any more, some customers stuck with it rather than convert when newer protocols were introduced. Digital Equipment Corporation in 1974 developed a data link protocol, based loosely upon bisync, called *Digital Data Communications Message Protocol* (DDCMP). It is still used in most DECnet networks.

Nowadays, IBM's flagship data link protocol is *Synchronous Data Link Control* (SDLC), which has essentially nothing in common with bisync. After SDLC was introduced in 1974 as part of IBM's very hierarchical *Systems Network Architecture* (SNA), a more generalized version, *High Level Data Link Control* (HDLC), was developed by the ISO. SDLC is effectively a subset of HDLC, which has become by far the most popular data link protocol family in use today.

The ISO definition of HDLC is quite flexible, leaving much to be filled in by others. Besides SDLC, one of the most common data link layer protocols is *Link Access Protocol–Balanced* (LAP-B). This was developed for packet switched networks and is described in CCITT Recommendation X.25 and in ISO 7776. When ISDN was first being developed, a data link protocol was needed for the D channel, and since LAP-B was already well established, the CCITT chose to use it as the basis of its new ISDN data link protocol, *LAPD*. The most important difference between LAP-B and LAPD (besides the hyphen in the name) is that LAPD has an address field that supports multipoint circuits, while LAP-B is limited to a simple two-point circuit. The newer LAPF is a LAPD variant used for Frame Relay networks.

The Edge-to-Edge Packet Level. Data link layer protocols sit atop the Physical layer, turning bits into frames and protecting against errors at the same time. If all of the devices that needed to communicate with each other were directly connected together at the Physical or Data Link layer, then there would probably not be much need for the next layer up. But allowing flexible interconnection of large numbers of computers requires additional capabilities. First, data must be routed between nonadjacent nodes. That's the principal function of Layer 3 in the OSIRM, the Network layer.

Packets versus Frames. In public data networks the protocol that operates across all of the hops together, from one edge of the network to the other, can be referred to as the *packet* level. A block of data becomes a packet at this point, when it acquires addressing information that goes beyond the point-to-point significance of a frame (see Fig. 2.9). In most networks, one frame encapsulates a single packet, so the distinction is more academic than real, but a few specialized protocols (such as the proprietary *T2* protocol used by Tymnet) achieve efficiency by packing more than one packet into each frame.

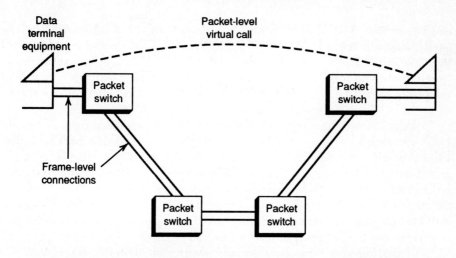

Figure 2.9 *In the frame and packet levels of X.25 networks, the frame operates between adjacencies, the packet across the network. Each frame level link may carry part of many packet-level connections.*

X.25 Packet Level versus OSI Network Layer.

In some simple networks, in which every computer is directly connected to the packet-switched network, the X.25 packet *level* is the same as the network *layer*. More often, though, a private network includes point-to-point circuits, LANs, and possibly private packet networks, so the packet level actually delivers only part of the end-to-end connection, making it a *subnetwork*. This distinction is not readily appreciated by some public network providers, though; since data and voice are not quite analogous, these providers do not appreciate the need for private network support in order to make use of a public data network.

What functions should be provided by the network layer or by a packet network filling the *subnetwork role* within the network layer? The most obvious ones are *routing* and *addressing*. Just as a telephone call is initiated by dialing a specific number, a packet is relayed to a destination noted by its address (or a corresponding connection identifier). Beyond this relay function, though, there's quite a bit of divergence of opinion about what a network should look like. The matter almost acquires the status of a holy war between advocates of the two major camps, supporters of a *connection-oriented network service* and supporters of a *connectionless network service*.

Are Connections Really Necessary? In the circuit-switched world the network's stock in trade is the connection. From the time a call is made until the time it's disconnected, a path is maintained through the network between the two ends of the call. This is a perfectly simple, natural way to model telephony. It can also be extended into the data world, where it is referred to as the connection-oriented model.

A packet-switched network doesn't deliver a fixed bandwidth circuit, but a connection-oriented packet network creates a path that packets follow whenever they're sent. This is called a *virtual circuit.* Like a connection-oriented data link protocol, a connection must be established before data can be transferred. From the public network provider's perspective this is beneficial: The network can charge for connect time, as a voice network does, as well as charging for packets. The virtual circuit protocol also provides *flow control,* so the overall level of traffic can be managed.

Virtual circuits have another advantage that benefits more than the network provider: Each individual packet doesn't have to carry the actual destination address; it just needs a connection identifier. The connection identifier just has to be big enough to distinguish between all connections that are present over any one data link at any given time, and it represents both the source and destination addresses. The actual source and destination addresses need be given only during the connection setup, and the network can remember routing decisions.

Connectionless networks do not follow the same model as telephone calls. Instead, they are more akin to letters or telegrams. If a network uses a connectionless protocol, each packet (called a *datagram*) carries its own source and destination addresses. The network is *memoryless* — each packet is carried independently. Two packets going from the same source to the same destination need not follow the same route and need not arrive in order. And (again like the post office) packet delivery is not guaranteed; the network operates on a best-effort basis.

Is this a disadvantage for the connectionless approach? While the advocates of virtual circuits might so argue, experience has shown that practical data networks often aren't as "reliable" as they claim to be. A connection-oriented network might claim to deliver packets in order, error-free and without loss, but data users are critical and will be reluctant to rely upon it. So it isn't actually necessary for the network to make these assurances; the user can make up for the network's failings with end-to-end protocols.

In some cases, though, connection-oriented subnetworks are advantageous because they provide flow control and local retransmission of lost data. When a connectionless subnetwork is used, end-to-end retransmission takes place across the entire set of subnetworks involved. If the level of loss across any one such subnetwork is high, significant increases in overall traffic can result.

CCITT Recommendation X.25 defines the user-to-network (edge) protocol for a connection-oriented packet-switched public network. This standard, first produced in 1976 and periodically revised, represents the apotheosis of virtual circuit ideology. Packets are delivered in order, reliably, with network-provided flow control and error correction. X.25 defines both the LAP-B data link protocol and the *Packet Layer Protocol* (PLP). Packet-switched data service with X.25 access is widely offered by telephone companies, especially in Europe.

It should come as no surprise, then, that networks based on X.25 are the basis of the primary packet-switching service used in ISDN. Indeed the term "integrated services" in large part refers to the integration of both circuit-switched telephone networks and packet-switched data networks into one infrastructure.

Connectionless networks are popular among many computer vendors and users. The prototypical packet-switched network, the ARPAnet built by the U.S. Defense Advanced Research Projects Agency during the 1970s and 1980s, used connectionless technology. The TCP/IP protocol suite, originated on the ARPAnet and now widely used in educational, industrial, and government applications, features the connectionless Internetwork Protocol (IP). Digital Equipment Corporation's DECnet products also feature a connectionless network layer.

Even public networks are beginning to phase in connectionless services. X.25 was developed during the analog era, when a 48 kbps data circuit was rare and precious. Some implementors consider it hard to scale well to the sorts of speeds that LAN users are now accustomed to. Some believe that there's just too much overhead involved in keeping track of all of those packets, guaranteeing their sequential arrival, and exercising flow control throughout the network. Connectionless network switches (and for that matter the simplified, though connection-oriented Frame Relay service) are widely viewed as being easier to scale to very high speeds. Besides, LAN protocols are generally connectionless, so a connectionless service is easier to use for LAN interconnection. That's a fast-growing market for high-speed network services.

The first connectionless service widely promoted by the Bell Companies in the United States is Switched Multi-Megabit Data Service (SMDS). First commercially deployed in 1991, it runs over copper access lines at 1.5 Mbps and over optical fiber access lines at speeds up to, and eventually beyond, 45 Mbps. SMDS was not developed as an ISDN service but will eventually be merged into Broadband ISDN, whose planned connectionless bearer service is suspiciously similar. In some other countries, public Metropolitan Area Networks are being deployed, offering essentially the same service as SMDS.

War and Peace among Packet Users. These divergent views of the proper nature of the Network layer are not impossible to resolve. While any given protocol tends to be in either the connection-oriented or connectionless camp, the Network *layer* found in the OSI standards supports a peaceful, if not quite friendly, coexistence between the two. The old "packet level" provided by public networks becomes one optional protocol for the newer subnetwork role (see Fig. 2.10). Other subnetwork options include the various LANs (Ethernet, Token Ring, Metropolitan Area Networks, etc.) and the simplest case, a data link protocol over point-to-point wire. The end systems, meaning the actual computers doing the communicating with each other, use a protocol of their choice in the internetwork role. So a network can use the connectionless network protocol over X.25, or for that matter the connection-oriented network protocol over an Ethernet subnetwork.

Both of these roles have addresses associated with them, but they need not be the same. A subnetwork address is typically assigned by the subnetwork provider, be it a public network or a LAN manufacturer. An internetwork address is typically assigned by the (private) network's owner from a block of addresses that may be assigned by some authority in order to guarantee uniqueness. The internetwork protocol is encapsulated within the subnetwork protocol, using rules (in a sense, an additional protocol) referred to as

Figure 2.10 *Relationship between the bottom three OSI layers and the older three-level X.25 model.*

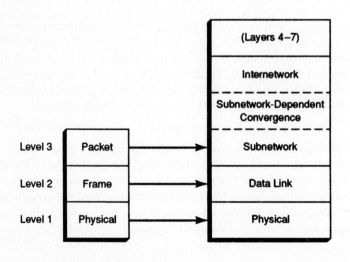

the *convergence role*. The nature of the convergence protocol can be summarized as "whatever needs to be done to provide the appropriate network service over the provided subnetwork."

This convergence principle is very liberating. It allows computer users to make peace with telecommunications network providers. It allows Local Area Networks (usually connectionless) to make peace with wide area networks such as ISDN (usually connection-oriented). It also isn't "free"; depending upon how divergent the subnetwork and internetwork protocols are, the convergence function may be simple or complex.

Even if the public subnetwork and private network are both connection-oriented, and even if both use the same basic network layer protocol (i.e., X.25 as the subnetwork and ISO 8208, the OSI connection-oriented network protocol, in the internetwork role), some convergence might be necessary, even if only to map one address onto another. This is an essential difference between the voice and data worlds. A private voice network might have its own numbering plan, but telephones still usually map 1:1 to telephone numbers or extension numbers. In the ISDN packet-switched service, X.25-like service is provided by using what are in effect telephone numbers, while the attached computers might use a privately assigned network address (see CCITT I.334 and ISO 8878). Note, however, that ISDN's *passive bus* feature, allowing multiple terminals to share a single line, further complicates the mapping process.

The Upper (End-to-End) Layers

What are all of these packets carrying around? Some packet-switched network applications are very simple. Public packet networks are widely used to enable remote terminals to log into computers. The most common protocols for this are quite simple. CCITT Recommendation X.29 defines a set of commands sent directly over X.25 by which a computer can command a *packet assembler-disassembler* (PAD). A terminal connected to a PAD can log into the remote computer. In this simplified model, end user data (keystrokes and displayed characters) are directly encapsulated within X.25 packets. X.29 commands are also encapsulated, with a single bit in the X.25 packet header to distinguish between data and commands.

But most data communication is more complicated than that! ISDN will have to accommodate many different types of payload. The suitability of the network to any given purpose and the requirements placed upon the network are in part based upon the nature of the data carried end to end across it.

The Network layer routes packets between computers, but as we have noted, some important functions still remain to be performed. These are handled in the upper end-to-end layers. Protocols that operate within these layers remain within the user data field of the packets that the network carries. The network has no business seeing them or, for that matter, even knowing about them. But the computers that are actually in contact with each other, that are actually using the network, rely upon them.

The OSI Reference Model leaves layers 4–7 to the end systems only. Other network models, such as TCP/IP and SNA, have a similar dichotomy between end-to-end protocols and those which the network itself sees. These models will be discussed below.

Why Use Packet?

Since essentially all private data networks, other than some used only for simple terminal dial-up functions, make use of a packet model, it might seem reasonable that data users would prefer to make use of packet-switched services rather than leased channels or circuit-switched network services. This is often not the case! Both performance and economic reasons often militate against the use of packet switching.

Packet switching isn't cheap. This stems in part from a fundamental difference between packet switching and circuit switching. With circuit switching, call setup takes place, and then a channel (in effect, a pipe) of some width is left in place for the duration of the call. The pipe can be narrow (Telex) or very wide; either way the amount of processor power required is the same. But with packet switching, an intelligent device must look at the header of each and every packet and route it along its way. Thus a faster circuit requires more computer horsepower.

Private line digital capacity is rated in bits per second. Circuit switch capacity is rated in ports; a large switch can have more devices attached to it than a small one. Packet switch capacity is rated in packets per second; more utilization or higher data rates require a larger, more costly switch.

Thus packet switching tends to be most economical when the average rate of traffic is low. Bursty, intermittent users with low overall traffic are the best candidates for packet-mode services. Many remote terminal applications are like this. So are credit card verification terminals, which typically exchange a few packets' worth of data every few minutes. Other likely packet users include remote branch offices, for which a dedicated circuit would be too costly.

In parts of Europe and in several other places, PTTs distorted their tariffs to encourage packet switching. Leased channel rates were set far above cost, while packet switching was priced below cost. In addition, private lines were usually restricted to connecting only locations belonging to a single customer. Thus intercustomer computer communications (i.e., electronic mail and document interchange) could use only packet-switched or circuit-switched (dial-up telephone) service. This led by the early 1980s to widespread use of X.25 within Europe. Had the PTTs been subject to competition, of course, such behavior would have been suicidal.

In the United States a different regulatory model was adopted. In the 1970s, packet switching was viewed as a *value-added* service and therefore not within the scope of telephone company monopolies. Packet networks were thus free to operate competitively but relied upon leased telephone company channels for access. This kept the price high, and packet networks were still rarely very profitable. If a customer had to pay for a leased channel, it would often be to the other site rather than to a packet carrier. Packet was thus most popular for "fan-in" applications such as dial-up time-sharing terminals in which a central point was connected to many remote users.

In the 1980s, when most basic services other than local exchange switching were made fully competitive, packet switching was reclassified as a basic service. Local telephone companies were allowed to provide service, but only at cost-justified rates. Among them, local telephone companies in the United States did very little packet business. It didn't help, of course, that the total volume of packet business was too small to really excite them.

One of ISDN's features, cheaper access to packet, may finally bring public packet switching to a larger cross-section of Americans. But since ISDN also offers fast digital circuit switching, and with leased digital channel rates lowered by the widespread deployment of digital transmission, packet services will still have tough competition.

The OSI Reference Model

The Open Systems Interconnection (OSI) project of the International Organization for Standardization (ISO) is roughly contemporaneous with ISDN. Both were conceived in the late 1970s; both were proactive standards efforts. While ISDN was a program to create a new framework for telecommunications that would operate across national boundaries, OSI was created as a new framework for data communications that would operate across vendor boundaries.

The X.25 standard for packet communications was introduced in 1976 and provided a three-level reference model. OSI sought to complete the picture, providing not just *interconnectivity* (the ability to pass bits) but *interoperability* (the ability to work together).

The first and most important contribution made by the OSI project was its reference model. The OSI Reference Model (OSIRM) created seven layers, as shown in Fig. 2.11. The first three layers were in large part based upon the physical, frame, and packet levels of X.25. The remaining layers were the

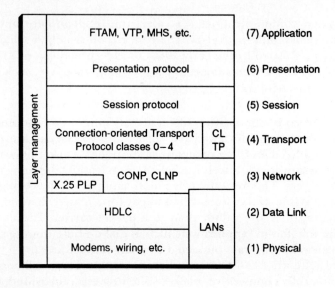

Figure 2.11 *The OSI Reference Model showing some of the protocols that may be found at each layer.*

framers' view of the functions that needed to be performed in end systems in a heterogeneous computing environment. In other words, OSI does not specify the minimum functions required for connectivity but includes functions that are oriented toward multivendor networks. Another way of looking at OSI is to view it as a universal second language for computers, a lingua franca for the computer era.

Like other attempts to synthesize languages that cross national boundaries, OSI has met with mixed acceptance. In the mid-1980s, many vendors publicly embraced OSI. Governments raced to put OSI procurement programs into place; several countries (including the United States and the United Kingdom) have GOSIP (Government OSI Profile) standards that are supposed to be met by any vendor offering to sell computers to that country's government.

But actual widespread use of OSI protocols has been slower to develop. Several factors have been suggested for this. OSI offers many options, such as two very different network layer services (connection-oriented and connectionless). Having OSI alone does not guarantee that compatible options are in place at both ends of a link. Another problem has been performance: OSI protocols must be flexible enough to accommodate many different styles of computing, but as a result, more narrowly focused protocols can often outperform OSI standards. And complete OSI protocol suites tend to be difficult to implement; it isn't OSI unless all seven layers are present!

By the early 1990s, enough practical experience with OSI has been gained to make reasonably efficient implementations possible. Internationally standardized profiles (ISPs) are being created to simplify the task of choosing the right set of options, and expectations have been trimmed to be closer to reality. OSI is now available and growing in popularity. Indeed, its growth curve has been rather close to that of ISDN, starting slowly and gradually building up steam in specific markets. While OSI networks per se are still not common, many OSI applications, such as message handling, are widely used, while some OSI protocols are the basis of other developments (including some of ISDN).

The Transport Layer (4). Within the OSIRM the next layer up is the Transport layer (4). This layer can provide either connection-oriented (COTS) or connectionless (CLTS) service to the layers above it. However, this decision is entirely separate from the CO versus CL decision at the network layer. Most applications require COTS, but some use CLTS. A very common technique is to provide the COTS atop the connectionless network service (CLNS).

The COTS delivers to its user (the next layer above it) a stream of error-free, sequenced packets (Transport Service Data Units). The amount of work that a Transport layer protocol has to do can be affected by the nature of the underlying Network service. If the user is satisfied with the reliability of a connection-oriented network for the application at hand, then the Transport layer may be fairly simple. If the end-to-end connection contains (anywhere within it!) a link that does not guarantee sequentiality or that may drop packets, then the required effort to provide the connection-oriented Transport service is more complex. The Transport layer also has to cope with segmentation: The underlying network may have a maximum packet size that's smaller than the higher layers need, so the Transport layer breaks up the packets into smaller ones.

The connection-oriented OSI Transport protocol is offered in five *classes*. Transport Class 0 performs little more than segmentation, it requires a reliable CONS to serve it. Classes 1 and 3 also rely upon the CONS but can recover from indicated network resets. Classes 2 and 3 provide *multiplexing*: A single network layer connection can carry multiple transport connections. Only the Class 4 protocol contains all of the capabilities (including packet resequencing and retransmission of dropped packets) needed to operate over a CLNS. It can, of course, also operate over a CONS; it is not much harder to implement than the simpler classes and uses many of the same protocol elements.

The connectionless Transport protocol is, as might be guessed, very simple. It provides multiplexing, segmentation, and an optional checksum. Packets are delivered to the upper layers in the same order in which they arrive, if and when they arrive. The CLTS is generally used for simple request-response applications.

The Session and Presentation Layers.

The upper layers are more narrowly focused. The Session layer (5) is somewhat controversial. Its principle function is to "control dialog" between the two ends of the link. Generally, this involves passing a *token*, granting the right to transmit, between the two ends of the connection. But since an application itself, as well as the Transport layer, can provide flow control, that function of the Session layer is often viewed as a needless one. (OSI applications specify the functions needed from Session; flow control is not left to the application.) Detractors have described it as a means of ensuring that in case the Transport implementation is broken and sends data more quickly than the Application is capable of receiving it, Session can stand in the way and slow everything down.

Session does, however, provide some useful functions. These include *major and minor synchronization points*, used for *checkpointing*. In case the transport connection breaks, the application can pick up where it left off. This is especially useful for transferring large files. Without it a large file could rarely be transmitted over an unreliable network, since it would have to start over again each time the network failed. Checkpointing is also useful for guaranteeing the integrity of some multipart transactions.

The Presentation layer (6) is also somewhat controversial. Its job is to facilitate translation of data between differing representations. At the time the OSIRM was being developed, two specific instances of this were widely understood. Videotex was considered a very important application, and there were several conflicting national standards for it. The other major example of the need for translation comes from IBM's historical use of the EBCDIC coding standard for its alphanumeric terminals, in contrast to most of the rest of the industry's use of the ASCII standard (now evolved into International Alphabet No. 5). The major activity of the Presentation layer is to negotiate context. For this purpose it makes use of a grammar called *Abstract Syntax Notation No. 1* (ASN.1). It can also be used to negotiate the encryption of data.

In practice, however, the Presentation layer is often viewed as carrying more overhead than it is worth. Applications themselves actually do most of the translation; Presentation is useful for negotiating this, but as a separate layer it must be present in every packet. Since it sits between the Application and Session layers, it also has to function as a conduit between the two. Likewise, ASCII-EBCDIC conversion is not so commonly needed that it should burden users who don't need it. And the Presentation layer never really solved the videotex problem; videotex vendors often prefer to keep their protocols proprietary.

The Application Layer (7). This is the highest layer defined by the OSIRM. What the Application layer is *not*, however, is the actual program that the user is running on each side of the connection. That is called the *Application Process* and is not part of the package; the Application Process is the eventual user of the OSI service! (Never, ever, call it "Layer 8" within earshot of OSI purists.) The Application layer instead is the protocol that provides specific services required for specific types of applications.

A few different Application layer protocols have been defined, with more to be developed in the future. *File Transfer and Manipulation* (FTAM) allows files to be copied, listed, created, and deleted. It supports both text-structured and binary files. FTAM is the best case for the existence of both the Session and Presentation layers, as it makes good use of their services. *Virtual Terminal Protocol* (VTP) permits users to log into remote computers. It is far more complex than earlier protocols (like the CCITT X.29 protocol often used over X.25 networks) and has seen relatively little use; its performance is questionable. *Job Transfer and Manipulation* (JTAM) supports remote batch job entry; it is sometimes viewed as a bit of an anachronism. *Message Handling Service* (MHS) provides for electronic mail, including multimedia as well as text formats. MHS began as part of CCITT Recommendation X.400 and is in effect the modern form of message switching! With over a century of progress, OSI has finally built a replacement for the telegram.

 One cannot do justice to the actual richness of the OSI Application layer in a small amount of space. While other OSI layers may involve more than one protocol working together, the Application layer has built a flexible and extensible structure for modular development.

Application Service Elements (ASEs) provide specific functions within the Application layer, while *Association Control Functions* coordinate the operation of the ASEs. These can in turn be nested into a *Multiple Association Control Function*, enabling two or more processes to be coordinated within a single application. A variety of general-purpose ASEs have been defined. The *Association Control Service Element* (ACSE) creates a context between the two ends of the connection. *Commitment, Concurrency, and Recovery* (CCR) provides checkpointing and other services. Other ASEs are defined for specific applications but may be recycled as the need arises.

If the OSI project is to be ultimately successful, its success will hinge on the utility of the Applications layer. As a general tool kit for distributed peer-to-peer processing, the Application layer offers power and flexibility. But the price of entry to OSI is not low. There are simpler ways to make use of packet switching, and they will remain in use until their users outgrow them.

The Internet Model and TCP/IP

While the world's leading standards bodies, including ISO and CCITT, have sworn their allegiance (at least in name) to the Open Systems Interconnection program, OSI is by no means the most widely used model of data communication as of the early 1990s. A more widely used set of protocols was developed in the 1970s and 1980s under contract to the Advanced Research Projects Agency (ARPA), part of the U.S. Department of Defense. ARPA was one of the pioneers of packet switching, having placed the experimental ARPAnet into service in 1972.

By 1982 the ARPAnet had adopted its second generation of protocols, which have come to be known as *TCP/IP*. This protocol suite is used on the ARPAnet's successor networks, including the Defense Data Network, the National Science Foundation's NSFnet, and a host of other government, educational, research, and commercial networks. Collectively, most of these networks are tied together as the *Internet*. (The Internet protocols can be described in terms of the OSI reference model, but this is made somewhat more difficult by the differences in the terminology. For consistency this text will use OSI terminology whenever possible.) Figure 2.12 shows a simplified Internet reference model.

The Internet protocol suite was originally adopted by ARPA but now has a life of its own. The *Internet Activities Board* (IAB) and its *Internet Engineering Task Force* are continuously improving the protocol suite, incorporating new subnet technologies like ISDN, SMDS, and Frame Relay, while new application protocols are also being adopted. IAB is unaffiliated with any major standards body, and its credibility is based upon public acceptance of its work, but the IAB is creating a new professional society, the Internet

Figure 2.12 *Simplified Internet (TCP/IP) reference model.*

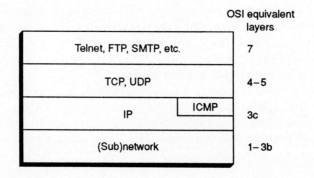

Society, to provide an open sponsor for its work. Internet protocols are essentially de facto standards, adopted by users without the imprimatur of an official standards body. This stands in marked contrast to the OSI and ISDN standardization processes.

Internets versus Subnets. In the Internet model the collective body of computers that can communicate with one another is referred to as an internet; this roughly corresponds to the OSI concept of a network. The Internet Protocol (IP) provides something very close to the connectionless network layer service. IP is in many respects similar to the OSI Connectionless Network Protocol (CLNP). It provides best-effort delivery of datagrams with no guarantee of sequentiality. The semantics of IP differ from OSI's CLNP in two major respects. IP addresses have a fixed-length (32 bit) address, and all header fields except for the last (*options*) have a fixed length. This tends to make it simpler to implement than CLNP, whose source and destination addresses can be up to 20 bytes long and which has other variable-length fields. With this simplicity comes a loss of flexibility, of course, but IP is still a long way from running out of unique addresses. (It has, however, run rather low on some kinds of addresses, owing to the way in which addresses are assigned.)

The Internet Protocol runs atop a subnetwork (called a *network* in traditional Internet dialect) that can be essentially anything. Many local connections use LANs, especially Ethernet. Wide area connections often use X.25, while others use the *Point to Point Protocol* (PPP), a variant of HDLC. A few, unfortunately, use *Serial Line Internet Protocol* (SLIP), a framing protocol that lacks error detection. SLIP users depend upon the weak arithmetic checksums in higher-layer protocols (TCP and IP) to detect transmission errors.

TCP Resembles the Transport Layer. While IP delivers datagrams across an arbitrarily complex network, the responsibility for reassembling the data back into order is left to the two ends of the connection. Sequential, reliable delivery is provided by *Transmission Control Protocol* (TCP), which bears a rather strong semblance to the OSI Transport Protocol Class 4. Again TCP and its OSI counterpart differ mostly in syntax; TCP again favors fixed-length header fields. One major difference is that TCP delivers a stream of bytes, while OSI Transport delivers discrete, bounded Transport Service Data Units. (In that sense, TCP incorporates a function of the OSI Session layer.) Applications are left to transform byte streams into records, as required.

TCP/IP does not have any equivalent of separate Session and Presentation layers. Most of the required capabilities of Session are performed within TCP, while any others, and Presentation, can be handled within applications that need them.

An alternative transport layer protocol, *User Datagram Protocol* (UDP), provides a connectionless service. This is used for applications that don't require sequentiality or that perform a simple task (such as looking up a name in a directory) for which the overhead of creating a TCP connection (virtual circuit) would be wasteful.

Several application protocols are widely used over TCP/IP. One of the most popular is the *Simple Message Transfer Protocol* (SMTP), which provides text-only electronic mail. SMTP is far simpler than the OSI equivalent (MHS, X.400), if again less flexible. *File Transfer Protocol* (FTP) provides both text and binary file transfers. It too is simpler than its OSI counterpart (FTAM), but it lacks a few of FTAM's features.

The *Telnet* protocol provides asynchronous terminal-to-host connectivity. It can be almost arbitrarily simple or complex on the basis of its many options; many computers use this for both local and remote logins. (It is slightly more complex than X.29, and much simpler than OSI VTP.) The *X Window System*[4] supports local and remote workstation computing using the Window, Icon, Mouse, Pointer (WIMP) style of human interface; while it can be run as an OSI application, it is more often used over TCP. It also requires considerable bandwidth: A 64 kbps ISDN connection is barely fast enough for an X Window session; most X Window System utilization does not extend beyond the LAN.

In many ways the Internet Protocols have filled the market niche for which OSI was intended: They are widely used, are available on many different computers, and provide the most-requested functions. It used to be fashionable to talk about migration from TCP/IP to OSI. Now it is more common to speak of their coexistence.

Systems Network Architecture

No discussion of packet-switched data communication would be complete without mention of Systems Network Architecture (SNA), the widely used premier data communications architecture of International Business Machines Corp. SNA was developed with a different premise than either TCP/IP or OSI. It is fundamentally hierarchical, designed to connect mainframe computers to terminals and other slave devices. Peer to peer operation has been added in recent years to support distributed computing.

The HDLC family of data link protocols began with SNA's SDLC, which uses polled (master/slave) operation. SNA networks can make use of X.25 or Frame Relay subnetworks. The upper layers are rather specialized too. Most IBM mainframe activity makes use of synchronous block-mode terminals that perform screen editing functions locally. Thus response time requirements are not especially stringent; the user perceives the delay only when the entire screen is being transmitted. On the other hand, these net-

---

[4] The *X Window System* was developed in conjunction with Project Athena at the Massachusetts Institute of Technology and is a trademark of MIT.

works require careful engineering to deliver any given level of performance and are thus rather labor-intensive.

IBM has more recently introduced *Advanced Peer to Peer Networking* (APPN), a first cousin to SNA that provides roughly the same services as OSI and TCP/IP. Within the SNA framework, peer-to-peer connectivity is provided with *Logical Unit 6.2.* (This isn't very mnemonic, but SNA terminology centers on *Physical Units* and *Logical Units* to refer to device and protocol types.)

Is the Public Packet Network Compatible?

Among the major data communication network architectures, OSI has an apparent head start toward becoming compatible with the types of packet service offered by ISDN. The OSI Connection-Oriented Network Protocol (ISO 8208) *is* essentially X.25. The CCITT even amended X.25 in 1984 in part to meet the requirements that had been adopted by ISO since the previous edition of X.25 (1980). And X.25's LAP-B protocol is also an OSI standard. But sharing a few protocols doesn't necessarily make a lot of difference once push comes to shove.

Many OSI users prefer the Connectionless Network Service, which treats X.25 as a dissimilar subnetwork protocol. Some of the features of X.25, such as order preservation and error recovery, are performed end-to-end in the OSI Transport Protocol Class 4, so X.25's efforts are, in some cases, potentially redundant and even possibly counterproductive. TCP/IP users are in the same class. Indeed, much of TCP/IP's success in recent years has come as a surprise to those who expected its users to migrate to OSI. If and when that migration does occur, it will almost certainly replace IP with OSI's CLNP (ISO 8473), not the X.25-oriented CONP.

SNA remains fully connection-oriented, but its hierarchical operation requires some effort to map into X.25 as well. The newer Frame Relay service, a streamlined packet mode that does not offer X.25's guarantees of low loss, may be a better match for SNA; it may also be useful for IP and CLNP-based networks.

Public packet switching in the ISDN era could find its greatest popularity in its original application: remote terminal to host dial-ins. Access to X.25, albeit at relatively low speed (less than 10 kbps) and with considerably more delay than a dial-up modem connection on an analog network, is available on the ISDN D channel. High-volume consumer-oriented dial-up services, not complex data communications, might remain the major users of public packet network services. The French experience with Minitels (millions of low-cost data terminals distributed to the home) is a good example of the sort of service for which a packet mode service will usually be the best solution. As other such services gain in popularity among personal computer users, packet services might finally experience real growth without depending upon subsidies.

Chapter
Three

Transmission Systems: The Digitization of the Network

The Impetus for ISDN

The course of evolution is replete with alternatives. Before any given outcome is reached, many crossroads are passed, many options are dismissed, and many details are settled in what might come to be viewed as an arbitrary way. But the overall direction somehow seems inviolable.

While many characters have played a role in it, the story of ISDN follows an obvious plot, with only the details left to highlight the authors' creativity. Telecommunications technology has been evolving toward an all-digital network for some years, and ISDN is in large part just the vehicle by which the many actors in the play can remain in harmony.

A network is built from *transmission* and *switching* components, which are held together by mutual adherence to a set of *protocols*. As the analog transmission and switching components were rendered obsolete by superior digital ones, a new set of protocols was needed to allow their full potential to be realized. ISDN provides a framework for the development of these components and protocols. But ISDN's own protocols are more a recent stage in the evolution of the digital network than an impetus for its continuance.

Message switching and packet switching have always been fundamentally digital technologies; circuit switching has only recently moved over to digital form. In the analog networks of the past, even digital switching, of both voice and data, had to be adapted to the requirements of analog transmission systems. In all-digital networks, such as ISDN, it is voice that has to be adapted to the requirements of digital transmission systems. This is not as difficult as it might seem; in practice, digital transmission systems provide better audio quality than the analog ones that they replace. Witness the digital compact disk; it has largely replaced the analog vinyl disk as the phonograph record of choice. The same principles lead telephony toward ISDN.

The Evolution of Digital Transmission Systems

The oldest transmission system in telecommunications is copper wire. The original telegraph wires strung across the landscape provided a digital medium that offered more than enough bandwidth for the human operators whose brass-pounding skill was so crucial to the early telegraph. The introduction of the telephone was also the beginning of bandwidth-limited transmission systems. The performance of the telephone was limited by the electrical properties of the copper conductors that supported it.

Voice-Frequency Loop Transmission

Any alternating current electrical signal is governed by the fundamental laws of electronics. In a simple, direct current circuit the amount of power that can be delivered is limited by the *resistance* of the conductors. Resistance, which converts electricity to heat, is constant at all frequencies. In an alternating current (AC) circuit, such as a telephone line, the equation grows more complex. Line *capacitance* (a property that tends to pass higher frequencies more readily than lower ones) and *inductance* (a property that tends to impede the flow of higher frequencies through a conductor) both serve to limit the ability to carry high-frequency signals. Capacitance between the two twisted conductors in a telephone line short-circuits some of the higher frequencies, while inductance restricts their flow. Thus the amount of *loss* in a transmission line tends to rise along with frequency.

In the early days of the telephone, loss alone was a major factor in limiting the range of telephone calls. All of the AC (signal) power was generated in the carbon microphone in the telephone instrument itself; enough of this had to reach the magnetic earpiece of the other party's instrument for the connection to be usable. Long-distance calls were sometimes made from special telephone booths equipped with extra-large mouthpieces!

A voice signal is carried across the telephone network within the nominal frequency range of 300–3400 Hz. This is certainly not hi-fi quality, but it suffices to make the human voice both intelligible and recognizable.

The first major development to extend the range of voice frequency telephone lines was the *loading coil.* This was an inductor placed in series with the line every few thousand feet. By canceling the capacitance at the high end of the audio frequency range, it improved intelligibility and allowed telephone lines to go more than a few miles. AT&T bought the patent on this invention just before its own original telephone patents ran out; this allowed it to develop a monopoly on "long-distance" (across a large city) telephony during the 1890s.

Vacuum tube amplification came into use during the early years of the twentieth century and made much longer ranges possible. Even then, each amplifier added *noise* to the connection, so the distant party's voice would eventually be lost even if more amplification could be added.

The development of transmission systems thus had to take into account a number of factors. Noise and distortion had to be limited, while cost had to be contained. The introduction of the negative feedback amplifier reduced distortion substantially, making it possible to have several amplifiers in a call, making even longer distances possible. This was followed by the development of a long line of transmission systems, the most recent of which use digital technology.

Analog Carrier

Before the introduction of digital technology, most long-distance telephone transmission made use of analog *carrier* systems. These are best understood by analogy to a radio: Just as you can tune a radio past many different stations, an analog carrier system puts many different telephone calls on a single wire pair or coaxial cable by modulating them onto different frequencies. This technique is called *frequency division multiplexing* (FDM). Long ranges are achieved by equipping the cable with radio frequency amplifiers, each capable of amplifying all channels at once.

The simplest FDM carrier systems run over simple twisted pair copper wire. Their channels are organized into a hierarchy. A *group* is 12 channels wide, providing 48 kHz of bandwidth. Higher-capacity systems combine five groups into a *supergroup* (see Fig. 3.1). Five or ten supergroups (depending upon whether you are in Europe or North America) can then be combined into a *mastergroup.* Even higher degrees of multiplexing can be accomplished. Were you to tap into one of these cables with a communications receiver, you could literally tune across the channels, one every 4 kHz (with certain spaces reserved).

The old Bell System deployed many thousands of miles of Type N carrier, which carried one or two groups over nonloaded cable-pairs, but its higher-density backbone routes were more likely to use Type L coaxial

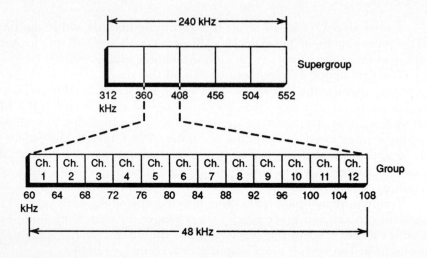

Figure 3.1 *Analog carrier system. Twelve 4 kHz channels are combined into a group, and five groups are combined into a supergroup.*

cable–based carrier systems. AT&T's lack of early enthusiasm for digital networks might have stemmed in part from its large investment in L carrier and similar microwave transmission systems. This transmission capacity was the most expensive part of the network; with many billions of dollars invested, moving toward digital networks would have meant a large write-off in still-working equipment. And it did; AT&T took a loss of several billion dollars (causing the one unprofitable quarter in its modern history) when it wrote off much of its analog plant in 1989.

Analog Microwave Radio. During World War II, microwave radio transmission equipment was developed for use in radar systems. After the war this technology was adapted for telecommunications use. Instead of superimposing many channels onto a cable, analog microwave radio systems use similar techniques to carried hundreds or thousands of individual channels through a single transmitter and receiver.

At its peak during the 1970s, over two thirds of AT&T's transmission capacity was in analog microwave technology. The bulk of this used frequencies in the 4 GHz and 6 GHz bands, where a reliable link could be established over distances of 30–40 miles, given a line-of-sight path. Shorter-haul links used higher frequencies (such as 18 GHz), while some low-density paths occupied a narrower frequency assignment near 2 GHz.

High-capacity microwave radio systems operate by a simple principle called the *heterodyne*. If you combine any two frequencies together in a nonlinear element (such as a simple diode), four frequencies are produced: Both originals are now joined by the sum and difference frequencies. So if a 1 kHz audio frequency is mixed with a 1 MHz radio frequency, the resulting signal will include components at 999 kHz and 1001 kHz (the difference and sum frequencies). That is in fact the principle behind amplitude modulation (AM), as used in broadcasting: Audio is mixed with a *carrier* signal, which is transmitted along with the two resultant *sidebands*.

Note that the sum and difference signals (*upper and lower sidebands*) are mirror-images of one another. If an audio signal were mixed with a radio signal, the resultant heterodynes would end up on both sides of the original carrier frequency, and the bandwidth used would be twice the original. (Note that in the above example the 999 kHz and 1001 kHz signals are 2 kHz apart, twice the bandwidth of the modulating signal.) In most analog transmission systems, one of these two sidebands is filtered out, effectively doubling the number of signals that fit into a given bandwidth. (The carrier is also suppressed by using a balanced mixer.) Thus it is very easy to map the sum of the audio bandwidths of all of the channels carried into the radio bandwidth of a carrier system.

In a microwave communications system the audio signals are mixed with low-frequency signals, and each is filtered into a single sideband, just as occurs with a cable-based carrier system. But in a microwave system the entire multiplexed bandwidth is heterodyned and filtered again to move it up to the microwave range. The relay stations needed every 30 miles or so can treat the entire signal as a unit, but complex multiplexing equipment is needed every time individual channels are used (at both ends of the multihop link).

Since the multiplexing and modulation processes occur at low frequencies, the radio system itself need not be limited to analog transmissions. This permits microwave radio systems to carry digital signals.

Data Under Voice and DDS. When demand for digital transmission began to build during the 1970s, AT&T (as both telephone company and manufacturer) introduced a way to combine analog and digital transmission on the same cable or microwave system. Called *data under voice* (DUV), it took advantage of "spare" bandwidth in the existing analog multiplex hierarchy to squeeze in a digitally modulated channel. Customers of *Dataphone Digital Service* (DDS) would receive channels from this "new" bandwidth, while the voice network used the original bandwidth. (Voice could not be carried at the fringes of the system's bandwidth because the transmission quality was inadequate. Digital systems needed only, of course, to properly regenerate 1's and 0's, so some distortion could be tolerated.)

AT&T was subject to strict rate regulation at the time and was facing serious competition for the first time. While an upstart originally called Microwave Communications Inc. (later MCI Communications Corp.) was concentrating on voice channels, Data Transmission Corp. (Datran) was building an all-digital microwave system and offering switched and unswitched digital transmission. AT&T hoped that by claiming that its DUV system utilized "spare" bandwidth, it would be allowed to offer DDS services at very competitive rates in order to meet the Datran challenge.

The FCC finally decided that DDS service should be priced the same as the equivalent analog channel and modem combination. DDS was thus preferable to analog services because it offered better quality, not lower rates. By 1977, Datran had gone bankrupt. AT&T's mostly analog network was king; competitors such as MCI and Sprint were also using mostly analog microwave. But this was the last gasp of analog radio; within a few years, digital transmission would rule the roost.

Modems: Digital Signals over Analog Transmission

While the bulk of transmission system development during the telephone's first century was analog, there was always a need to carry some digital data. Beginning with the telegraph and rapidly expanding once the computer era began, digital messages were a significant portion of telecommunications traffic.

The generic name for a device that encodes digital signals over an analog medium is *modem*, which is a contraction of the term modulator-demodulator. Claude Shannon proved mathematically that analog and digital information are interchangeable: Given a certain amount of analog *bandwidth* and a given *signal-to-noise ratio*, one can determine the theoretical limit of how many bits per second can be carried over the channel. In the typical case,

$$C = Bw \log_2 (1 + S/N)$$

where C is channel capacity in bits per second, Bw is bandwidth in hertz, and S/N is the signal-to-noise ratio, expressed arithmetically. For example, if a channel has a usable bandwidth of 3 kHz and a signal-to-noise ratio of 30 dB (i.e., a power ratio of 1000 to 1), then the channel capacity is 3000 * $\log_2$ (1001/1), or just under 30,000 bps. These numbers are typical of a modern telephone channel and slightly better than a typical transcontinental channel of the late analog era.

In practice, of course, no modem can achieve this theoretical limit; getting even halfway there is a challenge. Even that has taken years of development and improvements in semiconductor technology; the fastest modems use precision analog-to-digital converters and high-speed arithmetic circuits to perform digital signal processing (DSP).

Before the microchip era, typical modems were far slower. The very common Bell 103 Dataphone of the 1960s carried data at 300 bps over a single dial-up telephone line; private lines that provided fully independent transmit and receive channels ("four wire" circuits) could be stretched to 2400 bps by using different modems. Telex machines used modem speeds of

50–110 bps. By the mid-1970s, private line modems at 9600 bps and dial-up modems at 1200 bps were available, though costly.

Thanks to advances in DSP and large-scale integration (LSI) microchips that compress thousands of transistors onto a single chip, modern dial-up modems with a data rate of 9600 bps are now fairly common; CCITT Recommendation V.32 specifies the standard modulation technique, so many vendors' modems are interchangeable at this speed. A newer Recommendation V.32bis defines 14,400 bps modems. Proprietary modems and modems that operate over four-wire private lines can go even faster. Some vary their speed on the basis the line quality characteristics of the call and will take advantage of superior lines to raise the available data rate.

Be forewarned that some modems *appear* to be going faster than this but really aren't. Most transmitted data does not have a "random" bit pattern. Some bit patterns (for example, the letters *t* and *e* in English text and the null byte in computer data) are far more common than others. Some modems can take advantage of this fact to compress data before putting it onto the line. (The most common compression technique encodes the most common bit patterns as short strings, say, four bits long, while uncommon bit patterns are sent as longer strings.)

Data compression is possible on all-digital networks too, so a 64 kbps ISDN B channel can in some cases be given the appearance of, say, a 100 kbps channel. But the effectiveness of compression depends very much upon what is being transmitted. It tends to work well with plain text. In contrast, many computer bulletin boards store binary files in compressed, or "archived," form; there's little if any room for improvement when these are transmitted via a data compressor.

Digital transmission networks, and ISDN in particular, are sounding a death knell for modems, albeit a slow one. A network that can carry 9600 bps through a modem can carry 64,000 bps if converted to ISDN. Since the telephone industry has already replaced the vast majority of its long-distance transmission capacity to digital, the market for modems is declining. Already, private line modems are becoming a rarity as digital circuits replace them. But modems will remain important as long as ISDN is not universally available and as long as ISDN equipment is more costly than modems. Thus the death of the modem will be a long, slow one.

Digital Carrier Systems

The early telegraph wires carried signals at an effective rate of only a few bits per second. Telegraph networks were converted to use mostly automatic teleprinter machines early in the twentieth century. By the time switched teleprinter (Telex) service was introduced, the analog telephone network was quite advanced. Telex and other early data communications networks used modems to send bits over analog transmission lines.

T1 Carrier. The first digital transmission systems came into common use during the 1960s. AT&T's type T1 carrier system effectively set the standard for digitized voice, which has been carried through into ISDN.

T1 carrier uses unshielded twisted pair copper running at 1.544 Mbps, a rate formally known as digital signal level 1, or DS1. (The T carrier designation is more commonly used than the equivalent DS value, although the DS label is more generic. T carrier is actually the name of the transmission system; DS values designate data rates.) T1 carrier can go 6000 feet between repeaters; the repeater is itself a fairly simple device that can be mounted on a telephone pole, in a manhole, or in a pedestal.

The T1 carrier transmission system itself does not define how voice is carried. One can use T1 in many different ways. Some multiplexors use proprietary techniques to fit flexible combinations of voice and data onto it; others simply try to maximize voice capacity. The only requirements placed by the transmission system (and thus imposed upon customers of unswitched private line service, such as AT&T's Accunet T1.5) are those imposed by the transmission requirements.

T1 carrier sends information in *frames* of 193 bits, with 8000 frames sent per second. Most T1 transmission systems require that the user respect the framing and observe framing rules for the 193rd bit in each frame. The other 192 bits are available as payload. The pattern sent by successive framing bits defines a *superframe*. In old-style T1 the superframe is 12 frames long. A newer *extended superframe* technique uses 24 frames per superframe, with the framing bit available to carry both a maintenance channel and an error-detecting checksum (useful for monitoring link quality).

The T1 carrier modulation technique is called *Alternate Mark Inversion* (AMI). A digital 1 (called *mark* in telegrapher's terms) is transmitted as a three-volt pulse whose shape is rather strictly defined. A digital 0 (*space*) is sent as no pulse. Each mark is of the opposite polarity from the previous one, so the 1's balance out over time. It's important to note that the timing of the signal is carried by the pulses themselves. There is no separate clock signal, so the system is self-clocking (*isochronous*). Figure 3.2 shows a diagram of T1 carrier using AMI.

A minor problem with simple AMI is that a long string of spaces can lead to a loss of timing, since that would lead to a gap in transmission. So T1 carrier, in its oldest form, requires that at least 12% of bits be 1's and that no more than 15 consecutive 0's be sent. In a purely voice environment this isn't critical; standard (PCM) voice coding simply doesn't ever send the all-zero octet and uses all 1's for silence. But if an all-zero octet were sent into a T1 system, it would change the low order bit to a 1. In a data environment, of course, changing any bits is unacceptable.

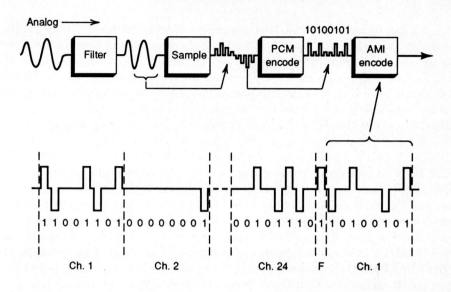

Figure 3.2 *T1 carrier as used for telephony. 24 voice channels, each sent as eight bits, are transmitted in sequence. Alternate Mark Inversion signaling is used. A single framing (F) bit identifies each 193-bit frame.*

A few solutions to this problem exist. One that has been implemented in most North American T1 systems is called *Bipolar 8-zero Substitution* (B8ZS). Whenever eight consecutive 0's occur in the transmitted pattern, they are replaced by a special pattern that includes a specific *bipolar violation*: A mark is sent with the same polarity as the previous mark, something that is normally forbidden in AMI transmission. While most bipolar violations are tagged as errors, this specific pattern is recognized as a special case, and the receiver treats it as a string of 0's.

Another solution that does not require B8ZS to be implemented is called *Zero Byte Time Slot Inversion* (ZBTSI). This works across a superframe, using framing bits to point to the first all-zero octet and using that octet to point to the next one. A rather complex scheme, it has found some use where the telephone company has failed to implement B8ZS.

A simpler solution, albeit a more wasteful one, is to simply limit data channels to use only seven out of every eight consecutive bits in a T1 frame. The remaining bit is always sent as a 1, guaranteeing both the 1's density and maximum consecutive 0's requirement. This technique gave rise to the 56 kilobit services that were prevalent in North America before ISDN became widespread; it is really a 64 kbps DS0 channel (eight consecutive bits in a frame) with one bit reserved. (The 56 kbps rate also comes into use because of bit-robbed signaling, described below.)

A somewhat more efficient technique is defined for ISDN in North America. A 64 kbps channel is allowed to carry any bit pattern *except* eight consecutive 0's. Some data protocols (notably the HDLC family) use bit stuffing for framing purposes; a 0 is inserted in every long string of 1's. This is backward from what T1 carrier requires, but inverting the bits (swapping 1's and 0's) allows HDLC to meet T1's requirements while running at a full 64 kbps. But most American telephone companies are ignoring this option.

CEPT-1 Transmission. These difficulties with T1 do not plague Europeans because T1 carrier is found mainly in North America and (with some variations) Japan. The Council of European Posts and Telegraphs (CEPT) some years ago developed an improved version of the T1 carrier system. Sometimes called CEPT-1, or informally E1, and defined in CCITT Recommendation G.703, AMI transmission is sent at a bit rate of 2.048 Mbps. This is exactly 32 times 64 kbps; each frame contains 256 bits. Recommendation G.704 describes its channel structure, with one of its 64-kbps channels devoted to framing, one to signaling, and 30 to digitized voice.

E1 systems have always used a bipolar violation scheme to provide complete bit sequence transparency. Not quite the same as North American B8ZS, E1's *HDB3* (High-Density Binary 3) technique substitutes a special bipolar violation pattern for every three consecutive 0's. The channel banks used with E1 systems also never used robbed-bit signaling (see below), so there are essentially no restrictions on data transmission.

The Channel Bank. T1 carrier was developed to carry voice, and the transmission system thus requires a companion device to digitize voice. The traditional telephone company device for doing this is called a *channel bank*. This combines the analog-to-digital (and back again!) conversion with multiplexing.

The oldest digital channel bank was AT&T's model D1, built before the integrated circuit was invented and thus quite bulky and costly. This split the T1 pipe into 24 channels, each eight bits wide. Each channel carried a seven-bit PCM voice sample and one bit for supervision (on-hook/off-hook and dial pulses). Later models (such as the popular D3, widely deployed during the 1970s and early 1980s) used eight-bit PCM, with the low order bit "robbed" only on every sixth frame. (This still provided over 1000 samplings per second, more than enough to indicate the condition of a switch hook or carry dial pulses.)

European (E1) channel banks began with eight-bit PCM, with signaling on its own channel and thus no bit robbing. In analog-based networks this signaling carries the same sort of on-hook/off-hook information as T1/D3. By adding a new protocol it also evolves nicely into the D channel of the ISDN Primary Rate Interface (European flavor).

Incompatibility across the Pond. The technique used for digitizing voice is called Pulse Code Modulation (PCM). Each audio channel is first filtered to prevent signals above 4 kHz from being carried. Then the audio is sampled 8000 times a second. In a typical modern implementation a 12-bit numeric value is then obtained. This value is then *compressed* for transmission as an eight-bit value and *expanded* on receive.[1] The transmission rate is thus 64 kbps (eight bits times 8000 samples per second).

But the *companding* (compression-expansion) formula used in North America is not the same one that is used in Europe. The North American standard (originally adopted by AT&T) is called μ255; the European standard (from CEPT) is called A-law. So a digital voice call that goes between Europe and North America must have its digital values changed to be compatible with the other companding scheme. A digital network therefore must know whether a call is voice or data: It *must* perform code conversion on some voice calls but must *not* modify the bit values on data calls! This becomes a significant issue in distinguishing between ISDN's different bearer services (see Chapter 4).

T1C and T2 Carrier. The next step in the evolution of digital transmission was to increase the speed of the carrier. To this end, AT&T invented the T2 carrier system. This operates at the *DS2* rate of 6.312 Mbps and carries four DS1 signals. T2 carrier was designed to operate over special twisted pair cable. While the basic modulation technique is AMI, it is even more sensitive than T1 to long strings of 0's, so it has always used a substitution pattern called *B6ZS* that replaces a string of six 0's with a particular bipolar violation pattern.

T2 has a data rate that is slightly higher than four times the DS1 rate, even though it carries only four DS1 signals. This accommodates the *asynchronous* nature of T2 carrier: The four DS1s are not expected to be timed according to the same clock as the T2, or for that matter each other. So one of the DS1s may be running a few bits per second slower than nominal, and another may be faster. T2 carries overhead to accommodate this; overhead bits may be added or thrown away as necessary.

The four DS1 channels are interleaved on a bit basis: Bits from each DS1 are transmitted one after the other. This contrasts with T1 carrier, in which the eight-bit samples from each channel are normally transmitted intact (byte interleaved).

T2 carrier never really caught on. While some was deployed, its existence is mainly theoretical, as a stage between T1 and the faster T3. DS2

---

[1] The digital μ255 compression algorithm in effect turns the 12-bit integer into an eight-bit floating point number, with a sign bit, a three-bit exponent, and a four-bit mantissa. This closely approximates the companding curve that is nominally specified, and can be easily implemented.

signals exist within multiplexors, and some low-capacity digital radios operate at the DS2 data rate, but few T2 carrier systems are in use. A later invention, T1C, carries 48 voice channels, placing it halfway between T1 and T2. While not a "standard," T1C has seen some use because it will run over a more common grade of cable than T2.

The CEPT/CCITT (European) hierarchy includes an 8.448 Mbps transmission system as the second level of its hierarchy, carrying four E1 carriers. This "E2" uses the same HDB3 coding as E1 carriers. Japan follows the speeds of the North American hierarchy as far as T2, though it diverges at higher speeds.

T3 and Faster Digital Carrier Systems. The next step up in the North American hierarchy is, not surprisingly, DS3, commonly referred to as T3 carrier system. Operating at a speed of 44.736 Mbps, it is generally configured to carry seven DS2 signals and thus 28 DS1s or 672 DS0s. Again it is asynchronous, allowing the DS2s to operate at slightly different frequencies.

T3 carrier was designed to operate over coaxial cable. It uses AMI coding with a three-bit zero substitution technique called *B3ZS*. T3 is not uncommon and is even offered as a private line service by many telephone companies. But at these rates, copper-based transmission is often no longer the most economical approach. Optical fiber systems have become more common. Many such systems operate at DS3 and multiples thereof, while providing T3 copper interfaces into higher-rate multiplexing equipment.

Level 3 of the European digital hierarchy is again a simple quadrupling of the previous level; E3 systems thus carry 480 voice channels with a bit rate of 34.368 Mbps. Copper-based E3, as defined in CCITT G.703, also uses the same HDB3 line signaling technique. Japan's own native multiplexing hierarchy departs from that of North America here too, and its level 3 rate (32.064 Mbps) is also designed to carry 480, not 672, DS0 channels.

The North American DS4 rate (274.176 Mbps, intended for 4032 DS0 or voice channels) was defined but never widely implemented. The European level 4 rate, 139.264 Mbps, is perhaps more widely seen, being again four times the previous level's rate and capable of carrying 1920 DS0 channels.

Digital Microwave Radio. With the bulk of long-distance traffic carried over microwave radio in the 1970s, the move to digital transmission didn't ignore this common medium. Analog microwave radio was popular because it made efficient use of that rarest commodity: bandwidth on the radio spectrum. With little more than 4 kHz of spectrum needed for each voice channel, single-sideband analog radio was hard to beat. But it didn't provide the high transmission quality of digital media and wasn't very efficient for carrying data. Digital radio systems have thus been developed to address both of these issues.

Since radio is an inherently analog medium, the techniques needed to build digital radios are essentially the same ones used in building modems. In effect, a digital radio system begins with a radio modem. These differ from wireline modems mainly in bandwidth: While most wireline modems are designed to fit into a 4 kHz wide channel, digital radios are allowed much larger bandwidths, often many megahertz wide. Depending upon the frequency band at which the radio operates, the allowable bandwidth of a point-to-point microwave radio link may be in the 80 MHz range. In contrast, digital cellular telephones carry a single voice channel using the same channel bandwidth as an analog cellular telephone, fitting into about 20 kHz. (However, these do not use 64 kbps PCM but instead use newer low-bit-rate voice coding techniques.)

A number of modulation techniques have been used to fit as many bits per second as possible into a radio channel. Shannon's laws that limit digital bit rate of an analog channel apply here with a vengeance: The signal-to-noise ratio of a radio channel determines the maximum bandwidth efficiency. Microwave radio channels are prone to fading from weather effects (such as "rain fade" and ducting, which diverts signals from their path). On an analog system these gradually reduce the quality of transmission. Digital radio systems show only a small increase in the bit error rate until the signal falls below a threshold level, below which point the error rate skyrockets until the signal is lost.

The simplest methods of modulating a digital radio transmit one bit at a time. Frequency Shift Keying (FSK), also used in the slowest wireline modems (typically running at 300 bps), will not even achieve an efficiency of 1 bps per Hertz of bandwidth. But it is cheap and easy to implement, so it finds use in some systems. Phase Shift Keying (PSK), which involves encoding bits by shifting the phase of the signal, can encode one or more bits at a time. Binary PSK (BPSK), the simplest form, shifts (or doesn't shift) the signal 180 degrees at a time to encode a single 1 or 0. But two bits at a time can be encoded by using 4PSK (four-phase PSK), in which the phase shift resolution is 90 degrees. Likewise, smaller phase shifts can encode more bits: 8PSK and 16PSK encode three and four bits, respectively. These use the same bandwidth as BPSK and thus provide better spectrum efficiency, but they cost more to implement and require better signal-to-noise ratios.

Most digital microwave radios actually combine amplitude and phase modulation in a scheme called Quadrature Amplitude Modulation (QAM). In wireline modems, QAM can fit 9600 bps down a voice channel. Similar efficiencies are possible on radio. The highest-capacity QAM radios encode nine bits into a single pulse, whose phase and amplitude translate to one of 512 possible patterns! This allows over 6 bps to be transmitted per Hertz of bandwidth.

As with the highest-performing wireline modems, high-capacity digital microwave radios do not turn all of their bandwidth over to usable payload. Some is devoted to error detection and correction. A common scheme, called *trellis coding*, reserves some of the possible bit patterns in the *constellation* of phase and amplitude combinations. If the receiver detects these, it knows that it has received an invalid value; it then attempts to compensate. Another part of the error correction strategy is to code blocks of bits into slightly longer blocks according to specific mathematical rules. These *forward error correction* (FEC) techniques allow some bit errors to be recovered, with no visible effect on the delivered payload.

Note, however, that if a block of data is severely errored (e.g., by serious interference or fading) such that the forward error correction fails, then a multibit error will occur. This doesn't occur on T carrier or optical fiber systems that transmit one bit at a time. But it does occur when modems are used over analog circuits.

Fiber Optics

While copper and radio waves were the transmission media of choice before the 1980s, that decade saw the telecommunications industry dramatically shift the bulk of its long-distance transmission into a medium that had been little more than a curiosity just a decade earlier. Optical fiber used to be a novelty item used for "lava lamps" and had a few other specialty applications such as medical imaging, in which it could carry light at most a few feet. But during the 1970s, new manufacturing techniques led to ultrapure glass that could carry light for many kilometers.

A fiber optic strand consists of a *core* surrounded by *cladding*, as shown in Fig. 3.3. The core carries light, while the cladding contains it by reflection and refraction. These are surrounded by structural support. Light, generated by either a light-emitting diode or a semiconductor laser, is then focused into

Figure 3.3 *Simplified cross section of an optical fiber. Light travels through the core, guided by the different refractive characteristics of the cladding. Single-mode fiber has the smallest core (about 10 microns).*

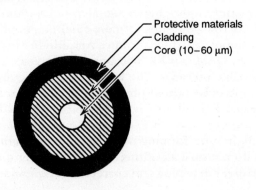

one end of the strand; the distant end feeds the light into a light-sensitive silicon diode.

Almost all fiber optic transmission systems are digital, carrying bits of information in the form of pulses. (Analog fiber optics exist but are rarely used for commercial telecommunications.) The information capacity of a strand is thus rated in bits per second. This tends to decrease with distance as the light loses its focus and the pulses tend to run together.

Fiber optics used in telecommunications can be divided into three basic types. The first two, *step index* and *graded index* multimode fiber, are relatively inexpensive; they differ in the design of the cladding. Graded index fibers are newer and support a higher bit rate than the step index type. *Single mode* fibers have a much smaller core and are more costly to manufacture and install but have a much greater range.

Step Index and Graded Index Fibers. The core of a multimode fiber is many times larger than the wavelength of light (which is about a micron, or a millionth of a meter, depending upon the color). In a step index fiber the cladding simply reflects the light so that it bounces along its way. The angle at which the light waves hit the cladding is not constant, which leads to *modal dispersion* and a reduction in useful bandwidth over distance. Graded index fibers have a cladding whose index of refraction gradually varies with distance from the core. The effect of this is to counteract modal dispersion and extend the effective range.

Multimode fibers now come in several standard varieties, with core diameters ranging from about 50 to 100 microns. Local telephone companies use graded index fibers for much of their interoffice plant. At DS3 rates, a graded index fiber can easily carry a signal for over 20 km without repeaters. This is also a good way to deliver high-speed private line services (T3 rate) to customers in lieu of copper local loops. It is also used to carry both analog and ISDN switched services to customers, with glass going to a field-mounted multiplexor and copper used only for the "last mile."

Single-Mode Fibers. The highest capacity fibers have the smallest core. In single-mode fiber optics the core diameter is only about 10 microns. This effectively keeps the light waves traveling the "straight and narrow" path, with little room for modal dispersion.

Single-mode fiber is more expensive to manufacture and significantly harder to install. But for high-capacity or long-range transmission it can't be beat. Single-mode systems can run for tens of kilometers between repeaters with a per-strand capacity measured in billions of bits per second.

Most major long distance carriers now depend upon single-mode fiber optics for most of their capacity. For many of them the challenge is no longer how to provide enough bandwidth. Instead, it's how to find markets for the huge surpluses that were created by the installation of single-mode fibers!

The familiar telephone rate structure was created during the era when long-distance transmission was very expensive. Long-distance switched services have historically subsidized local telephone service. In many cases, more than half of the price of a long-distance call is applied to cover the cost of local service. Technology, in this case single-mode fiber optics, has changed the underlying nature of the business faster than the regulatory system has been able to absorb it. This is beginning to change in the ISDN era, as competition's "invisible hand" forces rates to move closer to costs. But it's not going to happen overnight.

SONET and the Synchronous Digital Hierarchy

The traditional North American and CCITT digital transmission hierarchies evolved in an era when analog reigned supreme. Digital "islands" were surrounded by an analog sea. Virtually every service used to begin and end at channel banks, terminating in T1 signals; higher-rate digital carriers were simply a medium for more T1s.

In the mid-1980s, Bellcore led an effort to develop a new digital transmission hierarchy aimed at an all-digital network. They called it SONET, for Synchronous Optical Network (SONET). This technology was brought to the CCITT, where part of it was accepted into Recommendations G.707 through G.709, under the name Synchronous Digital Hierarchy (SDH). North American and European terminology differ somewhat, but the technology itself is gaining worldwide acceptance.

Compared to the multistep multiplexing needed to make use of even a single T3 carrier, SONET is the essence of simplicity. Only one step is needed to locate any DS0 channel in a SONET pipe of any capacity, ranging up to 2.4 gigabits per second! The basic SONET unit of capacity is the Synchronous Transmission Stream (STS). With a rate of 51.84 Mbps, STS-1 is designed as a replacement for DS3. The next higher rate, STS-3 (155.20 Mbps), is equivalent to three DS3s or four E3s. This "lowest common denominator" is thus the bottom of the CCITT SDH hierarchy and is called STM-1. (A Synchronous Transport Module is three times the equivalent STS rate. Thus STM-4 equals STS-12.)

Like practically everything else in digital telecommunications, SONET timing is based on the same 8000 frames per second used for T1. SONET uses a "two-dimensional" framing technique, as shown in Fig. 3.4. Beginning with one frame 8000 times per second, each frame is first divided into nine *rows*. Each row is then divided into *columns*, each eight bits wide. STS-1 has 90 columns. The leftmost (first transmitted) three columns are SONET overhead. Higher rates simply multiply the columns. STS-3 has 270 columns, with nine used for overhead; STS-12 has 1080 columns.

A single DS0 (64 kbps) channel can be located at the intersection of any column and any row. Traditional digital hierarchy signals can also be

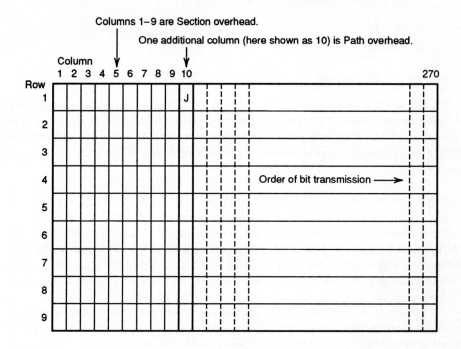

Figure 3.4 *In the SONET STM-1 frame structure, 8000 frames are transmitted per second, from row 1 to row 9. Each column represents eight bits; at 155.52 Mbps (STM-3), 270 columns are used.*

carried by creating *virtual tributaries* out of groups of contiguous columns. A DS1 stream requires three columns; E1 requires four.

In practice, SONET tolerates some variation in clock rates. The entire payload, in fact, may "float" slightly around within the frame; the overhead columns are then out of sync with the payload, and a pointer in the overhead indicates where the payload really begins. This is small change, though, compared to the complexity of, say, a T3 carrier system with all of its associated multiplexors.

SONET has other features that set it apart from earlier transmission systems. Its overhead includes alarm channels, *order wire* channels for carrier use, and reserved bandwidth for future applications. And by providing direct access to all of the channels within the frame it facilitates the provision of high-bandwidth services. A switching system designed for use with SONET can provide circuit-switched bandwidth in multiples of 64 kbps up to the full payload capacity of its SONET interface. Such flexibility was not anticipated in the early design of ISDN but will be seen in new multirate services. SONET has also been selected as the medium of choice for Broadband ISDN, in which STM-1 and STM-4 signals will be used for the local loop in some countries, including the United States.

Digital Loop Transmission

With digital carrier systems such as T1 and SONET dominating high-capacity transmission systems the last outpost of widespread analog transmission is also the oldest. The local loop, connecting the telephone set to the central office, has remained analog even after switching and trunk transmission have gone digital.

In many areas the local loop is already partially digitized. Digital loop carrier systems, often based on T1 or G.703 carrier technology but increasingly using optical fiber, carry groups of telephone lines from the central office to a neighborhood, office park, or other such area. These *subscriber line carrier* systems offer superior performance and lower costs in comparison to long runs of twisted pair copper loop plant. A multiplexing device, often mounted in a pedestal or manhole, converts back to analog for delivery to the subscriber.

This last piece of the puzzle is ISDN's to complete. Since the local loop affects the customer's choice of equipment as well as the telephone carrier's, it must conform to a standard that all vendors can meet. Just as there have been many options that the developers of trunk carrier systems have had to choose among, the selection of standards for digital loop transmission hasn't been easy.

ISDN actually encompasses three different types of digital local loop. The slowest, the *Basic Rate Access*, carries two channels of 64 kbps plus one 16 kbps channel. It is unique to ISDN; its characteristics will be discussed in Chapter 6. The *Primary Rate Access* offers higher capacity; its physical medium is T1 or E1 carrier, depending upon local custom. *Broadband* access will make use of SONET, but without the virtual tributary structure or any other fixed channelization. Instead, it is based on a novel technique called *Asynchronous Transfer Mode* and will be discussed in Chapter 8.

The Integrated Services

Three Categories of Service

Can a Swiss Army knife replace a whole toolbox? Probably not, but it can certainly reduce the number of times that one must dig into the toolbox. In designing ISDN the CCITT had to decide on a core set of services that could be more economically provided by a single network than by separate ones. In the time since that outline was settled, new services have been added to the list as the worldwide telecommunications industry used ISDN as its vehicle to modernize service.

If one were to study the CCITT I-Series Recommendations that define ISDN, an immensely detailed picture of its services would emerge. The standards process takes service definitions very seriously. Development of a new service begins with a decision by CCITT Study Group I that a service is worth studying. Then CCITT Study Group XVIII casts a full-scale service description. This follows a lengthy and somewhat rigid format that only a bureaucrat could love. The prose service description (Stage 1) is followed by a set of detailed information flows (Stage 2). Once this is complete, it is "thrown over the transom" to CCITT Study Group XI, which writes the required protocols (Stage 3).

In practice, of course, it isn't that simple. ISDN's most basic protocols were written without benefit of a service description, largely on the basis of historical practice. Service descriptions have thus been written to describe what already exists! The three-stage process is more commonly followed for supplementary services. And when protocols for new services are written, the service description is sometimes viewed as more of a rough guideline than as a rigid prescription. This doesn't occur for malicious reasons; rather, it's just often not practical to rigidly follow the service descriptions. Sometimes the service description is amended to reflect the final protocol.

Finally, the actual implementations of the services don't always come out exactly according to the standard. Equipment manufacturers and service providers both have a vested interest in preserving their pre-ISDN investment. Most of the cost of switching system development is in software; if a standard doesn't reflect a given vendor's existing implementation, the standard will often be ignored. It's just not practical, in all cases, for the services to be provided identically at all times, even if they are supposed to be based on a standard.

In defining services, the CCITT has broken them down into three categories. Most fundamental are the *bearer* services. These are the basic carrier offerings that carry voice and data; every call begins with selection of a bearer service. (In OSI terminology, bearer services operate between layers 1 and 3 but no higher.) *Supplementary* services operate in conjunction with bearer service. They're the "features" and the options that add value to a bearer service. Finally, there are *teleservices*. This category includes higher-layer services that involve computer processing of user data by the network. This last category is most controversial, since it extends beyond the traditional realm of the common carrier (although many PTTs have long provided similar services). Indeed, in the United States, local telephone companies aren't even allowed to offer teleservices, lest they impede competition, except under very tight constraints.

Bearer Services

In the CCITT's formal definition, ISDN evolves out of an *Integrated Digital Network* (IDN), an all-digital circuit-switched telephone network. In practice, the IDN never existed. Had it been built, it would have featured circuit-switched voice and data transmission as its bearer services. ISDN adds packet-switched bearer services, and Broadband ISDN will add novel bearer services of its own.

Bearer services are so called because they act as simple carriers, carrying information unchanged from end to end. This does not mean that the bits presented to the network necessarily come out unchanged; rather, the *information content* is unchanged, even if that necessitates changing the bits! (For example, telephone calls need to have their digitization format changed on calls between North America and Europe.) When a call is made, the caller has to specify which bearer service to use so that the network can give it the proper treatment.

ISDN bearer services provide a superset of what previous public switched networks offered. Circuit-switched services provide either a simple bit pipe or an audio pipe. (The differences are subtle but important.) Packet-switched services carry data with assurance of delivery, more or less. In general, the bearer service to be used for any given call is selected or negotiated at the time the call is originated, enabling a single interface to provide a wealth of choices.

The 64 kbps Clear Channel Bearer Service

The most fundamental ISDN circuit-switched bearer service, or at least the one that appears to be the simplest, provides a simple bit pipe at the standard rate of 64 kbps. Its formal name is *Circuit mode 64 kbit/s Unrestricted 8 kHz Structured Bearer Service*. This bit rate wasn't chosen arbitrarily, of course; it's the bandwidth that is most widely used for carrying voice. ISDN evolved from digital telephony, so this bandwidth was simply a given. The 64 kbps bearer service uses the standard DS-0 channel, which in ISDN is referred to as a *B channel* (where B stands for "bearer").

While this is largely intended as a data service, it isn't something that most data communications users would have asked for, had they been asked. It's more bandwidth than many applications, such as remote login using "dumb" asynchronous terminals, need. And it's less bandwidth than is required by many other applications, particularly the computer-to-computer connections which Local Area Networks specialize in. It's just the bandwidth that the telephone network offers.

But for many applications, 64 kbps is a fine value. It's several times faster than one can get from dial-up modems over analog telephone lines. Batch file transfer, electronic mail, and many other computer network functions are well suited to the 64 kbps speed. And the latest generation of remote computer terminals, using graphic protocols such as the *X Window System,*[1] can barely get by using 64 kbps. Low-bandwidth video conferencing systems and digital facsimile systems can also use 64 kbps channels.

---

[1] *X Window System* is a trademark of Massachusetts Institute of Technology.

The fundamental nature of this service, of course, is that the bits come out exactly the way they go in. The user presents 8000 octets (or eight-bit bytes) of data per second on a B channel on one interface, and they come out unchanged on a B channel elsewhere.

What if the user wants more than 64 kbps? Can two B channels be combined? By the definition of this service, no; each 64 kbps channel is independent of the other. It is *8 kHz structured* at only eight bits at a time. Two different calls placed at the same time between the same two points may end up being routed over different network facilities, or over different parts of the switch fabric, with different propagation delays, so they can't be viewed as one big channel.

H-Channel Circuit-Switched Bearer Services. While the 64 kbps B channel is ISDN's principal stock in trade, several higher-speed channels have also been defined. These are called *H channels* and are, by their nature, available only on the Primary Rate interface. H channels provide fixed increments of bandwidth that can be used both for circuit-mode services and to access packet-mode services.

The H_0 channel offers six times the capacity of a B channel, providing 384 kbps. Thus the 384 kbps bearer service provides 48 bits at a rate of 8 kHz. The H_{11} channel uses up all 24 slots in the North American T1 carrier, providing 1.536 Mbps of bandwidth; its European equivalent is the H_{12} channel, which provides 1.920 Mbps, 30 times the size of a B channel.

The astute reader will note that the European version of the Primary Rate has room for 31 channels (30B + D), while the North American provides only 24 (23B + D). So how does the H_{11} channel work? Initially, only one technique was proposed: A minimum of two Primary Rate interfaces would be needed, with the D channel on one controlling the H_{11} channel on the other (as well as its own, lower-rate channels). Europe, on the other hand, needed no such "kludge." So the H_{10} channel was introduced, offering 23 times the bandwidth of the B channel, leaving room for a D channel on a poor, lowly T1-based North American PRI.

2 x 64 kbps and Alternate Speech/64 kbps Bearer Services. The principle of being able to maintain exact bit ordering for all bits presented to an interface is sometimes called *8 kHz integrity*. The 64 kbps bearer service provides 8 kHz integrity for a single B channel. Since this is clearly inadequate for many users and the H channels are inflexible, some ISDN providers have added newer services that provide 8 kHz integrity across more than one B channel at a time. While these services are 8-kHz structured, they deliver more than eight bits at a time.

The 2 x 64 kbps bearer service allows two B channels to be treated as something not quite equal to single 128 kbps pipe. (This service is defined by the CCITT but not by ANSI, indicating that it is not generally accepted in North America. Its strongest advocates are the Japanese.) What distinguishes this from two separate calls, besides the possibility of a cheaper tariff, is the *restricted differential time delay*. The two channels need not be delivered exactly as one 128 kbps pipe, but the amount of time it takes to get across one channel should be maintained fairly close to what it takes to get across the other. In principle, if two independent calls are made between the same two interfaces, one could be routed via satellite and the other terrestrially; this service prevents that from happening.

This option is well suited to the Basic Rate interface, with its two B channels. But it doesn't really provide the sort of 128 kbps pipe that some users would find desirable.

Another variant bearer service defined by CCITT (in which the strongest support came from Belgium) but not by ANSI is the alternate speech/64 kbps unrestricted service. This is reminiscent of the old alternate voice/data private lines of the 1970s, allowing one circuit to switch between applications. In this new ISDN service the user selects it and the initial mode at call setup time; the user may then switch between the speech bearer service and the 64 kbps service without ending the call. This can be useful for some kinds of specialized applications, like multimedia telephone calls or giving speech introductions to fax images.

Multirate Bearer Service. One of the newest bearer services to be introduced to ISDN is the *Multirate bearer service*, which allows any number of B channels on the larger Primary Rate interface to be treated as a single bit pipe with 8 kHz integrity. This allows, for example, one call to specify 256 kbps while another specifies 192 kbps at the same time on the same interface.

These services have not come about without controversy; neither was in the 1988 CCITT Blue Book, nor in the original ANSI standards. Some switching equipment designed for telephony does not easily provide 8-kHz integrity across more than one channel, so some manufacturers were naturally reluctant to allow such flexibility.[2] In practice, these higher-rate services will not be widely available during ISDN's early years. Just getting them mentioned in the standards was hard enough!

Restricted Bearer Services. While the 64 kbps clear channel service seems simple enough, its availability in some instances will be delayed by an artifact of the old North American digital transmission hierarchy. T1 carrier was developed for voice transmission. In its original form, its self-clocking nature

---

[2] Northern Telecom introduced the multirate bearer service after developing the capability in its S/DMS switches, scheduled for initial deployment in 1991. Other manufacturers are expected to follow.

imposes certain requirements on what's carried over it. At least 15% of bits must be 1's, and no more than 15 consecutive 0's may be transmitted or the link can lose synchronization.

The long-term fix for this has already been identified and is being installed; the Bipolar 8-Zero Substitution (*B8ZS*) coding scheme provides total bit transparency (see Fig. 4.1). But until all T1 carrier systems and DS-1 interfaces are upgraded, some calls won't be able to use the 64 kbps bandwidth, or higher rates, without restrictions. The 64 kbps restricted bearer service is the result: It provides a 64 kbps bit pipe with the restriction that no *all-zero octet* be transmitted. The 255 other values are fine, but all zeroes is out!

Whether or not this is a problem depends upon the nature of the data to be transmitted. If the data uses any form of the HDLC protocol family, then it should have no problem because HDLC bit stuffing adds a 0 into every string of five or more 1's. To be sure, that guarantees 0's density, not 1's density, but that's solved by simply inverting all the bits for transmission! HDLC is by far the most popular family of data link protocols today and includes the LAPD protocol defined for ISDN D channels.

For other types of data the "64R" service is somewhat more limiting. Generally, one copes by simply using seven bits out of each octet, setting one bit to 1 in every octet, leaving unrestricted bandwidth of 56 kbps.

Figure 4.1 *Bipolar 8-zero Substitution applied to T1 carrier. With the illustrated sample data applied to straight AMI, 17 consecutive bit intervals with no signal would exist. This is unacceptable, so a special pattern, not otherwise allowed, is inserted in place of a block of eight consecutive 0's. Europe uses a functionally equivalent substitution pattern, HDB3.*

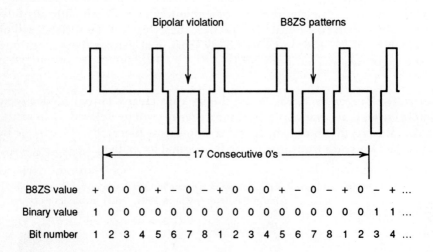

Restricted circuit-mode service exists only in North America and may not actually see much use; Bellcore prefers a 56 kpbs alternative. The ANSI standard service definition mentions it only in a footnote,[3] though it is supported in the call control protocol, in which it is not limited to the 64 kbps speed. The E1 (2.048 Mbps) carrier system used in Europe does not impose any restrictions on transmitted data. Most North Americans should never see it, since B8ZS upgrades are planned but may not always precede ISDN deployment.

A related service that is *not* found in CCITT standards but is actually implemented by several Bell Companies in the United States is, in effect, a 56 kbps bearer service. Old-fashioned T1 carrier systems use bit-robbed signaling, taking the low-order bit of every sixth octet away from the user. While bit-robbed signaling has no formal place in ISDN (Signaling System No. 7, a common-channel technique described in Chapter 7, is supposed to replace it), it lingers on. So users have to use *rate adaptation* protocols that mask out the low-order bit of every octet, allowing a net data rate of 56 kbps to flow. This arrangement is also useful for interworking with older switched 56 kbps services.

The Speech Bearer Service. ISDN draws its 64 kbps bearer channel rate from telephony practice, so why is telephony different from data? Several important differences in the way the network handles voice calls must be taken into account. Thus ISDN provides the *Circuit-Mode 64 kbit/s, 8 kHz Structured Bearer Service Category Usable for Speech Information Transfer*, or the speech bearer service for short.

Perhaps the most critical distinction between this and the 64 kbps service comes about because North America and Europe don't agree on how to encode voice into a 64 kbps channel. The North American technique converts a linear representation of the signal amplitude into a semilogarithmic one by applying a formula called μ255. Europe does the same thing by using a different formula, called A-law. To make matters worse, the European standard also inverts every other bit within each eight-bit sample. Both PCM dialects are found in CCITT Recommendation G.711.

If an ISDN speech bearer service call is made between the two domains, the network converts each digital voice sample value to the other side's nearest equivalent. Thus the bits are changed around, but the sound remains essentially unchanged. Audio is carried between the frequencies of 300 and 3400 Hz for a bandwidth of 3.1 kHz.

Voice calls are also capable of accepting audio tones and announcements. While ISDN's out-of-band signaling makes such things as dial tone and busy signal theoretically unnecessary (since the telephone itself can

---

[3] "During an interim period some networks may only support restricted 64 kbit/s digital information transfer capability, i.e., information transfer capability solely restricted by the requirement that the all-zero octet is not allowed. . . ."

generate them), who is to intercept a call made to a number that has been changed? When the speech bearer service is specified, audio tones and announcements may be provided.

And while the world's telephone networks have moved rapidly toward digital transmission, substantial numbers of analog channels and switches are still in service, particularly in remote areas. A speech bearer service call placed over an ISDN may actually be routed over an analog facility! It's not very likely, but it's allowed. This service also allows interworking with the analog telephone network.

Finally, there are certain liberties that may be taken with the quality of the audio when speech is specified. Digitally transmitted speech need not be carried in simple PCM format, requiring 64 kbps of long-haul transmission. The network is allowed to *transcode* the audio into a more bit-efficient format, such as 32 kbps Adaptive Delta Pulse Code Modulation (ADPCM) (CCITT Recommendation G.721). It's also allowable to packetize the voice, discarding the "silence" between words to further increase efficiency. This is fine for voice but not so fine for some other analog applications, such as interworking with voiceband data modems and fax machines — which brings us to another very similar bearer service.

The 3.1 kHz Audio Bearer Service. The only important difference between the 3.1 kHz audio bearer service (*Circuit-Mode 64 kbit/s, 8 kHz Structured Bearer Service Category Usable for 3.1 kHz Audio Information Transfer*) and the speech bearer service is in the way in which audio may be processed. If speech is specified, the network may take more liberties with the call! The 3.1 kHz audio bearer service uses standard PCM, with A-law to μ-law conversion as required. It prohibits silence suppression and low-bit-rate voice transcoding.

The analog telephone network, of course, did not make such distinctions. So when an ISDN interworks with an analog network, it defaults to this and not the speech bearer service! This is certainly a good idea now that fax and modems are so widely used.

Like the telephone network, though, ISDN might have to be told that it's not carrying voice. Modems and fax machines begin calls by sending a 2100 Hz tone into the network that disables audio processing. This crude inband signaling technique will remain necessary with the ISDN 3.1 kHz audio service.

ISDN may make modems and analog fax obsolete, but analog lines will remain with us for a long time. Thus the 3.1 kHz audio circuit-switched bearer service is likely to be the single most popular one that ISDN has to offer.

The 7 kHz Audio Bearer Service. When ISDN was first being developed, the only widely available technique for audio compression was 64 kbps PCM. Lower bit rates were sometimes used, but they suffered greatly in quality and generally couldn't even carry 2400 bps modems. But by the mid-1980s, AD-PCM had been perfected to the point that at 32 kbps, audio transmission was virtually indistinguishable from PCM. (Low-speed modems could pass through it too, but the act of converting between PCM and ADPCM was still a minor problem; more than two or three conversions per call could really scramble data.)

This led to a few subsequent developments. One sideshow was the Soviet Union's decision to build its national ISDN using 32 kbps instead of 64 kbps channels. Another was the realization that if 32 kbps could carry 3.1 kHz, the full 64 kbps of an ISDN bearer channel could carry higher fidelity. So a standard for 7 kHz audio transmission using ADPCM was developed and published in CCITT Recommendation G.722.

The average telephone handset can't provide this audio quality, and it's not needed for voice to be intelligible (although it may be very useful for some languages). But this fidelity, typical of AM radio broadcasting, is useful for applications like teleconferencing and audio program services. And given the competitive market, who's to say that some people won't pay a premium for a telephone with superior audio quality?

The 7 kHz audio bearer service was added to ISDN late in the game and has to play by a special set of rules. The network might be incapable of using it to send tones and announcements. When a call is initiated that specifies this bearer service, the terminal initially uses 3.1 kHz PCM. Only once the other side has connected will the two terminals attempt a handshake sequence that allows them to know that they are ready, willing, and able to switch to 7 kHz ADPCM. From the network's perspective this is very close to the 3.1 kHz audio bearer service during call setup and the 64 kbps circuit-mode bearer service once the call is connected.

The Packet Mode Bearer Services

ISDN provides a single jack for access to both circuit and packet switched networks. The range of options for accessing packet services is more complex than those for circuit mode. While a circuit-mode service always uses the D channel to set up calls and a bearer channel for the actual communications, packet calls can use just a bearer channel, just the D channel, or both to set up their virtual calls.

The services rendered are based on the connection-oriented model used in X.25. Most ISDNs will (eventually) gracefully interwork with X.25 nets just as they integrate with telephony. Some, especially in the United States, will also offer a newer, simpler service called Frame Relay. Some, especially in Europe, may offer Frame Switching, which falls somewhere between Frame Relay and X.25 in complexity.

Two philosophically different approaches were proposed for integrating X.25 packet switching into ISDN, as shown in Fig. 4.2. Characteristically, both were accepted, so networks may offer one or both options. These are

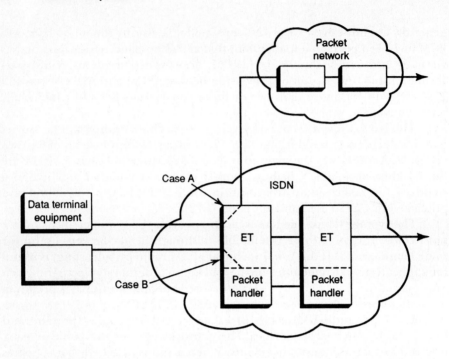

Figure 4.2 *Case A is access to packet, and Case B is packet integrated into the ISDN. In Case B, D channel call signaling may be used to establish some aspects of the packet service. Case A requires a circuit-switched call to be placed to the packet handler. Virtual calls are always initiated by using X.25 virtual call control.*

described in detail in CCITT Recommendation X.31 as well as in ANSI T1.608.

Case A. The first scenario for ISDN packet mode is actually easier to implement but somewhat more complex to use than the alternative. In *access to a packet-switched public data network* the ISDN is simply used as a circuit-mode network that provides access to a packet switch. This was originally called *minimum integration,* but its formal name in X.31 is now *Case A* packet.

A Case A user must first have an access connection to a packet handler in place before any packet calls can be made. A "nailed up" (permanently assigned) channel may be in place; otherwise, the initiator of the call first establishes a 64 kbps unrestricted circuit mode data call to an ISDN number assigned to a packet switch. Then one or many virtual calls may be made using X.25 procedures. The access connection may be a B channel or, in the case of a Primary Rate Interface, an H channel.

In Case A the ISDN number (essentially a telephone number) is used for the circuit-mode access connection between the packet handler and the terminal, but the older packet numbering plan (found in CCITT Recommendation X.121) is used for the actual packet mode virtual calls.

In Case A, a packet handler must of course be capable of completing the call to the destination address. If the packet handler closest to the destination already has a B channel connection in place to the recipient, then it may add the new call to that channel. Otherwise, it must first take the time to establish the call in circuit mode before switching gears into packet mode.

From the implementor's perspective, Case A is quite straight-forward. The packet network remains almost untouched, needing only to be able to support switched access connections. And that was often possible (using modems) in the pre-ISDN world (see CCITT Recommendation X.32). The computer network doesn't need to learn much ISDN either, since it's sticking to established X.25 virtual circuit procedures. Indeed, an X.25 user can migrate to ISDN by installing a circuit-mode terminal adapter and using this method of operation. And because the actual data doesn't touch the D channel, larger packet sizes are possible, up to about 4000 bytes on some networks.

But B channel packet is often more costly than the alternative, D channel packet; the latter is available only via Case B.

Case B. The other approach, the *ISDN virtual circuit service* (originally called *maximum integration*) now called *Case B* packet, treats ISDN packet-switched calls in somewhat the same way that it treats circuit-switched calls, as a service provided *within* the ISDN. Case A treats the two networks as separate.

In Case B the D channel may be used to carry both call control and user packets. The LAPD layer 2 protocol used on the D channel distinguishes between call control signaling and packet mode data. X.25 layer 3 call control procedures on the D channel are then used to initiate and receive virtual calls.

Every ISDN access line has the capability of handling some packets on the D channel, since that is required for circuit-mode call control signaling. The Basic Rate interface provides 16 kbps on the D channel and has only two B channels; this allows most of the 16 kbps to be used for packet-mode data transfer. Call control signaling has a higher priority, so heavy packet traffic can't block the D channel.

The available packet throughput on a 16-kbps D channel is often referred to as being 9600 bps, but that's just a round number that approximates the performance that can be expected. (Where but in data communications would 9600 be a round number?) The Primary Rate interface provides a 64 kbps D channel but has more channels to control and is often implemented differently, so it's less likely to support packet switching.

DMI Mode 3 had another innovative feature. Instead of setting up connections by using the bit-oriented on-hook/off-hook signaling usually found on T1 carrier, it specified an early snapshot of ISDN's DSS1 signaling protocol for its call establishment. In effect it was a prototype of an ISDN-style service. So AT&T made a serious effort to introduce the concept into the developing ISDN standards. Since it provided packet-switching service using only the LAPD frame protocol, the ISDN derivative of Mode 3 was dubbed Frame Switching.

In Frame Switching, ISDN call control signaling (CCITT Recommendation Q.933-1992[4]) is used on the D channel, while a new LAPD variation designed for frame modes, LAPF, may be used for information transfer on either the B or D channel. The network performs all LAPF functions, including flow control and error recovery by retransmission. If the network is unable to carry the offered load due to congestion, it may use LAPF procedures to throttle the virtual circuit.

Frame Switching has not gained widespread support among ISDN developers. Its main proponents were the French, who saw it as a way to support the low-cost videotex terminals (Minitels) that are so popular in France. But even AT&T's own network has abandoned the idea in favor of a different form of frame mode service.

Frame Relay. In the Frame Relay service, LAPD is stripped to its bare essentials and then stripped again. Frame Relay is based on the *Core Aspects of LAPD* protocol (ANSI T1.618), an extended subset of LAPD. Call control is typically on the D channel, using a form of DSS1 specified in CCITT Q.933 and ANSI T1.617.

While Frame Switching is a service based on the LAPD protocol, Frame Relay is based on the idea that LAPD per se isn't really what data networks want or need for an efficient packet-switched service. Frame Relay is even simpler, at least in terms of visible protocol elements (it uses fewer header bits). Some proponents consider it to be close to circuit switching. But that may be a bit optimistic; Frame Relay is more like packet switching with all of its armor removed. While it can be used to carry LAPF frames, it can also carry other flavors of HDLC, including those based on IBM's SDLC, or no other data link control procedures at all.

In the Core Aspects protocol, information is encapsulated within HDLC frames, using most of HDLC's essential elements: Frames are delineated by

---

[4] CCITT Recommendation Q.933, specifying call control for frame mode services, will be included with the 1992 White Book, along with Recommendation Q.922, specifying both LAPF and the Core Aspects protocol.

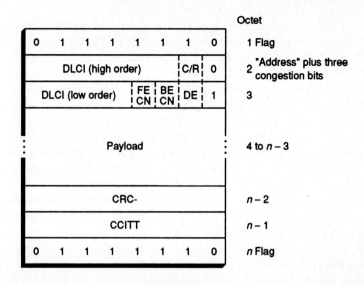

								Octet	
0	1	1	1	1	1	1	0	1	Flag
DLCI (high order)					C/R	0	2	"Address" plus three congestion bits
DLCI (low order)			FE CN	BE CN	DE	1	3	
Payload								4 to $n-3$	
CRC-								$n-2$	
CCITT								$n-1$	
0	1	1	1	1	1	1	0	n	Flag

Figure 4.3 *The Core Aspects frame used by the Frame Relay service is an extended superset of the LAPD frame used for D channel signaling. It does away with the LAPD elements of procedure but adds forward and backward explicit congestion notification (FECN and BECN) and discard eligibility (DE) indicators.*

flags, a 16-bit CRC is at the end of the frame, and a LAPF address (two or more octets) is at the beginning of the frame (see Fig. 4.3). But that's pretty much it. There are no HDLC control field, no sequence numbering, no flow control, and no error recovery within the network.

Unlike other ISDN packet services, the network doesn't offer a complete connection-mode data link service. While Frame Relay is connection-oriented, a frame either makes it across the network or doesn't. (Its address field, and thus the CRC, are local to each interface and are thus changed by the network.)

Frame Relay doesn't have any packet types. With no HDLC control field, the Core Aspects protocol treats all packets the same, as something to be delivered if possible. That not only means that the user has tremendous freedom in what can be sent across the network; it also means that the network has very little ability to communicate with the user. Such elementary functions as flow control and error recovery aren't addressed.

Is Frame Relay More Like Datagrams? In a connectionless network, individual packets are sent on demand; delivery isn't guaranteed either. Frame Relay isn't connectionless; it has two critical features that are clearly connection-oriented. First, each packet uses a data link connection identifier

(DLCI), not source and destination addresses. A DLCI is simply a number that identifies a virtual circuit, whose source and destination addresses are identified at connection establishment. Second, the network is allowed to enforce the *rate* at which data is sent across any given virtual circuit.

Rate enforcement is not entirely a new notion for packet networks. Good old X.25 includes the ability to specify an allowable throughput class, and the network may choose to enforce it. But in practice, almost no X.25 networks actually do. It's just not necessary. If the network is busy, it can send "Receiver Not Ready" messages to the sender. Actually measuring the flow of packets in real time (not billing time) for each virtual circuit adds cost for which most network designers haven't found the need.

Frame Relay networks lack the RNR capability. So to prevent any one sender from hogging the network, they can adopt a selective discard policy. The preferred technique is called a *leaky bucket,* based loosely upon this analogy: A bucket with a hole in it drips at a given rate. As long as it's not full, any water poured in will eventually leak out through the bottom. But if too much water is poured in, it will overflow the rim of the bucket. In Frame Relay, the bucket represents the right to send the largest burst of data that a user may send at any given time; the leak at the bottom represents the average rate. If a user hasn't been sending anything for a while, then the bucket is empty, and the user may send a burst of that size. Another way of putting it is to specify a burst size and an average *committed information rate* (CIR). The length of time over which the average CIR may be computed determines the largest burst that may be sent.

If a virtual circuit tries to send more than is allowed by the leaky bucket enforcer, the network has the option of setting a bit in the frame header to indicate that the frame is *discard eligible.* The frame may still be carried across the network, but if congestion is encountered at any point, a network has the option of discarding these frames first so that other frames (not discard eligible) are carried.

The network also has the option of discarding frames at the source if they exceed a given rate. This should generally be higher than what is needed to set the discard eligibility flag. In effect, it's a second leaky bucket: If the first overflows into the second (a small overload), then some frames are marked discard eligible. If the second overflows (a large overload), then frames are discarded then and there (see Fig. 4.4).

This rate-based mechanism is of course very much a connection-oriented concept. And in what telephone companies might view as a perfect world, with everyone's computer attached directly to the public ISDN, that computer might have the ability to control the rate at which it sends data so as not to exceed the rate negotiated for that call. That's fairly easy for individual remote terminal connections.

In practice, many or most users, especially those with Local Area Networks, will be consolidating many different virtual circuits (often found at

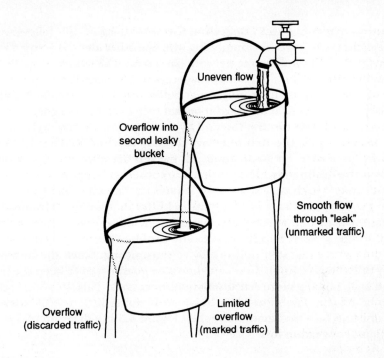

Uneven flow

Overflow into
second leaky
bucket

Smooth flow
through "leak"
(unmarked traffic)

Overflow
(discarded traffic)

Limited
overflow
(marked traffic)

Figure 4.4 *The "leaky bucket" algorithm is modeled on the approximate behavior of water. Offered traffic flow is uneven, but if it stays below an average value, the bucket doesn't overflow. If it does overflow, a second bucket separates modest overflow, which is marked "discard eligible," from severe overflow, which is immediately discarded. The actual data does not go through the bucket; the bucket represents the right to send additional data.*

the Transport layer) across the frame relay network. They are one user to the Frame Relay network, but the Frame Relay may be attached to a LAN with many users. The *bridge* or *router* connecting the LAN to the Frame Relay won't have any way to tell the actual senders to slow down!

So the bridge or router won't necessarily be worrying about the leaky bucket. It'll send what it can, hope that the network carries enough of it, and let the Transport layer handle the congestion. Or it can run a congestion avoidance protocol on an *edge-to-edge* basis across the Frame Relay network and discard excessive traffic by itself. Neither of these requires the customer equipment to even know about the leaky bucket. Both, however, are helped if the user follows a procedure generally required on connectionless networks, namely, *congestion control.*

Congestion Avoidance and Congestion Control. Imagine the following situation: Ten users (A–J) are communicating with one other user (K) across a Frame Relay network. Each node in the network has a buffer, 20 frames deep, on each of its output circuits. So when a frame is received, it's immediately queued into the appropriate output buffer unless that buffer is full. If the buffer is full, the frame is discarded, straight into the bit bucket (where else is it to go?).

Each user sends two frames, and by the time the last has arrived at the buffer leading to K, the first ten have already reached K. That leaves ten frames in the buffer. So far so good. All packets are either in the buffer or already at the destination. That's what's supposed to happen.

But what if each user sends four frames in the same time frame? Only ten can get to K, but 30 are left to fit into a buffer that is only 20 frames deep. Ten frames (say, one apiece) are discarded. K doesn't acknowledge these frames, so the senders all retransmit. The problem here is that the senders are adding to a congested network by retransmitting. Since the network is already full, the retransmissions can almost be guaranteed to keep the buffer full and keep making more retransmissions necessary. This situation is called *congestion collapse*. The network is busy, yet is doing little useful work, just retransmitting into the same bit bucket! Figure 4.5 is a diagram of a simple example of congestion loss.

Figure 4.5 *In this simple example of congestion loss the link from the network to terminal D is unable to carry the load coming from A, B, and C, so the buffer queue in the network discards frames. All four links are 64 kbps. Even if the link to D were larger, loss could still occur if D then sent data to A at a higher rate than A could handle.*

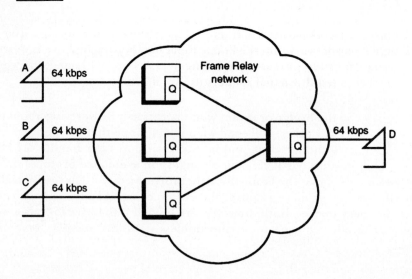

The LAPD protocol was designed to be used across a simple wire, not a packet-switched network. It allows a *window* of frames to be sent before one has been acknowledged, and if it receives a frame that doesn't follow in perfect modulo-128 sequence, then it solicits a retransmission beginning at the dropped frame, including all subsequently received frames. That's because it uses *go-back-N* error control procedures, which are designed for simplicity and a moderately low loss rate and transit delay.

So if a LAPD virtual circuit has a window size of eight, and the second packet is dropped, then seven packets will need to be retransmitted, not just one. It's easy to see how large window sizes can lead to congestion collapse. It's also not hard to prevent this from occurring by using a *congestion control* procedure.

The simplest congestion control procedure, which is implemented in several major Transport layer protocols and specified in LAPF, is called the *dynamic window*. Before this was made a mandatory feature, connectionless networks were prone to congestion collapse; with it, networks are generally stable.

The dynamic window is fairly simple: When a frame is dropped because of congestion, the window should suddenly and drastically shrink. (The American National Standard for Frame Relay's Core Aspects protocol, ANSI T1.618, recommends that it should fall to 1/4 of its previous size; TCP and OSI Transport Class 4 suggest going down to one packet.) When everyone who loses a frame does this, the load on the network drops, and the congestion is alleviated. Window sizes then creep up, adding one frame to the window size after a few frames have been carried without loss. Each virtual circuit's window size and data rate, when plotted over time, resemble a "sawtooth" pattern, but the network hums along.

 A better approach, though, is to try to avoid hitting the point at which loss occurs. That's called *congestion avoidance*. The ANSI Frame Relay standard specifies three different ways to do this! They're all optional, though, so users have to be sure that their equipment is compatible with the networks.

One technique is for the network to set the *forward explicit congestion notification* (FECN) bit in the Core Aspects header. This indicates that somewhere along the line, the frame encountered a congested node. (Congestion is determined on the basis of the average buffer size over a period of time.) If, during the period equal to a couple of window turns or round-trip delays through the network, at least half of the packets received have the FECN bit set, then the user should slow down by 1/8 or so, reducing either rate or window size. This scheme works best with destination-controlled protocols like ISO Transport Class 4, in which the receiver maintains a credit window, continuously updating the sender how much to send.

Another technique uses the *backward explicit congestion notification* (BECN) bit in the header. This is set in packets going *toward the sender* of packets that encountered congestion. That way, the sender can slow down without waiting for the receiver to pass the message back. This works with LAPF, whose window size is determined only by the sender. It does, however, require that traffic be flowing in both directions across the same virtual circuit, along the same path. These conditions apply to most, though not all, Frame Relay connections. (One-way traffic is possible, however, since there's no requirement that an acknowledged protocol like LAPD or LAPF be used.)

Finally, a Frame Relay network is allowed to send a *consolidated link-layer management message* (CLLM). This is a special packet, addressed to the maintenance DLCI, containing a list of all congested virtual circuits. A congested node originates this, and each node that receives it has to read out the list of DLCIs within it and shuffle them into new messages, each going toward its own destination. (That's because the virtual circuit numbers are lumped together in the payload of maintenance messages. Remember that there's no way for Frame Relay networks to communicate directly, in-channel, with users, since there's no control field!) The CLLM doesn't require two-way traffic, but it can add additional processing and traffic load to both the network and user.

All three of these congestion avoidance techniques, as well as the discard eligibility (DE) flag, are Frame Relay options. No network is allowed to *clear* the DE flag, the FECN, or the BECN, even if it doesn't know how to set or interpret it. Networks need not, however, carry the CLLM, since that requires additional processing.

Given all of this, is Frame Relay really any simpler than X.25? Ideally, yes. A user may send simple Unnumbered Information (UI) frames across the Frame Relay network and allow the Transport layer dynamic window to take care of congestion. The ISO Connectionless Network Layer Protocol [ISO8473] has a bit that corresponds (not coincidentally) to the FECN bit, allowing it to make efficient use of Frame Relay as well. These are fairly simple and don't slow traffic down as much as X.25's rather complex procedures. Frame Relay is also fairly easy to implement by using hardware assistance.

But X.25 is essentially bulletproof. Frame Relay's congestion control, on the other hand, depends upon the users' cooperation unless the network strictly enforces the leaky bucket. And that will not necessarily be simple to implement and could reduce efficiency by being unnecessarily limiting at times of light network loading. So neither is a panacea. Both of them, and possibly even Frame Switching (which simplifies X.25 without giving up LAPD's network-user flow control capability), will find many ISDN users. And neither will replace circuit mode, with its guarantee of bit-transparent delivery.

User Signaling Bearer Service

User-to-User Signaling is a supplementary service that allows small blocks of information to be sent between ISDN users as part of their D channel call control signaling. These messages are typically up to 128 octets long, if sent as part of call control message, or up to 256 octets if sent alone. The network is most likely to carry these messages over the Signaling System No. 7 network, but delivery is not guaranteed. Call control signaling messages are likely to have a higher priority.

The User Signaling Bearer Service (USBS) was created from the realization that some users don't need to send any more information than this. So if user-to-user signaling is sent with no other bearer service specified, then it *becomes* the bearer service! Thus this exists rather more by definition than by design. D channel layer 3 signaling messages are sent by using Digital Subscriber Signaling System No. 1(DSS1), which is an access protocol, normally used to request services from a network. The USBS actually uses DSS1 as a network layer protocol in the OSI sense, routing the packet across the network to a destination user.

It's not quite clear what applications this service is most suited for. Real data communication activities need longer messages and more of them; the USBS will typically offer a real bandwidth on the order of a few hundred, not thousand, bytes per second. Perhaps it will find a use for message-switching applications.

One use that has been described in more detail is the use of these messages to encapsulate other DSS1 messages to build private networks. PBX switches will presumably have the capability of speaking DSS1 to the network, but they can also use the USBS to speak DSS1 to each other.[5] That's not the only way to build private networks, but it has support among some PBX vendors, especially in Europe. USBS may also be useful for network management applications.

Supplementary Services

Man does not live by bread alone. Nor does ISDN live by bearer services alone. Supplementary services are the butter and jam that make the bread so much more desirable. Only offered in conjunction with bearer services, they are features and options.

Supplementary services cover a wide range of capabilities. Some are network options that are taken for granted in most packet-switched networks. Others are voice-oriented telephony features that are found in most PBX

---

[5] This is one of several scenarios described in the European Computer Manufacturers' Association Technical Report TR/NTW (ECMA, Geneva, 1987).

systems. Others are ISDN-specific. In general, public ISDN providers will offer them on an extra-charge basis, by subscription or per use. Some supplementary services affect the way in which basic calls are made. These may exist in pre-ISDN networks. Figure 4.6 lists the supplementary services provided with basic bearer services.

Number Identification Supplementary Services

The number identification services take full advantage of ISDN's message-oriented signaling protocol, so are likely to work better in an ISDN environment than over analog facilities.

Direct Dialing In. This service (also called *Direct Inward Dialing* in North America) allows a block of telephone numbers to be assigned to a single group of access facilities. This is typically used to enable every extension behind a PBX system to have its own telephone number. In the analog network this requires a special signaling technique using one-way trunk lines. In ISDN it is supplementary only because telephone companies charge extra for the numbers; the DSS1 protocol accommodates this quite naturally because it allows destination number to be specified on incoming calls. (It is essentially a symmetrical protocol, so the "from" and "to" numbers may both be included in the messages sent to and from the network.)

A very closely related service, *Multiple Subscriber Number*, allows more than one number to be pointed at a given ISDN line. This might, for example, allow a single line to have one number for an attached fax machine and another for telephone calls.

Calling Line Identification Presentation and Restriction. Not only does DSS1 allow a destination number to be specified, but it allows the originating number to also be sent to the recipient of the call. This is called *Calling Line Identification Presentation* (CLIP); it corresponds to the "Caller ID" features that are now appearing in many telephone networks.

While Caller ID has been quite controversial when applied to telephone networks, data networks have routinely provided this information. It is a required part of the OSI Network Service, which X.25 provides, and in any case, most computer network operators demand it for security reasons. Only in the case of telephone calls has this been controversial, but ISDN attempts to treat both data and voice calls equally.

Since many telephone users do not want their number sent to the recipient of their calls, ISDN provides the *Calling Line Identification Restriction* (CLIR) service. This blocks CLIP from being forwarded to the recipient of the call. The number is still sent through the network, so call tracing features (which provide the telephone company, but not the caller, with the number) such as the *Malicious Calls Identification* service will work. Emergency services

Supplementary Services	Circuit-Mode Bearer Services						Teleservices				
	64 kbps Unrestricted Demand	64 kbps Speech Demand	64 kbps 3.1-kHz Audio Demand	64 kbps Unrestricted Permanent	64 kbps 3.1-kHz Audio Permanent	1920 kbps Unrestricted Permanent	Telephony	Teletex	Telefax 4	Videotex	Mixed Mode
Direct Dialing In	X	X	X				X	X	X	X	X
Multiple Subscriber Number	X	X	X				X	X	X	X	X
Calling Line Identification Presentation	X	X	X				X	X	X	X	X
Calling Line Identification Restriction	X	X	X				X	X	X	X	X
Connected Line Identification Presentation	X	X	X				X	X	X	X	X
Connected Line Identification Restriction	X	X	X				X	X	X	X	X
Malicious Call Identification	a	a	a				a				
Subaddressing	a	a	a				a				
Call Transfer	X	X	X				X				
Call Forwarding Busy	X	X	X				X				
Call Forwarding No Reply	X	X	X				X			X	
Call Forwarding Unconditional	X	X	X				X			X	
Call Deflection											
Line Hunting	X	X	X				X				
Call Waiting	X	X	X				X				

Figure 4.6 *Association of basic and supplementary services.*   Reprinted with permission by ITU/CCITT (International Telecommunications Union/International Telegraph and Telephone Consultative Committee), CCITT Blue Book, vol VIII.7, © 1988. The full text may be obtained from the ITU Sales Section, Place des Nations, CH-1211 Geneva 20, Switzerland.

a indicates likely applicability for services not yet defined in the 1988 Blue Book.

| | Circuit-Mode Bearer Services | | | | | | Teleservices | | | | |
Supplementary Services	64 kbps Unrestricted Demand	64 kbps Speech Demand	64 kbps 3.1-kHz Audio Demand	64 kbps Unrestricted Permanent	64 kbps 3.1-kHz Audio Permanent	1920 kbps Unrestricted Permanent	Telephony	Teletex	Telefax 4	Videotex	Mixed Mode
Call Hold	X	X	X				X				
Completion of Calls to Busy Subscribers	a	a	a				a				
Conference Calling	X	X	X				X				
Three-Party Service	X	X	X				X				
Closed User Group	X	X	X				X	X	X	X	X
Private Numbering Plan	a	a	a				a				
Credit Card Calling	a	a	a				a				
Advice of Charge	X	X	X				X	X	X	X	X
Reverse Charging											
User-to-User Signaling	X	X	X				X	X	X		X

Figure 4.6 *(continued)*

(such as "911" in the United States) have precedence over CLIR and will receive the number anyway.

A subscriber may be able to request that CLIR be the default for all calls, in which case the subscriber must specify, on a per-call basis, when his or her number is to be presented. Conversely, a subscriber may simply invoke CLIR on a per-call basis when required. By following this service description, ISDN hopes to avoid the controversy that has plagued early Caller ID services that lack a universal ability to request privacy. (But the problem won't be solved if networks choose to offer CLIP without CLIR, which is also permissible.)

Subaddressing. Most connection-oriented data networks provide the caller with the ability to specify an arbitrary subaddress as well as the network-provided number. Applied to ISDN, this allows, for example, stations on a LAN to be addressed through a single ISDN address. The network does not in any way process the subaddress; it is simply passed along to the recipient of the call. The subaddress is long enough to accommodate a full OSI Network Service Access Point address, which can be 20 octets long.

Since the subaddress is supported in DSS1's basic call protocol, some factions (especially in the computer industry) object to having this classified as a supplementary service, which the telephone company can charge for. Telephone companies argue that passing this information along provides value to the customer and should not be free. Since telephone companies dominate the ISDN standards process, subaddressing is found here rather than as a feature of basic call control.

Charging Services: Reverse, Credit Card, and Advised Charging

The "collect call" is an ancient and venerable part of the telephone world, though it is not even permitted in some countries, such as France. Public data networks, on the other hand, are routinely set up to allow collect calling by default. Thus a user who dials in to a computer information service need not have an account with the X.25 network provider; the call is paid for by the computer service provider and billed along with the computer time. ISDN must provide this as a supplementary service, though details of how it is to be done are not included in the 1988 CCITT Blue Book.

The *Advice of Charge* service allows the caller to be informed immediately of how much a given sent-paid call cost. This is particularly of interest to users like hotels, which want to bill their guests for their telephone calls. But it's a feature that can be useful to business and residential customers as well.

The *Credit Card Calling* service allows calls to be billed to an account belonging to neither the caller nor the called party. While this too has not been described in the Blue Book, it is widely implemented (and often automated) in the analog world, so interim procedures are likely to be implemented by networks before the completion of a standard.

Call Completion Services

These services allow calls to be made even when one of the parties' lines is already in use. While all exist in some form or other in the analog network, ISDN adds to their capabilities.

Call Hold. One of the oldest features in the world of analog telephony, in which it was typically implemented with relays, *Call Hold* takes on a special role in ISDN. The DSS1 protocol allows each individual call appearing at any given interface to have its own identification number (*call reference value*). This allows more than one call at a time to be on hold at that interface, while zero or more (up to the number of available B channels) circuit-mode calls may simultaneously be in a connected state. The user may then *retrieve* held calls selectively.

With this feature an ordinary ISDN interface is (at least theoretically) capable of juggling a large number of simultaneous calls. When would this be useful? In stock trading, for instance: In the analog world, stock traders often have large "turrets" with dozens of lines. With ISDN the interface needs merely to be given the right to put many calls on hold at a time. Then, if the telephone instrument (which may be a computerized workstation) provides an adequate human interface, the trader may rapidly switch from call to call. One possible human interface, of course, is a multibutton telephone set. Just because the different calls occur on the same physical line and possibly on the same telephone number doesn't mean that they can't be displayed like the "lines" on a traditional multiline telephone instrument!

How many calls can a given line have on hold at a time? ISDN subscribers are each authorized to have a certain number of call IDs[6] active at any given time. Calls may then be active or held. If a Basic Rate interface is allowed five call IDs and uses one B channel (typical of a voice instrument), then it can have four on hold or in other nonconnected states (i.e., ringing).

In many analog telephone systems a call must be put on hold before call modification features can be invoked. How else can the user get the dial tone needed to dial the feature code? With ISDN and its out-of-band signaling, that problem is eliminated, and some features can be invoked without putting an active call on hold. ISDN's Call Hold service is thus not an exact substitute for the analog hold service; it is a powerful tool with many possible applications. It is also a part of many other supplementary services, such as conference calling.

Call Waiting. Of all of the services that are improved by ISDN, Call Waiting must rank near the top. This service allows a party to be notified that someone is attempting to call, even though the line is already in use. In the analog telephone network the only way to notify the caller is to interrupt the connection, often with a beep tone. This is tolerable for voice but disastrous for voiceband data, since it causes errors and usually causes modems to disconnect.

With ISDN's out-of-band signaling, call waiting is simply an application of the DSS1 protocol. Incoming call notification is given on the D channel, even though one or more B channels is already in use. The recipient can

---

[6] While service descriptions use generalities like "call ID," the DSS1 protocol uses a specific information element called call reference value.

then choose to hold the original call, disconnect the first and go to the second, or simply ignore the waiting call.

Other supplementary services, such as Calling Line Identification Presentation and Call Deflection, can be used in conjunction with Call Waiting. For example, the recipient of the waiting call may find out who is calling and decide to deflect it to someone else.

ISDN's definition of "busy" introduces another wrinkle. Not only can the network define the user as busy, in which case call waiting may be invoked, but the user may define himself or herself as busy after the call has been offered. Thus a call can be simply rejected. If the caller is on an ISDN too, then the reason will be given; a caller on an analog line is likely to simply receive busy tone.

Call Completion to Busy Subscriber. Someone who does receive a busy signal then may choose to have the network help put through the call. *Call Completion to Busy Subscriber* (CCBS) is the ISDN version of the "Camp-On" or "Ring Again" feature found in many PBXs, extended across the network. Upon receiving a busy indication the caller requests this service. When the called line is free, the network notifies the caller and completes the call.

Multi-Level Precedence and Preemption. The U.S. Department of Defense has operated its private telephone network, Autovon, since the 1960s. Autovon offers many features that are not found in conventional analog networks, including end-to-end four-wire switching and a nonhierarchical routing technique designed to survive the destruction of some of its switching centers. For Autovon to evolve over to ISDN, one feature unique to its hierarchical military heritage was needed.

Multi-Level Precedence and Preemption (MLPP) allows some telephones to be more equal than others. If a call cannot get through to its destination, then it may be dialed with a precedence code. While ordinary calls are classified as *Routine,* four special precedence levels (*Priority, Interrupt, Flash,* and *Flash Override*) are provided, each more powerful and made available to fewer and fewer callers. A call can *preempt* a call of a lower level, seizing, as required, congested trunk facilities and breaking in (following a warning tone) to a busy line.

In analog Touch-Tone telephones, the four precedence levels above Routine are selected with the fourth column on the keypad, which is not found on civilian (or low-ranking) phones. In ISDN these precedence levels are defined in the DSS1 protocol. These allow important calls to get through during an emergency.

Community of Interest Supplementary Services

These services, carried over from pre-ISDN days, enable a large customer to make use of multiple ISDN facilities as a specialized resource.

Closed User Group. Public data network customers often do not want strangers to be given access to their computers, so these networks provide the *Closed User Group* (CUG) service. This allows callers to specify that the call they are about to make is being made to a fellow member of a specified CUG; the call will be rejected by the network if the destination is not part of that group. A recipient will also be informed if the call is being made via a CUG so that the recipient can selectively accept such calls.

A given interface can be a member of a specific CUG by default, with the ability to belong to multiple CUGs as well. Some CUGs restrict incoming access *to* themselves; others restrict outgoing access. Restrictions may also be placed on calls within CUGs.

Private Numbering Plan. A customer with multiple locations, such as a large corporation, may request that the network provide a "virtual private network" service in which users do not dial the regular public network number, but instead dial a customer-specified location code plus extension number, for calls between company locations. Typically, a company may have a private numbering plan that allows users to dial a three-digit site code and a four-digit extension number to reach any other company extension anywhere in the world. (Outside of North America, formats other than 3 + 4 digits may also see widespread use.) Like most other call offering supplementary services, this isn't specific to ISDN but is considered an ISDN supplementary service, and the DSS1 protocol allows users to specify whether a given number is part of the public or a private numbering plan.

Multiline Business Group and City Wide Centrex. In North America, Centrex is a popular telephone company service that simulates a PBX using central office lines. The North American ISDN standards label it *a Multiline Business Group*. Some supplementary services may be limited in scope to lines within this group. The *City Wide Centrex* service extends this to cover locations served by more than one central office. Features that are normally restricted in scope to one switch, such as abbreviated dialing, work transparently between switches as well. While many ISDN supplementary services are not restricted by definition to a single switch, City Wide Centrex implements a greater degree of transparency than might otherwise be provided. (These features are not defined by the CCITT.)

Message Waiting Indication. Most commonly found in hotel rooms but increasingly popular in businesses as well, the *Message Waiting* feature allows a designated station, which is typically an attendant or a voice mail system, to provide an indication to a telephone user that a message is waiting to be retrieved. On analog instruments this is usually a neon bulb that flashes when about 100 volts (current limited) is superimposed across the telephone line. With ISDN a telephone instrument will have some kind of indicator (implementation dependent) that, under control of DSS1 messages, indicates whether or not any messages, and possibly how many, are waiting to be retrieved from the designated answering point. This service is being defined in North America but not yet by CCITT. It also poses some regulatory issues, since it treads closely to the line between telecommunications and information services.

Call Offering Services

These supplementary services are more typical of the features accessible from modern PBX instruments or available as extra-cost Centrex options from telephone companies. Early ISDN implementations typically did not follow developing standards; instead, they simply allowed ISDN lines to access the existing services. Often this required "star code" access; others defined proprietary protocols to invoke them with.

Some of these features work much better on ISDN than on analog networks, or would if the standards were implemented in full. The additional signaling flexibility provided by DSS1, in contrast to the limited capabilities of analog telephone sets, allows them to be more useful than before ISDN. For users to benefit from this, however, telephone equipment manufacturers will have to solve the perennial problem of the human interface. Complex features are relatively hard for most users to comprehend, and considerable effort will have to go into the ergonomics of these features before they reach their potential.

Call Forwarding Services. Call forwarding occurs when the network causes a call to be presented to ("ring") a line other than the one that was called. Several supplementary services fall into this category.

Call Forwarding Unconditional causes all calls made to one number to ring on a different one. Its most obvious use is for parties who are away from one location to have all of their calls go to the location where they will be. If there is a charge associated with the call from the dialed number to the destination number, the customer who requested call forwarding pays for that portion of the call; the party who made the original call pays only for the call to the dialed number.

Call Forwarding Busy allows calls to be answered for a line that is engaged. A typical application is to allow calls to be forwarded to one's secretary. The ISDN definition of *busy* is a complex one, though. Since a given interface has more than one B channel, is a line busy if one channel is busy or if both are busy? These and other options helped to make this service a difficult one to define in relation to analog lines for which being busy is a simple matter. Indeed, this is one of the few services in which ISDN's message-oriented DSS1 protocol could make someone (especially someone trying to write or implement ISDN standards) look back fondly upon the old analog network.

Call Forwarding No Reply takes care of telephones that are temporarily unattended. If a call has not been answered within a defined period of time (typically in the range of 10–15 seconds), then the call moves to another line, such as an answering machine, message service, or secretary.

Call Deflection is a service that exists on a few pre-ISDN PBX systems that support proprietary instruments but never on analog lines. It allows a ringing call to be moved to another line at the request of that line. On an analog network the call would have to be answered before it could be moved, which would constitute the *Call Transfer* service. But an ISDN user might determine who the caller is (via the CLIP service) and decide to pass it to someone else, using deflection. Some PBX vendors referred to this as *snub forwarding*. But it has other applications as well, such as moving a call to another person who is better suited to answer it or between an automated attendant (a computer examining incoming calls) and a live person.

Line Hunting. While an ISDN Basic Rate interface can handle two circuit-mode calls (or a large number of packet calls) at once and a Primary Rate can handle many more, many users require multiple interfaces to handle their incoming call loads. This service, used by essentially all multiline (analog) business telephone customers, is *Line Hunting*. A group of lines (a *hunt group*) shares a telephone number, and callers do not receive busy signal unless all available channels on all access arrangements are busy.

This is one of those services that is much simpler to define in the analog world than in ISDN because of the difficulty in determining what busy means. For circuit-mode calls, this is relatively straightforward; for packet calls, it requires more attention.

Call Transfer. Like most PBX systems, ISDN allows users to transfer calls to other parties. The ISDN *Call Transfer* service supports the different flavors of call transfer. The call to be transferred is placed on hold, and the second call is made. The user then transfers the held call to that second destination before (unscreened) or after (screened) the second destination answers. A variation allows the call to be transferred "blind," without even putting the first call on hold and waiting to find out whether the second destination rings.

Hot Line. This service, which is being defined in North America, allows a line to have a tightly restricted calling capability. Three options are provided. In one the line can call only to a list of designated numbers; another option allows it to receive calls only from a list. Finally, both sending and receiving capabilities may be restricted. This may be useful in conjunction with various special applications, such as emergency telephones in public places and direct lines to hotels and taxi services from airports. It doesn't really depend upon ISDN but gains flexibility due to ISDN's use of Signaling System No. 7

for its internal call setup. It can also be implemented within customers' equipment.

Multiparty Services (Conference Calling)

The conference call is another feature that is improved by ISDN. Many PBX systems can make conference calls, but the analog telephone instrument is very limiting. With ISDN, each call added to a conference has a Party ID of its own. The station that requests the conference calling service, the controller, can then make new calls and add them to the conference, up to the number of parties specified when the service is first invoked.

What makes ISDN conferencing so powerful is that the controller does not lose control of the individual parties. They can selectively be *split* from the conference and either held, disconnected, or joined with the controller for a private side conversation. While this is going on, the other conferees can still hear each other. The conference continues until the controller disconnects.

The best analogy for this is to imagine an old cord switchboard with an operator capable of plugging individual calls into a multijack conference circuit. Jacks can be inserted or removed at will. ISDN does it digitally, using the DSS1 protocol.

While the *Conference Calling* service provides maximum flexibility and allows large numbers of conferees, the *Three Party Service* provides a restricted subset. It appears to have been created to simplify transition from earlier analog three-party calling features — the older, more limited feature was simply defined as being part of ISDN. Of course, by being a separate feature it may be tariffed at a lower rate, under the "value of service" principle that is so popular among telephone monopolies.

Another variation on the conference call, not yet found among CCITT recommendations, is the *Preset Conference* (*meet-me conference*). With this service, the subscriber provides the network with a list of numbers, and at a designated time the network simultaneously calls all of them. When they answer, they are connected to a conference bridge. This is intended for large group-style meetings when the conference call can be prearranged.

Multiline Key Telephone Service

This is arguably one of the most commercially important supplementary services, required to make ISDN Centrex a viable alternative to PBX systems. Yet it is defined only in North America, and existing implementations don't follow any standard. European PTTs are less interested in Centrex, and European PBX users are less accustomed to using multiline telephone sets.

Electronic key telephone sets give the user the appearance of multiple lines on one instrument. Given other ISDN services such as Call Hold, Multiple Subscriber Number, and Call Waiting, it may be possible to create a multiline instrument without defining a special service for the purpose. But by defining a key telephone supplementary service, users can more easily order the combination of features needed for applications like secretarial line coverage.

Before electronic PBXs took hold in the late 1970s, almost all multiline telephone sets depended upon huge relay collections and complex wiring. A six-line keyset required a 25-pair cable, and each line required a *key telephone unit* (KTU) mounted in a *key service unit* (KSU). Electronic PBXs introduced proprietary electronic telephone sets, using one to three pairs to provide equivalent service, with software in the PBX performing most of the KSUs functions. Ideally, the electronic keyset will match old-fashioned electromechanical sets for easy access to features; many to date have been rather weak in the human factors department.

By the mid-1980s, electronic keysets had replaced the standard electromechanical ones for almost all new installations. Even small business telephone systems were dominated by "electronic key." But Centrex required published interfaces. Initially, Northern Telecom and AT&T both made public the specifications for their proprietary electronic key telephones, but ISDN standards will be available for their replacements.

Teleservices

What is an ISDN used for? For that matter, what is the telephone network used for? In some eyes, the answer to at least the former question can be summed up in the word *teleservices*. These are higher-layer services, essentially applications in the OSI (layer 7) sense, that make use of ISDN bearer services.

The role of teleservices is one of the major differences between the U.S. view of ISDN and that of most CCITT members. In the United States, telephone companies (those that provide bearer services) are expressly *forbidden* by regulation from offering higher-layer services, except as strictly separate unregulated operations. In most other countries, PTTs are allowed to offer any service they want. And in some they have had the right to claim a monopoly or at least to subsidize it with revenues from monopoly services. While the PTTs have been reigned in somewhat, that's exactly the sort of scenario that the United States is seeking to avoid!

Only a handful of teleservices are defined by the CCITT. Backers of the standards say that by standardizing them, users will be guaranteed international compatibility. Detractors note that this stifles progress; computing, after all, changes at a much faster pace than simple telecommunications.

How much of a threat to competition do teleservices pose? Some ISDN old-timers remember a scenario that some early European ISDN pioneers might have been planning. With "interconnection" of customer-owned modems, PBXs, and station equipment still prohibited in some countries, computer users had a loophole: The jack on the back of the modem allowed free interconnection of data terminal equipment, such as computers and display screens. After all, the PTTs didn't own the computers. But what if they could? If ISDN were really as powerful as they dreamed it might be, then could not ISDN teleservices replace privately owned computer time-sharing? In this vision, privately owned computers would be relegated to isolated batch processing and perhaps limited desktop functions.

Most observers today would consider such a scenario to be impossible. But the computer industry and the telephone industry harbor a long-standing distrust of one another. Teleservices are just one area of conflict. What's most important is that ISDN bearer services may be used however the subscriber sees fit. If the user chooses not to make use of PTT-provided offerings, teleservice standards are merely a few suggestions.

So even to an American a teleservice description may serve a purpose. The teleservice becomes a means of providing *interoperability* between different makes and models of TE. The carrier may provide only a bearer service, but the customer makes use of a teleservice. In this scenario, the main question becomes one of authority: Whose teleservice descriptions are applicable? Market forces are likely to be more important than the CCITT; de facto standards, and de jure standards from other bodies, could emerge.

The Telephony Teleservice

In the European model of ISDN, telephony itself is a teleservice, offered over the speech or 3.1-kHz bearer service. This definition might be a disingenuous one, designed to demonstrate that the U.S. regulators cannot prevent the telephone companies from being in the teleservice business! But in the United States, telephony is defined as being essentially synonymous with the bearer services that support it, and not a teleservice.

Videotex

This computer time-sharing service, allowing menu-driven access to databases, is offered by many PTTs. The French are perhaps the most familiar with it; their PTT distributed millions of small computer terminals at no charge to its subscribers, ostensibly to replace telephone books. The many information providers attached to the network, which divide their revenues with the PTT, range from business and travel databases to the many popular "pink" services that provide interactive soft-core pornography.

With many PTTs and other carriers, including U.S. telephone companies (not as part of ISDN, but through separate subsidiaries or with strict accounting separations to prevent cross-subsidies), providing videotex services, it was natural to define this as an ISDN teleservice. In the world of personal computers this is the most successful remnant of computer time-sharing. Not only does this provide access to static databases, but interactive applications like electronic mail and game-playing are also provided. Text and graphic images are both supported.

Telex, Teletex, and Telefax 4

Teletex is a modernized form of *Telex* message switching. Originally operating at 1200 bps in several European countries, Teletex networks are now able to interconnect to ISDN as teleservices. ISDN can also provide speeded-up access to Telex networks, exchanging messages and providing speed conversion. Many other electronic mail systems exist as well and are likely to be added to the ISDN Teleservice roster in the future.

Telefax 4 is based on Group 4 facsimile, a CCITT-defined 64 kbps all-digital fax service that requires about two seconds to transfer a typical page. *The Mixed Mode* teleservice combines Telefax 4 and Teletex into one call to provide both images and text.

Message Handling

CCITT Recommendations of the X.400 series define an electronic message-handling service that has been widely implemented. It too is an ISDN teleservice. Many non-PTT networks (such as MCI Mail in the United States) provide X.400 services, and it is widely implemented in private computer networks as well. The X.400 protocols are referred to as *Message Oriented Text Interchange Systems* (MOTIS) within the context of OSI, where they are now accepted by ISO as well.

Many other teleservices may also be defined or are currently in the process of being defined. In theory, teleservices can have supplementary services of their own, but no supplementary services for teleservices have been defined to date.

Chapter
Five

ISDN Architecture and Reference Model

The ISDN Reference Configuration

ISDN has a language of its own. Its terminology is an important part of the architecture that the details are built upon. And just as ISDN's services reflect the heritage of the telecommunications industry that spawned it, ISDN's architecture is a framework for continuing evolution. The role of individual components is defined so that each can be designed separately with some hope of the finished system's succeeding as a whole.

One of the most fundamental expressions of the ISDN architecture is the *reference configuration,* a schematic diagram that models the relationship between the various *functional groups* and *reference points.* Shown in Fig. 5.1, the reference configuration should not be confused with a real network topology; it is simply the minimum diagram needed to show its components.

A *functional group* is a representation of a group of functions that might be found in a typical device in a real network. Any given functional group, like any real device, provides a certain set of functions. By defining them in

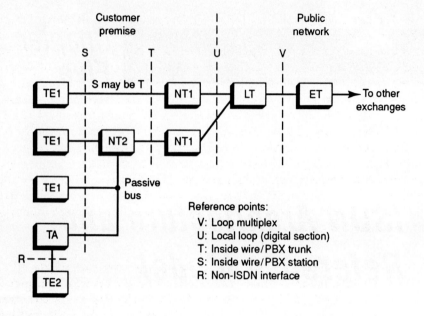

Figure 5.1 *The ISDN Reference Configuration shows functional groups and reference points.*

the abstract, ISDN's reference configuration allows for future developments to be inserted into the architecture and doesn't constrain implementations.

A *reference point* is the interface between two functional groups. It typically corresponds to a point on a wire but could conceivably exist only in software or in theory. Services are typically defined by their behavior at a reference point.

The Network Terminators

The most obvious place to begin to explore ISDN is at the point at which most of its services are defined, the *user-network interface* (UNI). But there is no such animal in the CCITT reference configuration! That's because there are three possible sites for the UNI, the applicable one depending upon national regulations and customer configuration.

ISDN's digital local loop terminates at the customer premise on a functional group called NT1 (network terminator 1). This is conceptually quite simple, having only physical layer and maintenance functions. It corresponds most closely to the pre-ISDN Channel Service Unit (CSU) and Data Service

Unit (DSU), the devices that terminate digital private lines in North America and some other countries.

As defined in ANSI T1.601-1988, the Basic Rate local loop uses a two-wire (one pair) interface and a fairly complex line code capable of supporting 160 kbps for a typical maximum distance of 18 kilofeet. (Where else but in the North American telephone industry would a standard unit of measurement be created by appending the metric prefix *kilo* in front of *foot*?) The corresponding intrabuilding transmission system on the user side of the NT1 uses four wires and a simpler line code at a rate of 192 kbps. The extra bandwidth (48 kbps) is needed for local functions. NT1 provides loop-around testing to the central office and other test signals, while providing a separate set of functions needed to support the four wire internal interface. The Primary Rate requires some NT1 functions too, even though there is no line rate or signaling code conversion.

CCITT Recommendations define the user side of the NT1 as reference point T. The network side, however, is conspicuous in the CCITT reference model for *not* having a reference point attached to it. That's a political decision: In the ANSI standards the network side of NT1 is reference point U. The U.S. Federal Communications Commission ruled that NT1, like the CSU, should be customer provided, so in the United States the user-network interface is at reference point U. Most other countries allow the telephone company to provide the NT1, so the customer does not get access to what would be the "U interface."

In most countries the UNI occurs at reference point T, but some administrations still supply their customers with local switching equipment, such as PBX systems, as well. In such cases the UNI may be at reference point S. Functional group NT2 is any device between NT1 and the TE that intercedes in ISDN signaling above layer 1; it usually provides local switching service.

Typically, NT2 is described as being a PBX or a Local Area Network, but only a hard-core devotee of integrated voice and data switching could possibly take a typical implementation of NT2, or any other PBX, for a LAN! In some cases, however, it may be possible to use a LAN as part of a distributed NT2 entity, especially one whose application is limited to data. The NT2 in such an installation would consist of the collective ISDN to LAN gateways, plus the LAN itself. The ISDN-standardized S and T reference points would not actually touch the LAN.

The S reference point occurs at the terminal side of the NT2. Coincidentally, S and T can be taken to refer to *station* and *trunk* on an ISDN PBX. In terms of protocol and electrical characteristics the two reference points are identical; a telephone set cannot tell S from T. They are distinguished only by their relative position: At the T reference point, layer 2 and 3 signaling toward the TE is provided directly by the network, while at S it may be provided by the NT2. The two points may be coincidental, as when there is no NT2 provided.

Terminal Endpoints and Terminal Adapters

The TE1 (terminal endpoint 1) functional group includes all manner of native-mode ISDN terminal gear, ranging from telephones to computers to fax machines. By definition a TE1 attaches to the S or T reference point and does not provide a switching function to support other gear. A corresponding concept in X.25 networks is *Data Terminal Equipment,* or DTE. But ISDN, of course, is not limited to data, so it simply has "TE," which can stand for terminal equipment or terminal endpoint.

If only TE1s could make use of ISDN, the service would not be very popular! Some business telephone users would buy the service, but hardly any computer users: The early ISDN vision of integrated telephone-computer workstations died long before the first ISDN came on line, sunk by the lack of customer demand. Instead, virtually all early ISDN data communication is based on use of the *terminal adapter* (TA) functional group. This provides whatever functions are needed to attach a non-ISDN device to the S reference point. A TA typically provides all of the ISDN-specific functions: DSS1 signaling, ISDN physical layer protocols, and often the *rate adaptation* needed to support any data rate other than the unrestricted 64,000 bps. A TA is the nearest ISDN equivalent of a modem.

The user side of a TA is reference point R, and any device attached to it is classified as a TE2. Reference point R refers to *non-ISDN* and older interfaces, such as RS-232C, V.35 and even the analog telephone line.[1] It's whatever the TE2 requires, and the TE2 is whatever the customer has. This is the "escape hatch" from ISDN to the real world of customer-provided devices.

The Passive Bus

A key feature of the S reference point at the Basic Rate is that it permits up to eight devices, TE1s and TAs, to be attached to a single line. This differs from previous digital PBX technology, which could support only a single device per line. The details of the passive bus will be discussed in Chapter 6.

At first glance the passive bus looks a bit like a Local Area Network. The semblance, however, is quite cursory. Devices on the bus use an arbitration technique to share access to the network, not to communicate with each other. A telephone, fax machine, and computer within an office might share the line; since there are two B channels, two B-channel calls can be active at

---

[1] The formal CCITT definition of reference point R used to be restricted to CCITT-standardized interfaces, such as V.24 and V.35, and did not include the analog telephone. However, this reference point is the logical home for all non-ISDN devices.

once, independent of each other. In some offices, two adjacent desks share a line but have separate telephones. That enables ISDN to get by with fewer lines than an equivalent analog PBX or Centrex system. But contention can be a problem, so few customers have actually installed more than two devices per line.

The nature of the passive bus is particularly important in considering the impact of ISDN on residential telephone service. Today, in most countries, several telephones can be plugged into one analog telephone line; all will ring together, and more than one can be *bridged* onto a single call. Someone can answer the kitchen phone and shout to someone else, who will join the call in the bedroom. This type of operation is not supported by the passive bus! Several TEs may ring, but the first one to answer the call owns it. *Privacy* is inherent. Telephones in Germany work this way, but for most people, ISDN will not provide a satisfactory residential service without either a small NT2 (to transfer and bridge calls) or, more likely (and cheaply), a TA and analog telephones. Subscribers who use ISDN for their home computers may end up needing to pull at least *three* pairs through their homes, one for the analog telephones and two for the ISDN.

Inside the Network

The UNI represents the edge of the ISDN cloud, the contents of which are nominally of no concern to the user. But they are certainly of concern to the telephone company! ISDN standards exist not only to help customers acquire NT and TE equipment, but also to help network providers build their own networks.

ET, LT, and Reference Point V. Analog telephone lines often, but not always, terminate directly at a central office switch. Analog local loops perform quite well for a few miles, and their range can be considerably extended by inserting series loading coils. These cancel the line capacitance at audio frequencies, while severely limiting high frequency response. A loaded copper line can provide adequate voice quality for 5–10 miles, depending upon the gauge of the copper.

ISDN is more finicky. The Basic Rate interface at reference point U (which requires unloaded lines) has a shorter range than an analog line, while the North American Primary Rate uses T1 carrier, which requires repeaters every 6000 feet. The European PRI, using "E1" carrier (2.048 Mbps), is similar. If ISDN were available only to customers who were within that distance of the central office, it would not be very successful.

Even to serve analog customers, long local loops are often not the best choice that a telephone company can make. Copper wire is expensive, and the local loop often represents most of the total cost of providing telephone service. So multiplexors are frequently used to reduce the number of copper pairs required, as well as to improve transmission quality.

In an ISDN the functional group that provides the network end of the local loop, at reference point U, is called the *line terminator* (LT). The functional group that provides the actual switching and layer 3 signaling is called the *exchange terminator* (ET). Reference point V separates them. Most central offices contain both ET and LT functions, but LT can also be separate.

When remote LTs are used, the LT may be realized as a pedestal-mounted outdoor equipment cabinet, equivalent to an analog subscriber line carrier system. It may also be installed at a customer's premise; for example, an indoor LT may be created to serve an industrial park or office building.

Reference point V is not fully defined as of this writing. This pleases the central office manufacturers, since it often forces the LT to come from the manufacturer of the ET. (Such isn't always the case; a PTT or telephone company can always require its suppliers to adhere to its own standards.) It is notable, though, that the CCITT initially put more effort into defining the interface at V than at U. The former is defined for their benefit, the latter for the customer's. The PTT simply maintains a monopoly on the supply of NT1s and in turn can acquire them from the supplier of the LT, knowing that they will be compatible. Besides, if reference point U were defined internationally, other countries might adopt competitive supply, weakening the PTT's role.

Other Reference Points. Quite a few other reference points are named by, CCITT but are not defined in detail. These include N, between two ISDNs; K, to an analog telephone network; P, to specialized resources within the network; and M, to specialized service providers outside the network.

For the most part these have not been defined as well as the user-network interface reference points; some exist only as labels for a point on a diagram. Other reference points are the subject of future standardization. A link between two NT2s, for example, is called reference point Q in Europe; in North America that point is described as simply another instance of T if there is no special signaling in use and is reference point B if it provides a tandem switching function. Another set of reference points is being defined as part of a network management architecture.

The Control Plane and the User Plane

An ordinary analog telephone line has only one pair of wires, which carries both the actual conversation and the signaling messages that are needed to establish its connections. An ordinary packet-switched network access, using either the common connection-oriented approach typified by X.25 or a connectionless approach typified by the Internet, interleaves control information among its messages. ISDN, on the other hand, breaks with this tradition. It separates the functions needed to make connections from the actual connections themselves.

The *control plane* in the model is where ISDN's signaling takes place. It is typically referred to as *out-of-band* signaling because separate bandwidth is used for signaling and the connection itself. Most of the time, actual communications between end users occurs in the *user plane*, whose bandwidth is relatively unencumbered by the requirements of connection establishment.

In Fig. 5.2, observe the ISDN protocol stack for ISDN circuit switching compared with the X.25 protocol stack. The connection establishment phase of ISDN X.25 is sometimes divided into B channel and D channel portions. The D channel may be used to create the connection to the packet handler, enabling the B channel to support the X.25 protocols.

 It becomes clear that for data applications, ISDN's two-plane approach is more complicated than non-ISDN packet switching. It wasn't created because data users demanded it, or even because data users wanted it at all. Indeed, the fact that ISDN

Figure 5.2 *ISDN call control compared with X.25 packet call control. Note that ISDN separates the call setup procedures from the data transfer phase. ISDN Circuit and Frame Relay services operate this way; ISDN Packet Mode service (X.31) retains X.25 virtual call setup procedures.*

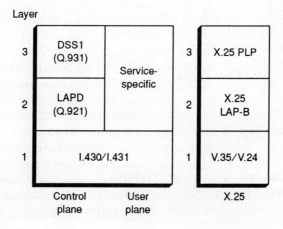

packet mode (X.31) uses traditional X.25 call control procedures (after the connection to the packet handler has been established) reflects both the preference of X.25 users, who see no reason to change, and the carriers' investment in X.25. ISDN Frame Relay (a "new packet mode"), on the other hand, uses the D channel to set up its virtual circuits. That reflects its creation as part of the ISDN standardization process: There are fewer pre-ISDN Frame Relay users. And some pre-ISDN Frame Relay systems do have their own inband signaling systems.

Out-of-band signaling is favored for ISDN because it works better for voice calls. It enables the B channel to have full bit transparency during connections. An analog telephone line hangs up a call by opening the circuit, preventing the flow of current, which is detected by a relay. An X.25 network disconnects a virtual call when a Clear Request packet tells it to. What does one do with a digital voice network except create a separate signaling channel? And if the voice network is to be able to carry other services, should they not do things in the same way?

This doesn't reflect disregard for data users' wishes so much as it reflects the inevitable compromises that take place when disparate services are combined onto a single network. Economy of scale, it can be argued, outweighs economy of specialization. One network is better than two, even if some of its features look a bit odd. Out-of-band signaling for data is at worst a petty inconvenience, but it opens up a whole range of voice features that could never have been accommodated without it.

Three Planes in Private ISDNs?

An interesting variation upon the two-plane ISDN architecture is found in the modeling done on behalf of private network standardization. ISDN is defined as a private network whose internal protocols are invisible to users. Within the cloud, Signaling System No. 7 is generally used. But the vast majority of PBX systems don't support Signaling System No. 7: It is far more complex than DSS1, and very few PBX customers have any use for it.

But what about large corporations that have private voice networks? "Blue Book" ISDN provides them with no support. PBX vendors are free to define their own proprietary interswitch protocols, but they can't find much help in the ISDN subscriber interface protocols. In the United Kingdom, PBX vendors are encouraged to support British Telecom's own Distributed Private Network Signaling System (DPNSS), a pre-ISDN out-of-band signaling protocol for PBXs. DPNSS has little support elsewhere, though; most suppliers and users would prefer to see ISDN extended to include private nets. Three large European PBX manufacturers — Alcatel, Siemens, and Ericsson — are cooperating on a newer ISDN-based protocol, IPNS.

The European Computer Manufacturers' Association (ECMA), a private body that has been instrumental in many aspects of early ISDN development, published a Technical Report on private networks (TR/NTW), which set up a framework for applying ISDN methodology to private networks. This has led to some development work on an inter-PBX protocol called Q-sig. And the OSI standards body, ISO/IEC Joint Technical Committee 1, now has a group working on private telephone network signaling, picking up in part from the ECMA work.

One of the features of these private ISDNs is a *three*-plane model for private ISDN (see Fig. 5.3). Not only is there a user plane carried between end systems, but two control planes are needed. One is needed to enable the PBX (or NT2) to communicate with other PBXs, the other to enable the PBX to communicate with the public ISDN, as required, in order to maintain these signaling connections to other PBXs.

Three Layers

The early development of ISDN protocols occurred during the early 1980s, at the same time that the OSI project was getting seriously under way at ISO. OSI proclaimed the importance of layering, and ISDN followed suit. The result is an ISDN layered model that pays some heed to the OSI Reference Model while really being based on earlier concepts, especially telephony and X.25 packet switching.

One important difference between ISDN and OSI layering is that the latter operates in one plane, while ISDN layering is applied differently to the control plane and user plane. It's the control plane that uses three layers all the time. With circuit-mode bearer services the user plane rarely goes above Layer 1 until it leaves the ISDN.

Layer 1: Physical

The Physical layer, sitting at the bottom of the stack, is responsible for the same functions as the OSI Physical layer. It conveys bits. But its multiplexing function is required to separate the D channel from the other channels; thus the control plane separates from the user plane above Layer 1. It also provides a collision detection scheme for passive bus arbitration.

The Physical layer protocols include a number of maintenance functions, while the Basic Rate S and T reference point protocol includes support for passive bus arbitration as well.

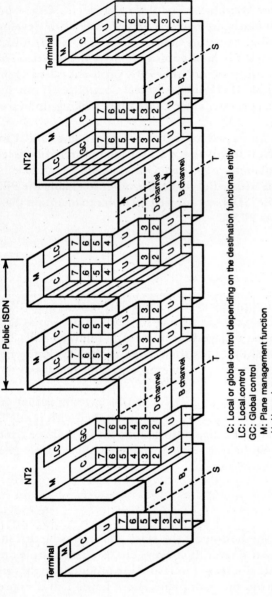

Figure 5.3 *Private ISDN protocol reference model, based on CCITT I.320. In addition to the transfer of user information (U), separate control mechanisms operate between the private ISDN and the local network interface (LC) and between the switching systems that support the end users (GC).   Reprinted courtesy of the exchange Carriers Standards Association (ECSA), T1S1.1/89-562. Note that this is derived from a working document and may be subject to change.*

C: Local or global control depending on the destination functional entity
LC: Local control
GC: Global control
M: Plane management function
U: User plane

Notes: 1. For simplicity, U reference points and NT1 functional units are not shown.
2. The protocol used across "T" reference point for basic call setup is the protocol specified in Q.931.
3. This example pertains to a circuit mode bearer connection on a basic rate interface or on a primary rate interface using associated signaling with user-user information and supplementary service control.

Layer 2: Data Link

The Data Link layer operates on the Control plane, again serving essentially the same function as the OSI Data Link layer. But the LAPD protocol used in ISDN includes a multiplexing function that is not found in the LAP-B protocol more commonly found in OSI stacks (thanks to its inclusion in X.25) and an address negotiation scheme to allow TEs to automatically choose a unique TE Identifier.

The User plane for packet mode services specifies a Data Link layer protocol as well. The D channel requires LAPD because it needs to distinguish signaling from user data, while the B channel usually uses LAP-B because that's inherited from the X.25 standard. Circuit mode services don't have a specified Layer 2 protocol in the user plane; it's the user's choice. It is possible in DSS1 to inform the recipient of a call what Layer 2 protocol will be used, but it's transparent to the network.

Layer 3

Here's where OSI and ISDN diverge a bit more. In OSI, Layer 3 is the Network layer, routing packets to the specified network service access point (NSAP). It provides a service directly to the Transport layer and may internally consist of separate protocols occupying different *roles*. For example, an X.25 network may provide the *Subnetwork Access* role, with the OSI Connectionless Network (Internetwork) protocol occupying the *Subnetwork Independent Convergence* role.

ISDN lacks such subtlety. Indeed, its Layer 3 protocol, DSS1, only loosely corresponds to X.25 Level 3 when providing a packet-mode service. In ISDN frame mode applications, DSS1 replaces the equivalent X.25 connection establishment protocol, specifying the address and call parameters.

In the case of circuit-mode services the OSI Reference Model is rather inappropriate: OSI doesn't address telephony or its equivalent at all. Indeed, one can easily view any circuit-mode service as simply a bit pipe operating in the physical layer. In such a case, ISDN's Layer 3 call setup function doesn't correspond very well to the OSI Network layer. Instead, it's somewhat like an Application layer protocol, in which the application is making or breaking a connection! Its addressing function, however, fits squarely in Layer 3.

To verify this, perform a simple thought experiment: Can you imagine using call control protocols to set up connections between, say, railroad tracks or electrical conductors? It's not hard. The fact that we're dealing with a telecommunications network doesn't change the nature of circuit establishment. ISDN's Layer 3 isn't really OSI Layer 3; it's just the layer that sits atop Layer 2! And it doesn't need a Layer 4.

ISDN purists wince at that thought; the OSI Reference Model was even changed to accommodate out-of-band signaling and other ISDN innovations and now defines such connection control as a Layer 3 function. So officially, call control belongs in Layer 3. But the proof of the pudding is in the eating: The DSS1 protocols for supplementary services, beginning with CCITT Q.932, are modeled on the OSI Application layer protocols, not those of the Network layer. It's pretty hard to imagine how a technical distinction between "basic" and "supplementary" service can be four layers apart. (The opposing viewpoint, to be fair, considers the use of Application layer–derived protocols for call-related service control to be a needless complication.)

Thus ISDN's signaling protocols, while three layers high, are often really equivalent to OSI layers 1, 2, and 7. At other times they're 1, 2, and part of "3a." This doesn't mean that ISDN is wrong; it just points out the futility of trying to adhere strictly to the OSI model when it really isn't very helpful.

Addressing and Numbering

Most people think they understand pretty well what a telephone number is. In the simple case that's no doubt true. But when one deals with complex network interfaces and multiline telephone sets, the concept of number can get quite confusing.

The familiar analog telephone network evolved from cord switchboards and electromechanical switches, which provided a simple paradigm: Each telephone line has a number of its own; each number refers to a single line. But there have long been variations. Party lines, for instance, were based on having multiple numbers per line, while hunt groups allowed several lines to be reached via a single number. Multiline key telephone sets provided access to multiple lines (and thus numbers) from a single instrument while sometimes also allowing multiple appearances of any given number.

Still, the behavior of an analog telephone line is fairly obvious. What has proven less obvious is the behavior of a proprietary electronic multiline telephone set, as found in many PBX systems. And ISDN adds a few wrinkles of its own.

Is a Number Just an Address?

One view of the concept of telephone number is to treat it as an address by which a call is routed to an intended destination. Such an address is significant only for *incoming* calls. So a telephone set may have several "line" buttons on it, each capable of supporting a separate call, but all sharing a single telephone number. AT&T, for instance, designed the first release of its System 75 PBX to operate that way; only later did its multibutton instruments gain the ability to have different numbers on its buttons.

A second approach is to treat a number as an address for *one* call at a time. Such a telephone set may have several line buttons on it, each requiring a different number, though typically arranged in a hunt chain. Such an arrangement is more familiar to users of electromechanical key telephone sets and is found in many PBX installations. A few PBXs even allow the user to choose either "single-call appearance" or "multiple-call appearance" for its directory numbers. The former is busy when any one appearance of the number is in use; the latter is not busy until all appearances are in use.

ISDN numbering also provides a lot of flexibility. Any given UNI can have a single unique number associated with it, its *ISDN address*. That number may support more than one call at a time, depending upon its subscription option. It may also support more than one TE at a time, using the passive bus. All devices on the bus are offered all incoming calls. But once a call is connected to one TE, that TE alone owns the call; analog-style bridging is not provided. Other options for the bus are possible, though; individual TEs or jacks may have separate numbers, and a TE can have a *subaddress* to which it knows it should respond. (Subaddresses can also be used to identify devices beyond the ISDN interface, or a full OSI NSAP address.)

But other options are possible. Using one supplementary service, several numbers may be assigned to a given UNI; incoming calls are then presented with the destination number included, so only TEs that recognize the called number as their own will answer. That is the Multiple Subscriber Number service. The Direct Dialing In service provides a block of numbers to a multiline UNI group with the expectation that an NT2 sorts them out.

It is also possible to simulate an electronic key system with ISDN by putting individual numbers on whichever lines the subscriber chooses to make them appear on. A secretary's line may receive calls for every number in the department, while other individuals' phones have only their own numbers.

What's in a Name?

The data world normally operates a bit differently from the voice world. Though ISDN treats voice and data in essentially the same way, some related concepts can be applied to ISDN addressing.

A computer network locates things by *address*, where address is typically a numeric value of some sort. Within the Internet protocol suite (TCP/IP), the *IP address* is a 32-bit value that identifies a computer or an interface into a computer. Within the OSI network layer the Network Service Access Point (NSAP) address uniquely identifies a binding between Network and Transport layer entities, thereby locating the latter. Usually, the syntax of the NSAP address includes fields to identify a computer system and a selector to indicate an NSAP within that system.

In both the OSI and Internet cases, as well as in most other protocol suites, applications don't have to actually identify computers by number; names are used instead. Internet mail, for example, is typically addressed, by humans, to names like "goldstein@systemname.companyname.com." The mail application then consults a directory program of some sort to translate the host name, "systemname.companyname.com," into a numeric address such as 16.20.0.67. (Internet addresses are typically represented by the decimal values of their four octets.)

ISDN numbers don't correspond to either name or address. An ISDN interface may have many computers (i.e., a LAN) behind it; each computer may then have its own OSI, IP, or other host address. The ISDN number that reaches that address is, from the computer's view, a *subnetwork point of attachment*, a way to get partway to its destination. An ISDN address can also be used in the *Initial Domain Part* of an OSI NSAP address.

Considerable effort has gone into finding ways for applications to translate names into addresses. This *directory* function is discussed in CCITT recommendations of the X.500 series. A simpler but somewhat less powerful scheme, the *Domain Name System*, is widely used within the Internet community.

ISDN Numbering Plan, CCITT E.164

The CCITT ISDN numbering plan, found in Recommendation E.164, is based upon the telephone numbering plan (E.163) but allows for 15 digits, rather than E.163's 12. It generally contains the CCITT-assigned country code, the city or area code, and the local number. These numbers are assigned by telephone companies, either as ISDN addresses or as other numbers. Since the ISDN numbering plan includes the telephony plan as well as a mechanism to escape to the packet numbering plan (X.121), an ISDN interface is always a part of the existing worldwide voice and data network. ISDN numbering is evolutionary, not revolutionary.

Interworking

One of the popular myths about ISDN, especially in its early years, was that ISDN subscribers could use it only to communicate with each other. If that were true, who would want to be the first ISDN customer? While many data applications are limited to a single customer's lines, the telephone world, like many fax and data users, depends upon being able to make connections with large numbers of other users. Witness the fax machine, whose popularity soared once it became ubiquitous. When only a few businesses had fax machines, they didn't see much use.

So considerable effort has gone into determining how ISDN can *interwork* with other networks. This isn't difficult in principle; ISDN is functionally a superset of telephone, packet-switched data, and circuit-switched data public networks that came before it. But the details are tricky, mostly because ISDN users expect more information than they can get from non-ISDN networks.

For example, ISDN provides *answer supervision* on telephone calls: The caller receives positive notification, via DSS1 signaling, of whether and when the other party answered the call, or if not, why not. Busy signal, network congestion, number not in service, and various other *causes* are all reported back to the caller in DSS1 in the event that a call attempt failed. But what happens when the called party is a telephone on a step-by-step exchange? The ISDN itself doesn't attempt to listen to the call progress tones and translate them, though the terminal may and probably should. Instead, the interworking procedures allow the ISDN to notify the caller that the call has left the ISDN. The user must then switch to other procedures, such as actually *listening* to the call.

A different set of problems exists for data calls. While E.164 is a superset of the older E.163, packet-switched data networks use a different numbering plan (CCITT Recommendation X.121). Interworking procedures provide, among other things, a way for X.121 numbers to be passed along to ISDN users and vice versa. It also maps the various cause codes, for example, the reasons for call failure, from X.25 into DSS1 equivalents. (DSS1 provides a different set, reflecting both data and voice needs.)

A considerable portion of the body of ISDN standards is devoted to interworking. This is not a temporary aberration; analog telephony is likely to remain with us for many years to come, and ISDN will always be limited to a small portion of data networking, though it will provide a major part of the telephone companies' data offerings. And as broadband ISDN comes into being, interworking between it and narrowband ISDN will require additional efforts.

That's why ISDN architecture is, in effect, open-ended. Not only does it include the architecture used to build the ISDN and its own TEs; it also requires definition of the way ISDN interacts with the rest of telecommunications. Like the architecture of a building that must take its setting into account, ISDN is an architectural model whose success hinges upon its ability to blend into the telecommunications environment around it.

The ISDN Hop-by-Hop Protocols: Layers 1 and 2

The Bottom of the Stack

If any one subject defines what is uniquely ISDN more than anything else, it is probably ISDN's set of protocols. While service definitions and reference models are of great academic value and were instrumental in getting ISDN developed, its actual implementation depends more upon the protocols, since they define "where the rubber hits the road" and determine what is actually possible.

A few of ISDN's protocols are based on earlier ones, but many were cut from whole cloth by members of the various committees that created ISDN. The best example of the former category is LAPD, the D channel Data Link layer protocol, which is a variant of the LAP-B protocol found in CCITT Recommendation X.25. A good example of the latter is the Digital Subscriber Signaling System No. 1 (DSS1) Layer 3 protocol used for ISDN call control; it has little in common with anything that preceded it.

ISDN follows a nominal three-layer model, with separate protocols defined within each layer. They were not developed in any particular chronological order; rather, protocols were simply considered completed when adequate consensus formed. Early versions of several protocols were published in the 1984 CCITT Red Book, but many changes were made in preparing the 1988 Blue Book. This latter document is considered the definitive one, with many additions made since its publication, but no changes that would lead to incompatibility.

Layer 1: Physical

It might seem a bit odd at first to speak of a Physical layer protocol, since the simple bit-oriented operations at this layer might not appear at first to have the complexity of the higher layers. But the Physical layer is home to several types of protocols.

At the bottom of this layer is the actual *line signaling:* How are bits represented by an electrical signal on the wire? This is part of the *physical media access* function; some ISDN interfaces have additional access requirements. Once individual bits are handled, the various channels need to be separated via the *multiplexing* function. Finally, the ISDN physical layer has several other functions, including layer *management,* and is generally considered the home of *rate adaptation,* which is needed to run services of different speeds over ISDN's fixed-rate channels.

The Primary Rate Interface

Certain aspects of the Physical layer, other than just speed, differ between the Primary Rate and Basic Rate interfaces. The Primary Rate uses familiar techniques for its line signaling and multiplexing functions. In North America and Japan it is derived from T1 carrier; in Europe and most other places it is derived from the equivalent "E1" format in CCITT Recommendations G.703 and G.704.

North American T1 Carrier. T1 carrier operates at a line speed of 1.544 Mbps (the DS1 rate); in its original application (the D series channel bank) it provided 24 channels of 64 kbps (the DS0 rate) apiece. (Eight kbps are used for framing and line maintenance functions.) Each of those channels was intended for one voice connection. In the most common variation of the North American ISDN PRI, one channel is reserved for the 64 kbps D channel, and 23 are used as B channels. That's pretty straightforward; ISDN simply adopted the original multiplexing scheme and adapted it to its own purpose.

The line signaling for the PRI is also adapted from T1 carrier. It uses a fairly simple technique, *Alternate Mark Inversion* (AMI). This takes each logical 1 and sends it down the line as a 3-volt pulse (mark); successive 1 pulses are of the opposite polarity from each other. A logical 0 is signified by no pulse at all.

AMI signaling has a few interesting properties. It's fairly simple to generate and receive yet has fairly good range: At reference point U the maximum range of a T1 carrier system is 6000 feet between repeaters. (By contrast, the original RS-232 interface was specified for only 50 feet at only 9600 bps.) And because it always inverts the polarity of its pulses, it has DC balance: The positive and negative signaling pulses always cancel each other out over a short period of time. Thus connections do not need to pass DC values, simplifying the interface. Finally, it can be tailored to operate over shorter distances by changing the shape (*template*) of the pulse. Thus the S/T interface, designed for short-haul intrabuilding use, uses a set of pulse templates optimized for shorter distances. This is derived from the well-established DSX-1 interface used for intrabuilding T1 carrier connections.

But AMI requires a sufficient density of 1's, or the receiver will lose its synchronization. That's the reason for the Restricted Digital bearer services. To get around that restriction, ISDN standards recommend the use of Bipolar 8-zero Substitution (B8ZS), a technique that replaces a string of eight 0's with a special pattern that would otherwise be an error because it has two successive pulses of the same polarity. Telephone companies are phasing in B8ZS, which is supplied with most new equipment, but there's a lot of older non-B8ZS transmission gear in the field taking its sweet time to depreciate.

Another potential incompatibility between different flavors of T1 carrier, and thus different primary rate services, is the technique used for framing. Given a stream of bits, how does the receiver know which one is the first bit of the first channel? That's handled by the last bit in each 193-bit frame. A repetitive pattern (1 0 0 0 1 1 0 1 1 1 1 0) in the framing bits indicates not only which bit is the first, but also which frame is which in a 12-frame *superframe*. The receiver must hunt for this pattern in every 193rd bit; after it has confidently found the pattern, the signal channels are usable.

A newer technique is called the *extended superframe* (ESF). It stretches a framing pattern over 24 frames, using only every fourth framing bit for frame alignment. The remaining framing bits are used for a 4 kbps maintenance channel and a 2 kbps error-detecting checksum. ESF is also recommended for ISDN, though some interfaces built from older equipment may omit it.

European E1 Carrier. AT&T was installing the earliest T1 carrier systems in the early 1960s, but the nearest European equivalent wasn't standardized until the late 1970s. Originally defined by the Council of European Posts and Telegraphs (forerunner of today's European Telecommunications Standards Institute, but a lot less open) and informally called the CEPT-1 system, it is the 2.048 Mbps carrier system found in CCITT Recommendation G.703. (That Recommendation also includes several other carrier systems, so just calling this system "G.703" is insufficient.) It is nicknamed the "E1" system, though that term seems to be most popular among Americans accustomed to T1.

Having learned from American mistakes, E1's designers included the High-Density Bipolar 3-bit (HDB3) line signaling variation on AMI, a bipolar violation technique like B8ZS in principle, though different in detail. Thus there is no need here for a Restricted Digital bearer service. They also adopted a higher line speed, providing 32 channels of 64 kbps apiece. One of those channels was reserved for timing (in lieu of the odd framing bit in T1); the other was reserved for signaling (in lieu of the robbed-bit signaling found in most T1 channel banks). This latter signaling channel became the D channel in the European PRI. Thus the most common PRI configuration in Europe is 30B + D, in which the B and D channels are all 64 kbps.

It might have been nice for ISDN to unify the transmission standards across the Atlantic, but that would have been impractical for several reasons. ISDN has to evolve from the existing national telephone networks. Since the multiplexed digital transmission hierarchies differ between countries, neither side could have reasonably afforded to adopt the other's. Equipment manufacturers can either sell into limited markets or provide both forms of PRI. ISDN's goal of "terminal portability" is imperfectly met, but ISDN's goal of becoming real was accommodated nicely by adopting existing transmission systems for the PRI. The European and North American hierarchies rejoin at the STM-1 level (155.52 Mbps). (See Chapter 8.)

The Basic Rate Interface

Unlike the PRI, the Basic Rate interface (BRI) was a novel development, only loosely based upon prior practice. And in many respects, the BRI is the single most distinctive element of ISDN, since it digitizes the last mile in the network for the ordinary telephone set, providing the last link for the transition away from analog transmission facilities. Since the BRI was developed anew, it didn't have a chance to be split into totally incompatible North American and European flavors — at least not at the S and T reference points. Though some variations exist, the same chips (integrated circuits that implement the functions found in CCITT Recommendation I.430) can be used worldwide.

A few important characteristics of the BRI are applicable at reference points S, T, and U. Two B channels (64 kbps) are provided along with a 16 kbps D channel, hence the nickname "2B + D." Unlike some instances of the North American PRI, the B channels themselves on a BRI do not impose any restrictions on digital transmission. And the interface itself must provide some degree of management and timing information.

But there are many critical differences between the BRI at the S and T reference points (which are themselves identical) and at the U reference point. They are different Physical layer protocols that are both capable of delivering the 2B + D service. The S/T protocol is optimized for short-haul inside building wiring use, while the U protocol is optimized for local loop applications.

The S/T Basic Rate Interface. CCITT Recommendation I.430 defining the Basic Rate interface at reference points S and T was completed quite early in the ISDN development process. Few changes were made after the 1984 Red Book version was published. This is remarkable in that the CCITT had to invent it from scratch.

Transmission is simplex: Separate pairs are used in the NT to TE direction and the TE to NT direction. Thus four wires are needed, compared to two for most analog telephone sets. This was not viewed as a serious burden for intrabuilding operation, since the S/T interface operates only to a distance of half a kilometer or so. But nowadays it could turn out to be a problem, since most modern PBX systems need only a single pair to connect even their fanciest instruments. Thus BRI customers might need to rewire their facilities.

Another possible problem with the BRI found in I.430 is potential for electromagnetic interference (in some cases interfering with radio transmissions). The passive bus option adds the need to maintain polarity on transmit and receive wires, a requirement for terminating resistors at the far end of the bus and nowhere else, and a set of somewhat confusing design rules that depend upon wiring configuration. One should not then be surprised if this BRI has not been a smash success!

The line signaling used here, called *pseudoternary coding,* is a variation on our old friend AMI, with the logical 0 transmitted as a pulse (mark) and the 1 transmitted as no pulse. An example is given in Fig. 6.1. No special transparency arrangement, such as B8ZS or HDB3, is required, though. An adequate density of 0's is guaranteed by the frame structure.

Multiplexing is based upon a frame structure that was developed specifically for this application (see Figs. 6.2 and 6.3). Each BRI frame is 48 bits

Figure 6.1 *Pseudoternary line code is used on the Basic Rate interface at reference points S/T.*

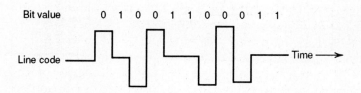

Bit value   0   1   0   0   1   1   0   0   0   1   1

Line code   Time ⟶

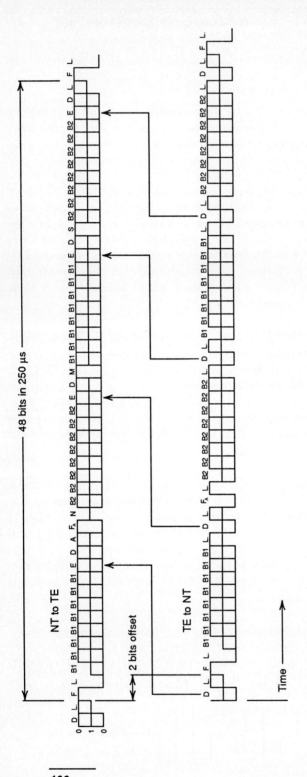

Figure 6.2 *Basic Rate frame format at reference points S/T.* *Reprinted with permission by ITU/CCITT (International Telecommunications Union/International Telegraph and Telephone Consultative Committee), CCITT Blue Book, vol. III.8, © 1988. The full text may be obtained from the ITU Sales Section, Place des Nations, CH-1211 Geneva 20, Switzerland.*

TE to NT Bit Position	Group
1 and 2	Framing signal with balance bit
3–11	B1 channel (first octet) with balance bit
12 and 13	D channel bit with balance bit
14 and 15	F$_A$ auxiliary framing bit or Q bit with balance bit
16–24	B2 channel (first octet) with balance bit
25 and 26	D channel bit with balance bit
27–35	B1 channel (second octet) with balance bit
36 and 37	D channel bit with balance bit
38–46	B2 channel (second octet) with balance bit
47 and 48	D channel bit with balance bit

NT to TE Bit Position	Group
1 and 2	Framing signal with balance bit
3–10	B1 channel (first octet)
11	E, D echo channel bit
12	D channel bit
13	Bit A used for activation
14	F$_A$ auxiliary framing bit
15	N bit
16–23	B2 channel (first octet)
24	E, D echo channel bit

Figure 6.3 *Bit utilization within the frame structure of the Basic Rate interface at reference points S/T.*   *Reprinted with permission by ITU/CCITT (International Telecommunications Union/ International Telegraph and Telephone Consultative Committee), CCITT Blue Book, vol. III.8, © 1988. The full text may be obtained from the ITU Sales Section, Place des Nations, CH-1211 Geneva 20, Switzerland.*

NT to TE Bit Position	Group
25	D channel bit
26	M multiframing bit
27–34	B1 channel (second octet)
35	E, D echo channel bit
36	D channel bit
37	S: the use of this bit is for further study
38–45	B2 channel (second octet)
46	E, D echo channel bit
47	D channel bit
48	Frame balance bit

Figure 6.3 *(continued)*

long, carrying 16 bits from each B channel plus 4 bits from the D channel. Interleaved with this are 12 other bits. With 4000 frames transmitted per second, the total bit rate is 192 kbps.

Those bits outside of the B and D channels, with a total bandwidth of 48 kbps, perform a number of functions. Some are used for framing purposes. Others are set to whichever value is required to preserve DC balance over part of the frame. Others are available for maintenance functions. But the most novel, and in some ways controversial, portion of the BRI is the technique that it uses to permit passive bus operation.

Of the bandwidth sent from the NT to the TE, 16 kbps are used for *echo* (E) bits. Each echo bit reflects the value of the previously transmitted D channel bit in the TE to NT direction. Thus each TE can tell whether its D channel transmission was properly received. When the D channel is idle, it sends a stream of 1's, transmitted as no pulse. The first TE to have a non-idle D channel fills in the empty pulse slots after listening to enough idle E bits. If two devices attempt to seize the D channel at the same time, they stop transmitting and listen for more idle E bits.

This creates a simple priority mechanism. Signaling traffic gets priority over packet-mode data traffic because the former may be sent after waiting for fewer blank E bits. This is important because signaling has a real-time component to it that would cause serious problems if it were delayed. Packet traffic is also more persistent than signaling traffic: If the user were transferring a long file, packet traffic could be present for hours on end. Thus it has to remain in the background!

All told, the I.430 Basic Rate interface is fairly complex, but it has been implemented in silicon by several vendors. Thus its most important characteristics, to users, are the simple ones: It supports the passive bus, has a limited range, requires four wires, and provides 2B + D to the TE. A number of simpler transmission systems have been implemented by using fewer nanoacres of silicon, requiring only one pair, and covering greater distances; the BRI carries a heavy burden because of its bus configuration.

Reference Point U Has a Tougher Job. While the S/T reference point was enshrined in standards first, the U reference point — the local loop between the customer's NT1 and the telephone company's LT — was so controversial that it was removed (in 1981) from the CCITT Recommendations, never mind having any standards associated with it. The PTTs that dominated CCITT were so protective of their planned monopoly of the NT1 (which terminates the local loop at point U) that they refused to admit that it could possibly be standardized.

But in the United States the Federal Communications Commission stood by a 1984 ruling (ISDN, based upon the earlier *Digital NCTE* ruling about network channel terminating equipment) that NT1 had to be customer provided and couldn't be bundled with the service. Thus ISDN could not be deployed without a public specification for the user-network interface at reference point U. This led to a lengthy standardization effort at ANSI-accredited Technical Subcommittee T1D1.

Coming to agreement for the line signaling technique to be used here was not easy. Several requirements had to be met, including a range of 18 kilofeet, tolerance for a limited number of bridge taps, and mixed-gauge wiring. These are the hazards of the real world of what telephone companies call *outside plant*.

Early on, it was agreed that only a single twisted pair could be used, so both directions had to be multiplexed onto it. Some early proposals called for *time compression multiplexing* (TCM). That technique, nicknamed "ping pong," allows the full bandwidth of the line to be used in one direction at a time, switching back and forth rapidly to give the illusion of full duplex transmission. TCM seems simple because there's no problem with interference between the signals being sent and the signals being received. But it requires that the bit rate be more than doubled; each two-way frame requires time for each side to transmit its frame, and a guard interval needs to be left to account for the time it takes the frame to travel from one end to the other.

To send 160 kbps, the bit rate of each burst would need to be around 400 kbps; higher bit rates tend to shorten usable range. Thus TCM was dismissed from consideration because it didn't seem to be able to reach the desired range (18 kilofeet).

The alternative to TCM is *echo cancellation*. This takes a bit more work on the part of the line transceiver chips but has proven practical and is used in high-performance modems (such as those described by CCITT Recommendation V.32). Each end of the connection sends and listens at the same time. It's easy to cancel out the signal that is being generated locally, but transmission lines aren't "perfect": Some of the signals are reflected back to the source from various points in the transmission line, including the destination. These echoes also have to be cancelled out in order to get accurate signals.

Having decided to use echo cancellation, T1D1 needed to choose a line signaling technique. Two proposals were offered. Northern Telecom and AT&T both wanted to adopt AMI coding to the Basic Rate U interface. Both were designing AMI into their early ISDN equipment; virtually all ISDN in North America through 1990 used AMI.

Siemens and Bellcore both favored a technique called *MMS43*, or *4B3T*, which has been adopted for use in Germany. This uses three voltage levels on the line, like AMI, but treats + and − as separate signals (*ternary* coding). Three of these can collectively represent 3^3 (27) different combinations, more than are needed to carry four bits worth of data (2^4 or 16 combinations). Thus four bits (4B) are mapped into a codeword of three ternary signals (3T). DC balance is achieved by using four *alphabets* of 3T signals, such that a codeword that was imbalanced would be followed by a codeword from an alphabet that tended toward the opposite imbalance.

The rationale behind 4B3T coding was that it required only 3/4 as many signals as AMI; it would signal at 3/4 of the bit rate and could thus go farther. This didn't impress the North American manufacturers who preferred the cheaper AMI technique. An impasse lasted for over two years before a compromise was reached: Both schemes were scrapped in favor of one developed by British Telecom and its Canadian subsidiary, Mitel.

This new *2B1Q* scheme mapped two bits into one four-state *quat* (see Fig. 6.4). A quat could have a value of roughly +3, +1, −1, or −3 volts. DC balance was achieved through scrambling of the raw bits, a technique that is widely used in modems (and also found in MMS43). Note that while the signaling rate of 4B3T was only 3/4 that of AMI, 2B1Q's was only 1/2 of AMIs, or 80 kbps. In practice, though, it's not clear that 2B1Q will outperform 4B3T, since it requires receivers to distinguish among four, instead of three, voltages.

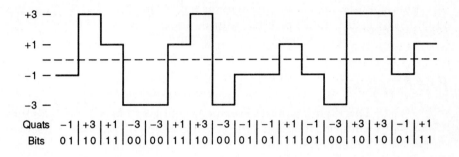

Figure 6.4 *Example of pulse sequence using 2B1Q line code.* Reprinted courtesy of the Exchange Carriers Standards Association (ECSA), ANSIT1.601, 1988. Note that this is derived from a working document and may be subject to change.

Once the decision was reached in mid-1986 to adopt 2B1Q, the rest of the details fell into line. The line signaling rate of 160 kbps provided 16 kbps for timing and maintenance functions in addition to multiplexing the 2B + D channel structure. The maintenance functions were basically Bellcore's doing and reflect a telephone company perspective. The central office (ET/LT) could poll the NT1 for maintenance, put it into loopback mode, and so on. If the customer wanted to test the line, the procedure was somewhat less than symmetrical; basically, the customer was expected to call up the telephone company's repair service number and ask them to perform the test!

Thus we arrived at the standard North American ISDN Basic Rate interface specification for reference point U, found in American National Standard T1.601. This will be used for all major ISDN BRI deployments in the United States and Canada. It might be adopted by some European countries as well, but most PTTs are not compelled to use any one type of line signaling, as they will usually bundle the NT1 with the ISDN service. In such cases the network side of the NT1 is of interest only to the PTT in making its procurement specifications for LTs and NT1s.

To be sure, the CCITT has actually published Recommendations concerning the Basic Rate local loop. Recommendation G.960 describes this *digital section* as ending at reference point T, with a reference point designation (the letter *U*) conspicuously missing from the transmission system. Recommendation G.961-1988, however, discusses the "Digital Transmission System for Metallic Local Lines for ISDN Basic Rate Access" at that unnamed point! It doesn't make any decision, though: It has *six* appendixes (technically not part of the Recommendation), describing MMS43, 2B1Q, AMI, AMI with time compression, a binary biphase technique, and the SU32 group code. (At least they didn't pick favorites.)

Rate Adaptation

This topic is generally lumped with Layer 1 because it deals with a bit-level function: How can data at one bit rate be carried over a higher-speed stream of bits? And while much of the rate adaptation effort has dealt with this issue, the actual protocols have gotten quite complex, handling additional functions as well. Rate adaptation usually takes place end-to-end across an ISDN, not within the network. Thus these protocols are generally a user option, not a network choice, except when the network is providing an interworking service, such as carrying data outside of an "ISDN island."

Serial line data interfaces generally come in two flavors: *synchronous* and *asynchronous*. A synchronous interface requires separate clock and data connections: One bit of data is delivered with each pulse on the clock connection. When a synchronous computer interface is connected to a modem, the modem generally supplies the clock; the interface might not even have to be told how fast it will be going. The modem might also be able to adjust its own speed, as necessary, to accommodate varying line conditions. (Noisy analog lines are, of course, a major reason to adopt ISDN!)

Asynchronous interfaces don't have clock connections. Instead, the computer and the device attached to it (possibly another computer, a modem, or possibly a peripheral device such as a display terminal) have an a priori agreement as to the speed at which the interface is operating. Each character (generally an eight-bit byte) is preceded by a *start* bit, which "wakes up" the other end. A *stop* bit follows the character, for a typical total of ten transmitted bits for each eight-bit byte. As long as the two ends of the line have a reasonably close (a few percent) approximation of the line speed, the receiver will be able to sort out all eight bits of the received character, based on timing after the start bit.

ISDN offers neither option! Like most digital wide area transmission media, ISDN is *isochronous*, or *self-clocking*. There are no start bits or stop bits and no separate clock wire, but timing (effectively equivalent to synchronous operation) can be derived from the line signaling, provided that the rate is agreed to a priori. In ISDN the B channel rate is of course exactly 64,000 bps, within reasonable tolerance.

For most purposes, ISDN circuit-mode data transmission is effectively a synchronous 64 kbps pipe. That's fine for many synchronous protocols: When a block of data (such as an HDLC frame) is ready to be transmitted, it is strobed out onto a succession of bits. When no data is ready to be transmitted, a filler pattern known to the synchronous protocol (such as HDLC flags, or a string of 1's, or Signaling System No. 7's Fill-in Signaling Units) is sent. ISDN is in that regard little different from a modem.

But it's not always possible to operate that way. Asynchronous transmission depends upon bit timing at the agreed-upon speed, such as 9600 or 1200 bps. Even with synchronous transmission an ISDN sometimes has to interwork with a lower-speed network and provide a transparent bit pipe whose effective speed is that of the slower network. A good example of this is a 9600 bps modem pool attached to an ISDN Centrex arrangement, providing connectivity between ISDN users and the vast analog network beyond.

The process of fitting one flavor or rate onto another is called *rate adaptation.* (In the fractured English of CCITT standards it is often called *rate adaption,* using an otherwise-obscure variant form of the same word.) Several standard and proprietary forms of rate adaptation have been in use ever since digital networks began to be built; ISDN has increased their importance.

One form of rate adaptation is *flag stuffing.* This is standardized for X.25-style networks and is defined in CCITT Recommendation X.32 (dial-up access to X.25 packet switching). But this is really just a natural consequence of packet switching, in which the packet network naturally decouples the low-layer operation at either end of a connection. (Only Level 3 has significance across a packet network.)

Another common and early form of rate adaptation occurs in North American circuit-switched data networks. The transmission hierarchy delivers 64 kbps service, but robbed-bit signaling interferes with the low-order bit, so only the seven high-order bits in each transmitted octet are available to the user. This is both the standard method used by ISDN to interwork with these 56 kbps services and the principal reason why these services offer only 56 kbps in the first place! Such rate adaptation is quite natural.

When the first integrated voice-data PBXs appeared on the scene, their designers faced the need for cheap, efficient rate adaptation schemes capable of carrying low-speed data over the 64 kbps isochronous channels typical of voice-oriented switches. Each PBX manufacturer generally created its own technique, encouraging or requiring its customers to purchase rate adapters (generally hidden inside proprietary telephone instruments) from that PBX vendor.

The simplest rate adaptation scheme, *blind sampling,* simply maps each low-speed bit into several successive high-speed bits. When 9600 bps are mapped into 64 kbps, each low-speed bit covers six or seven of the high-speed bits. This usually works, provided that the oversampling rate stays above five or so, but that's not very efficient. Another technique that has actually been proposed for low-speed ISDN rate adaptation is to use modems.

A somewhat more sophisticated scheme was developed by Northern Telecom for its SL-1 Add-on Data Module, introduced in 1979. Now called *T-link,* this provides a set of mappings for low-speed data rates into 64 kbps.

Each transmitted octet may contain both data and control bits. At speeds of up to 9600 bps, each low-speed data bit is transmitted three times. The receiver can then correct for single-bit transmission errors by "voting." T-link was never submitted for consideration as a CCITT standard but was licensed to several other vendors. In the early 1980s it was used by Digital Equipment Corp. for its CPI-32 Computer-PBX Interface, and it is still found in some ISDN terminal adapters (TAs).

AT&T's Digital Multiplexed Interface (DMI) program not only led to the development of frame-mode ISDN bearer services, but also includes its own rate adaptation schemes. DMI Mode 0 provides unadapted 64 kbps connectivity, and Mode 1 provides 56 kbps using the usual seven out of eight coding. Mode 2 maps one or more bytes (arriving asynchronously or synchronously) into HDLC frames and rounds up the speed using HDLC flag stuffing. Mode 3 goes beyond simple rate adaptation and uses X.25 procedures atop LAPD frames. DMI rate adaptation (modes 2 and 3) is used in some AT&T ISDN TAs and voice/data telephone sets.

CCITT Recommendation V.110

The earliest CCITT standardized method for ISDN rate adaptation is found in Recommendation V.110. This was originally designed to allow various pre-ISDN synchronous data rates (such as 2400 and 9600 bps) to be carried over 64 kbps channels. V.110 rate adaptation takes place in two or three steps. A block of 80 consecutive bits is defined by a framing pattern (see Fig. 6.5). Several 8 kbps streams are then identified by using synchronous TDM, with up to 48 of the 80 bits used for data, and the remaining bits used for framing and control purposes (indicating line speed, the state of the terminal adapter's control leads, etc.). The low-speed data is then mapped into one or two of these streams.

It would appear possible to map more than one low-speed stream into a single B channel using V.110, but this support is only latent; V.110 does not fully support multiplexing. (This may, however, be extended in the future.)

Asynchronous data support was added to V.110 in the 1988 Blue Books, using a technique originally published by the European Computer Manufacturers' Association in its standard ECMA-102. The asynchronous stream, with its start and stop bits intact, is first mapped into a synchronous stream at the next higher standard data rate. Then synchronous V.110 procedures are applied to the results.

Several European PBX and central office vendors and a few North American, European, and Japanese TAs support V.110, but it is far from universally accepted. Its characteristic 80-bit block pattern requires specialized hardware (or complex software) for implementation. HDLC-based alternatives are preferred by some suppliers, if only because HDLC chips are more common than V.110 chips.

Octet number	Bit number							
	1	2	3	4	5	6	7	8
0	0	0	0	0	0	0	0	0
1	1	D1	D2	D3	D4	D5	D6	S1
2	1	D7	D8	D9	D10	D11	D12	X
3	1	D13	D14	D15	D16	D17	D18	S3
4	1	D19	D20	D21	D22	D23	D24	S4
5	1	E1	E2	E3	E4	E5	E6	E7
6	1	D25	D26	D27	D28	D29	D30	S6
7	1	D31	D32	D33	D34	D35	D36	X
8	1	D37	D38	D39	D40	D41	D42	S8
9	1	D43	D44	D45	D46	D47	D48	S9

Figure 6.5 *V.110 rate adaptation uses an 80-bit block structure. Bits D1 through D48 may be used for either data or stuffing, depending upon speed. E and S bits provide control functions.*   Reprinted with permission by ITU/CCITT (International Telecommunications Union/International Telegraph and Telephone Consultative Committee), CCITT Blue Book, vol. VIII.2, © 1988. The full text may be obtained from the ITU Sales Section, Place des Nations, CH-1211 Geneva 20, Switzerland.

The Newcomer: V.120

While DMI rate adaptation per se was never accepted by any major standards bodies (AT&T instead created its own DMI/ISDN Users' Group), an HDLC-based rate adaptation technique has been adopted by the CCITT as an alternative to V.110. Recommendation V.120 defines rate adaptation using statistical multiplexing. It's philosophically close to DMI Mode 3, updated to reflect its principal use on ISDN instead of earlier voice-data PBX systems.

The V.120 rate adaptation scheme was originally developed by ANSI T1D1 (as ANSI T1.612, *Terminal Adaptation with Statistical Multiplexing*), based upon a combination of an IBM proposal and AT&T's DMI. Both organizations had made a strong commitment to HDLC (IBM patented it), and neither was enthusiastic about V.110. They met a receptive audience when they decided to pool their efforts within the framework of standards. Once the work was moving in North America, it was forwarded to CCITT Study Group XVII, which helped to finish the project.

V.120 defines methods of mapping both synchronous and asynchronous data into LAPD frames with both protocol-sensitive (HDLC) and bit-transparent modes. One of its trickier aspects is defining how to carry HDLC data streams, since LAPD itself uses HDLC bit stuffing and framing and the 16-bit HDLC checksum. HDLC was not designed to encapsulate itself! Thus V.120 requires users to select the right mode or performance will be degraded. It also requires several other options to be agreed upon.

More than one low-speed stream may be accommodated (statistical multiplexing), with the LAPD address (data link control identifier, or DLCI) used to separate them. Before a DLCI is used, its characteristics are identified using DSS1-like signaling. DLCI 0 is reserved for use as a sort of inband D channel, and a subset of DSS1 (Recommendation Q.931) circuit mode procedures is used.

While Q.931 is not trivial to implement, V.120 was designed with ISDN in mind. ISDN terminals and TAs will presumably already have Q.931 implemented, so the V.120 subset can reuse existing software. HDLC controller chips are becoming ubiquitous (after all, the D channel requires one for its own LAPD), so V.120 doesn't require specialized hardware either. Thus it is likely that V.120 will become a very popular protocol for rate adaptation, especially in North America.

Which Is More Applicable?

Both V.110 and V.120 have their own strengths and weaknesses. V.110 is more straightforward for synchronous communications, and it provides shorter delays. V.120's synchronous modes can be downright tricky to get going. But for asynchronous terminal-to-host links, V.120 is possibly the more natural fit. These are typically price-sensitive and thus favored by cheaper HDLC chip-level support. Whether the statistical multiplexing feature catches on remains to be seen.

Layer 2: Data Link

Once Layer 1 separates the D channel from the B channels, the D channel needs a Layer 2 protocol to support its call control and packet-handling functions. Before ISDN the most common type of packet-switched network interface protocol widely used by telephone carriers was the type described in Recommendation X.25, whose principal data link protocol is LAP-B (Link Access Protocol–Balanced). LAP-B could not, however, support all of the functions required for the D channel, so it was modified to produce LAPD, the Link Access Protocol for the D channel.

LAPD must provide several services. Like any Layer 2 protocol, it must provide framing and error detection. Like LAP-B and most others, it must provide error recovery, which is accomplished through retransmission. Like

LAP-B, it must run in balanced mode, not polled in a master/slave relation-ship like its cousin SDLC. But like SDLC and unlike LAP-B, it must be capa-ble of multiplexing multiple users on the same channel. Once these requirements are given, the design decisions that go into LAPD become more obvious.

The HDLC Protocol Family

LAPD belongs to a family of protocols that conform to the specifications in ISO3309, which outlines the common characteristics of *High Level Data Link Control* (HDLC). This family of protocols began with IBM's invention of *Syn-chronous Data Link Control* (SDLC) and was subsequently generalized by ISO into a more generic family of standards. ISO4335 specifies a set of procedures that operate within the HDLC frames specified by ISO3309 and provided a framework that eventually led to the development of LAPD.

Flags and Bit Stuffing. What all HDLC-family protocols have in common is a framing technique based upon use of the *flag* octet to delineate frames. As shown in Fig. 6.6, every frame begins and ends with a flag, whose binary value is 01111110. HDLC must be able to deliver to the higher layer any possible bit pattern, though, so it also specifies a technique for providing *transparency,* separating its own flags from data that happens to have the same bit pattern.

Transparency is accomplished by using *bit stuffing:* If the serialized data being transmitted contains five 1's in a row, then the transmitter automat-ically inserts a 0 immediately thereafter. Thus the arbitrary bit pattern 0101111101 is transmitted as 01011111001. Notice the extra 0; even though this particular pattern only had five 1's, a 0 was inserted for transparency. The receiver, seeing the pattern 0111110, assumes that the 0 immediately following the five 1's was inserted for transparency and strips it before con-tinuing to process the frame. In practice, this adds on average about one bit for every 63 or so bits of random data. Note that this means that the number of bits transmitted is *not* an even multiple of 8, even though the frame payload must be an integral number of octets. For this reason, HDLC is referred to as a *bit-oriented* protocol.[1]

Normally, HDLC permits flags to be sent freely in between frames, but it's not always necessary; only one frame is needed at either end of a frame. (The same flag can be used as the end of one frame and the beginning as the next. This feature is not, however, universally implemented in HDLC hardware.) In some circumstances, flags are used as an interframe filler that indicates the availability of the channel. On the D channel, though, with multiple devices contending for the link, TEs normally send an idle pattern

---

[1] A good discussion of data link protocols is found in *Technical Aspects of Data Communications* by John McNamara (Bedford, MA: Digital Press, 1988) and in *Telecommunications: Protocols and Design* by John D. Spragins (Reading, MA: Addison Wesley, 1991).

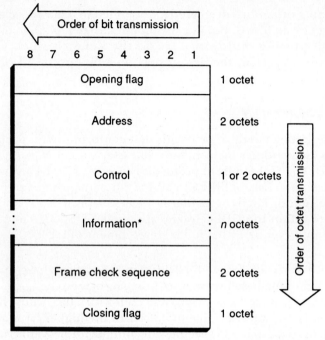

Order of bit transmission

8 7 6 5 4 3 2 1

Opening flag	1 octet
Address	2 octets
Control	1 or 2 octets
Information*	*n* octets
Frame check sequence	2 octets
Closing flag	1 octet

Order of octet transmission

* Not present in some types of frames

Figure 6.6 *Basic LAPD frame format. One or more flags separates frames.*
Reprinted with permission by ITU/CCITT (International Telecommunications Union/International Telegraph and Telephone Consultative Committee), CCITT Blue Book, vol. VI.10, © 1988. The full text may be obtained from the ITU Sales Section, Place des Nations, CH-1211 Geneva 20, Switzerland.

of all 1's, which at Layer 1 at reference point S is sent as zero volts. Thus a non-idle device puts data on the line, while several devices can be idle at the same time without causing interference.

Checksum for Data Integrity. The HDLC specifications allow either of two cyclic redundancy checksums (CRC) to be used to detect transmission errors. The most commonly used CRC is 16 bits long and is called *CRC-CCITT*. (The name *CRC-16* is used to refer to a 16-bit CRC that uses a slightly different generator polynomial; it was used in some older protocols such as bisync.) LAP-B, LAPD, and SDLC all use CRC-CCITT. This checksum maintains a *minimum Hamming distance* of 3 up to a frame size of 4095 octets, which means that a minimum of three bits must be in error before the CRC can give a false reading that an errored frame is correct. *Any* possible two-bit error is guaranteed to be detected. Furthermore, *any* combination of bits in error will be detected if the first and last errored bit are within 16 bits of each other. The likelihood of a three-bit error pattern going undetected is also quite slight (2^{-16}).

HDLC also allows for an alternative checksum, *CRC-32*, which as the name implies is 32 bits long. CRC-32 is an option in some forms of HDLC, including the Point to Point Protocol (PPP) specified for use in TCP/IP networks, and is found in most (non-HDLC) Local Area Networks, including Ethernet, FDDI, and the Token Ring. The CRC-32 has a minimum Hamming distance of 4 for frame sizes of up to 12K octets, as well as superior error detection characteristics in the face of extremely high raw error levels. But it is viewed as overkill for ISDN signaling and is not specified in LAPD.

The HDLC checksum always goes immediately before the closing flag. Typically, a single integrated circuit provides both the framing and CRC generation and detection functions for HDLC. When a flag pattern is received, the first test is to see whether or not the received frame (after removing inserted 0's) is an integral multiple of eight bits long; if not, it's in error (in LAPD and some forms of HDLC). Then (in LAPD) the 16 bits immediately preceding the flag are used as the checksum. The receiver compares the value that it has computed with the value that it received; if there's a match, the frame is presumed to be valid.

Note that there is a bug in HDLC that theoretically lowers its Hamming distance from 3 to 1, wherein a *single* bit error may go undetected! If a bit is changed in transmission from a 0 to a 1, and it happens to create a string of exactly six 1's, then the receiver will falsely detect a flag where none was sent. The 16 bits immediately preceding that flag will be treated as a CRC, and if the resultant short frame happens to be an even multiple of eight bits, the CRC has a 2^{-16} chance of falsely showing a correct frame. The rest of the original frame, of course, will also be subject to possible misinterpretation, since truncating it from the front will cause the transmitted CRC to be equally ineffective. This problem is minimized by including a frame length indication, something that is not used in most forms of HDLC but is found in some higher-layer protocols.

Addressing. The first octet (after the flag) in an HDLC frame belongs to the *address* field. In SDLC this is generally one octet long and is used to identify the different stations that may share a multidrop circuit. SDLC procedures specify that every circuit has exactly one master and one or more slaves. Each frame can be identified by its message type as being either a poll or final (response) message. Figure 6.7 illustrates the LAPD address field format.

Before LAP-B was developed, the first peer-to-peer version of LAP found in early editions of X.25 required two separate asymmetrical connections, each one polling the other side. LAP-B combined the two onto one connection, a more efficient arrangement. LAP-B, though, does not support multidrop lines. So the address octet is unused except for the low-order command/response bit, which is principally used for certain error recovery functions. The poll/final bit in the control field is a *poll* if the address field indicates *command* and *final* if the address field indicates *response*.

Coding for this bit is not always symmetric. The network and user sides usually use opposite values to indicate a command. This confusing feature of both LAPD and LAP-B is believed to be an artifact of analog modems, as it helped to detect accidental remote loopbacks. LAPF (Recommendation Q.922), a newer variant designed for end-to-end use in Frame-mode services, uses symmetrical coding for its command/response bit.

LAPD takes advantage of the fact that HDLC allows the address field to be extended beyond a single octet. (The low-order bit in the address octet is set to 1 to indicate that it is the last octet or 0 to indicate that another address octet follows. Thus seven bits are actually usable in each octet.)

The first address octet in LAPD is the *service access point identifier* (SAPI). Six bits are available, followed by the command/response bit and the address extension bit. The SAPI generally indicates which protocol the datalink connection is supporting. If the frame carries DSS1 Layer 3 signaling, then the SAPI value is 0, and if the frame carries X.25 packet-switched data, the SAPI is 16. Layer management uses SAPI value 63 (all 1's). Most of the remaining values can be used for Frame Relay connections.

The second address octet is the *terminal endpoint identifier* (TEI). This field is required because up to eight different TEs may be attached to the same BRI at reference point S/T in a passive bus arrangement. Each TE requires a separate TEI, of course. TEI values of 0–63 are nominally reserved for manually assigned TEIs, wherein the TE is assigned a value at subscription time, and it is the user's responsibility to ensure that no two TEs share a TEI

Figure 6.7 *In the LAPD Address field format the 13 address bits collectively form a DLCI, which consists of the six-bit SAPI and the seven-bit TEI.* Reprinted with permission by ITU/CCITT (International Telecommunications Union/International Telegraph and Telephone Consultative Committee), CCITT Blue Book, vol. VI.10, © 1988. The full text may be obtained from the ITU Sales Section, Place des Nations, CH-1211 Geneva 20, Switzerland.

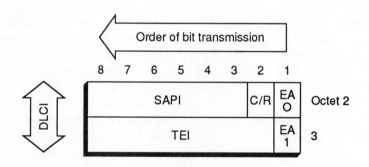

on the same bus. TEI 0 is used for point-to-point links. Values 64–126 are reserved for automatically assigned TEIs; LAPD includes a complex protocol of its own for automatically assigning TEIs to devices as they are attached to the bus. Not all ISDN TEs support automatic TEI assignment. TEI 127 is the broadcast value. It is used for ISDN call offering, as well as for use during automatic TEI assignment.

The address is followed by the *control* octet, which indicates the type of frame. This may be followed by additional control information, such as sequence numbers, depending upon the specific type of message and the nature of the connection. If the frame carries information, this comes next; finally, a checksum precedes the closing flag.

Balanced Procedures. Besides the framing and error detection functions, HDLC family protocols have control functions that provide error correction and link flow control. The various members of this family offer different options, the two major variants being the master/slave, or *unbalanced,* procedures and the peer-to-peer, or *balanced,* procedures. Only the latter are found in ISDN protocols.

Every HDLC connection begins with a two-way handshake. The initial command specifies the mode. SDLC, an unbalanced procedure, begins by sending the command *Set Normal Response Mode.* (SNA advocates would not like to be viewed as unbalanced! Instead, the term "normal response" is used.) LAP-B, found in X.25, instead begins with *Set Asynchronous Balanced Mode.* The respondent then accepts the connection with an *Unnumbered Acknowledgment* (UA) response or refuses with *Disconnected Mode* (DM) frame.

Both SABM and SNRM commands are used to initialize connections in which the *modulus* is 8; that is, every *Information* (I) frame is numbered 0 to 7, then starts from 0 again. LAPD differs from the default LAP-B format by requiring (as of the 1988 Blue Book; this was an option in the Red Book) the use of extended numbering, in which seven bits, instead of three, are used to identify each frame. Thus the modulus of LAPD is 128. LAPD connections are initialized with the *Set Asynchronous Balanced Mode Extended* command (SABME).

Once the connection is established, data transfer may occur. LAPD uses a *sliding window* for both flow control and error recovery. Every I frame is numbered sequentially, modulo-128. Frames can be acknowledged in returned I frames, since the I frame carries both transmit (its own) and receive (acknowledgment) sequence numbers. The received sequence number is the number of the *next* frame after the last one successfully received; that is, it is the number of the frame that the receiver is expecting.

Frames can also be acknowledged, absent returned I frames, in *supervisory* frames. The *Receiver Ready* (RR) frame, besides carrying an acknowledgment sequence number, tells the sender that the receiver is able to accept more data. The *Receiver Not Ready* (RNR) also carries an acknowledgment, but it tells the sender to immediately stop transmitting. Frames that are already in transit (up to the window size) are still accepted, but any additional frames received after RNR and before another RR can be expected to go straight into the bit bucket.

The number of frames that may be transmitted before being acknowledged is the *window size*. For example, in the case of a TE connected to an ET, if the window size is 3, the TE may send frames 11, 12, and 13 after receiving acknowledgment for frame 10. Once frame 11 is acknowledged, frame 14 may be sent. The transmitter maintains the window, which is typically negotiated a priori; CCITT Recommendation Q.921 defines the appropriate window size for various ISDN D channel applications. A station must cease transmitting when either an RNR frame is received or it has exhausted its window.

Error Recovery. Like all HDLC-family protocols, LAPD frames include a cyclic redundancy checksum, in this case using the 16-bit CRC-CCITT polynomial. If the checksum fails at the receiving end, then the frame is simply discarded. There is no explicit negative acknowledgment. Since the error may be anywhere in the frame, including the address or control field of the header, the receiver might not be sure whom the errored frame came from.

LAPD provides two basic techniques for recovering from frame loss errors. If a frame is received out of sequence, then the receiver can assume that an intervening frame was dropped, and it sends a Reject frame, specifying the number of the missing frame. If, on the other hand, the lost frame is not followed by another one in short order, then a timer at the transmitter expires, and the frame is retransmitted. This timer is typically set to 1.5 seconds for D channel applications, though it is nominally changeable. Satellite circuits require longer timers, typically 2 1/2 seconds. All frames following the missing frame are also retransmitted: All of these common HDLC procedures use *go-back-N* procedures. Frames received after a gap are discarded by the receiver. This is not a serious shortcoming for the D channel, but go-back-N protocols are generally inefficient over satellites and other long-delay circuits and at high speeds, since the entire window must be retransmitted after a single error.

In unbalanced procedures a *primary* station sends *commands* (using the poll bit), while *secondary* stations send *responses*. In balanced procedures, either side may transmit at any time. Either side of a LAPD connection may, under certain circumstances, poll the other side.

Upon receipt of a valid I frame that is not a poll, a receiver may either acknowledge it with RR or RNR or piggyback its acknowledgment onto another I frame. But upon receipt of a poll, that poll must be immediately acknowledged with RR or RNR. All retransmitted frames are sent as polls. All frames that acknowledge polls must have the *final* bit set. A retransmission will be repeated for a predetermined number of times, and if it is not acknowledged, the connection is terminated.

   LAPD itself does not make use of selective reject procedures enabling individual lost frames to be retransmitted, although they are optional in the broader HDLC context. Error recovery in LAPD always uses go-back-N procedures (see Fig. 6.8).

Figure 6.8 *LAPD acknowledged flow of information. Note that several frames might have to be retransmitted even if only one is lost, since selective retransmission is not provided.*

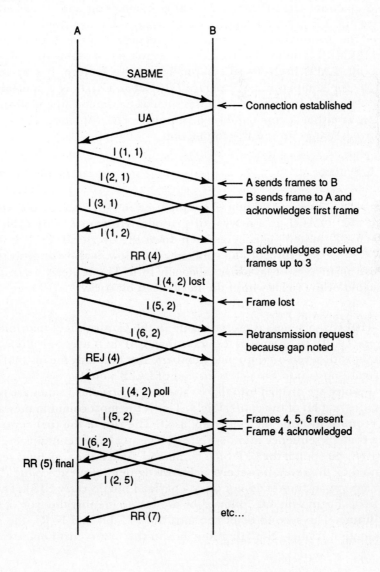

Unnumbered Frames. In addition to the procedures outlined above for sequenced transmission, some LAPD operations have no sequence numbers attached to them. These are used for both control purposes and information delivery. While the I frame provides assured delivery of sequenced frames, *Unnumbered Information* (UI) frames provide a simpler service. UI frames are not acknowledged. They have several uses. In DSS1 signaling, a call is offered to the group of TEs attached to a passive bus by sending a UI frame to the broadcast TEI. UI frames can also be used in conjunction with some packet data applications, in which either the data is not critical or acknowledgment comes from a higher layer.

The *Reset* function, sent with the same SABME frame type used to initiate connections, reinitializes an existing connection and its associated sequence numbers and state machines. This may occur as a result of errors that exceed the protocol's normal capacity to recover. Another frame type, *Frame Reject* (FRMR), is defined in HDLC as a response to certain types of protocol error, but LAPD itself doesn't normally use this feature. It may accept it, though, for compatibility. *Exchange Information* (XID) is a special HDLC frame type used for various purposes such as parameter negotiation; it may be sent as either a command or a response. The *Disconnect* (DISC) frame effectively "hangs up" on the connection.

HDLC Syntax.

The actual bit-level coding used in HDLC protocols, including LAPD, is a marvel of protocol efficiency. Nary a bit is ever wasted! This helps keep down the overhead, though it makes the protocol a bit confusing to follow. It also obviously predates modern principles of layering, especially in its Frame Relay variants, since the layout of the fields within the header is a bit tricky.

HDLC's terseness is most notable in the Control field that follows the address. LAPD, to be sure, is less terse than LAP-B: It uses only the extended formats, with seven-bit sequence numbers. But that only means that control information fits into two octets instead of LAPB's one!

Frames are divided into three varieties. *Information* frames are noted by a 0 in the first bit of the control field. This is the most common message type and requires just one bit to identify itself! The rest of the first control octet is the frame's sequence number (N(S)). The next octet contains the poll/final (P/F) bit (poll if the C/R bit is command, final if the C/R bit is response) followed by the seven-bit receive acknowledgment sequence value (N(R)).

Supervisory frames do not carry a payload but do carry N(R). Their control fields begin with 1 0, followed by two bits to identify the type of supervisory frame. The second octet contains the P/F bit and N(R), the same as Information frames. Note that four bits in the first control octet are spare!

Not everything adds up to an even integral number of octets, even in LAPD. (Note that there are no spare bits in any LAP-B control octet.)

Unnumbered frames are denoted by a control octet that begins 1 1. These do not carry any sequence numbers, so there is no need for a second control octet; enough bits remain in the first control octet to identify all required unnumbered message types. These include the various initialization (mode setting) commands, as well as special functions like XID and FRMR.

LAPF and the Core Aspects Protocol. Frame-mode services use HDLC-based protocols to provide service across the network, not just between two physically adjacent nodes. Two bearer services are based upon this: Frame Switching and Frame Relay.

In the less popular of the two, Frame Switching, the TE at each end establishes a Layer 2 connection with the network, allowing the network to provide sequenced, flow controlled delivery of I frames. In Frame Relay, the network doesn't get involved in Layer 2 procedures at all but instead only uses the HDLC address field to communicate with the TEs.

Originally, these services were to be based upon LAPD, but the LAPD protocol was already complete, and it lacked certain features required for edge-to-edge (or end-to-end) use. So a variant of LAPD, called LAPF, was created; it will be found in CCITT Recommendation Q.922 in the 1992 White Book.

The most important difference between LAPD and LAPF is in the address field. Collectively, LAPD's SAPI and TEI are replaced by a single field, the *data link connection identifier* (DLCI). This is usually just an arbitrary virtual circuit identifier. But when LAPF and LAPD coexist on the D channel, some DLCI values are reserved so as not to cause confusion with reserved SAPIs.

The Frame Relay bearer service makes use of a subset of LAPF called the Core Aspects (ANSI T1.618, also Annex 1 of Q.922). This was created by taking LAPF and leaving off the control field on the assumption that the control functions could be handled by the end systems without network involvement. The *network* looks only at the core aspects (flags, bit stuffing, DLCI, checksum), while the *elements of procedure* that use the control field are left to the end users. The network does not, then, intervene in the error control procedures, does not look at sequence numbers, and does not assure delivery. Here is where layering becomes tricky too: The C/R bit is not used by the network and is effectively treated as payload, even though it is located in the middle of the DLCI field. The Core Aspects frame is shown in Fig. 6.9.

Core Aspects is simpler than LAPF, but Frame Relay itself isn't entirely simple. A major problem with Frame Relay is that it takes away all flow control from the network. The network can't send Receiver Not Ready frames, since the end user needn't be running any form of the HDLC procedures. (The user could, for example, be encapsulating Internet Protocol packets directly

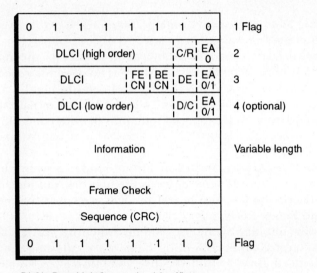

| 0 | 1 | 1 | 1 | 1 | 1 | 1 | 0 | 1 Flag |

DLCI: Data Link Connection Identifier
C/R: Command/Response (used by Q.922)
EA: Address Extension (1 for last address octet, 0 if not last)
FECN: Forward Explicit Congestion Notification
BECN: Backward Explicit Congestion Notification
DE: Discard Eligibility Indicator
D/C: DLCI/Control Indicator (for future use)

Figure 6.9 *Core Aspects frame used for Frame Relay service.*

within the Core Aspects frame.) So how does the network communicate to the user that it is congested in order to reduce the likelihood that packets are lost and to reduce the average delay through the network caused by long internal queues?

In a classic case of standards compromise, the Core Aspects provides three different explicit ways of indicating congestion to the end users and a separate method of prioritizing frames within the network. All of these are optional. If the network and its users can agree upon a technique, then performance is optimized. (For good measure, some pre-standard Frame Relay implementations use yet another signaling technique, but it is not standardized in ISDN.)

Three bits of the second address octet are not used for the DLCI; they are instead recycled for Frame Relay congestion control. (This leaves only ten bits for the DLCI, but a third and even fourth address octet may be added as required. Only the second octet, not necessarily the last, is used for congestion management.)

One bit is used for *forward explicit congestion notification* (FECN), set when the frame encounters a congested resource, such as the internal queue of a network node leading from a router to a transmission facility. A second bit is used for *backward explicit congestion notification* (BECN). This is "piggybacked" onto passing frames in the opposite direction from the ones that encountered congestion. Thus they arrive directly at the sources of the excessive transmission.

A third bit is used to mark frames for *discard eligibility* indicator. This may be set by the *first* node that a frame encounters within a Frame Relay network if the average rate of data sent exceeds the negotiated value (which is set during call establishment). Then, if congestion is encountered, any node may choose to first discard frames whose DE bit is set.

The Core Aspects protocol also defines a *Consolidated Link Layer Management* (CLLM) message as yet another congestion control option. The CLLM is encoded as an XID frame, and its payload contains a list of congested DLCIs. Each switching node within the network must interpret the payload of the CLLM in order to figure out what to notify next; a single CLLM message from one congested node may thus end up as quite a few separate ones as it makes its way toward the edges of the network. The CLLM is addressed to SAPI 62, which is reserved for network-to-user signaling.

Thus three new one-bit fields are added to the address field, and a special message is defined to make up the Core Aspects protocol, while the control field (and its associated sequence numbers) is omitted. Its LAPD heritage remains, but the details have changed quite a bit.

The ISDN Call Control Signaling Protocols

User and Network Protocols

The "cloud" model of ISDN separates the protocols used inside the network from those seen outside but coordinates them into a single working whole. Layer 1 and 2 protocols are significant only locally, but higher layers have impact across the network. Here, two very different protocol suites come into play. The Digital Subscriber Signaling System No. 1 was invented for the express purpose of *requesting* ISDN services across the user-network interface. Riding inside LAPD frames, it enables a TE (or NT2) to make requests of the serving ET within the network. Signaling System No. 7 is the protocol suite used *within* the network to facilitate the *provision* of that service.

These two protocols have some aspects in common, owing largely to their common origins in the CCITT and their need to work together, but they are fundamentally quite different. Signaling System No. 7 (SS7) is far more complex. It is used for non-ISDN as well as ISDN applications, so while much of ISDN depends upon its provision, the provision of SS7 by network operators doesn't hinge upon ISDN's acceptance. SS7's protocol stack is also more complex than that of DSS1. Neither quite follows the seven-layer OSI Reference Model, but SS7 has a more detailed layered structure.

Digital Subscriber Signaling System No. 1

In the three-layer ISDN protocol reference model, the user-network interface is occupied by a protocol that is formally called the Digital Subscriber Signaling System No. 1 (DSS1). Officially, the name applies to all three layers of the suite, including LAPD, but protocols below Layer 3 have other names by which they are better known. This name is actually quite a recent development, having been attached at the last minute to the 1988 CCITT Blue Books. Before that time, the "Layer 3" protocol was known by its original CCITT Recommendation number, Q.931. That name still sticks in common usage.

But only part of DSS1 is contained in Recommendation Q.931. That part deals with *basic call control* and includes both a general syntax and a detailed set of messages and procedures. DSS1, however, also includes the signaling required for invoking supplementary services. In the Blue Book a general syntax for supplementary services is defined in Recommendation Q.932. In the 1992 White Book and in subsequent editions, detailed service-by-service protocols will be grouped into the Q.95x series.

Basic call control protocol definition for circuit-mode and most packet-mode services was completed by 1988, but the supplementary services portion of DSS1 is an open book. New services are constantly being developed. They will no doubt make use of the protocol elements that were defined in Q.932 but will each have their own nuances. Telephone companies and switch vendors alike are seeking to improve their competitive positions, and it's here, in DSS1, that the rubber finally hits the road.

In theory, ISDN protocol development at the CCITT follows a fixed process. A service is approved by Study Group I and defined in detail by Study Group XVIII; then the protocol to implement it is written by Study Group XI. That has indeed been the case with many of the supplementary services. But Q.931 itself was largely written by Study Group XI during the 1981–1984 Study Period, years before anyone bothered to write a service description for "basic call." And that seminal work helped to define the nature of ISDN as much as anything that followed. The service has often tended to follow the protocol, not the other way around.

Something Old, Something New

At first glance, Q.931 appears to be an entirely novel protocol. Its syntax is unique, an intricately woven hierarchy of protocol elements. At the top is the *message*, encapsulated one per Q.921 frame. Each message in turn is composed of *information elements* (IEs), selected from a common pool, containing pertinent details of the message.

If LAPD and the other HDLC protocols are optimized for terseness, then they may have been part of the inspiration for Q.931. Another predecessor was the Facility field in X.25. Q.931 sacrifices clarity (at least to the human reader, but then protocols aren't meant for human readers) in the interest of keeping messages as short as possible. It even adopts some concepts from HDLC while adding some of its own. But Q.931 syntax was really created anew for the ISDN basic call control protocol.

Something Borrowed

It ended there, too. By the time Q.932 was being written, the wisdom of Q.931 syntax was already being questioned. It was of course too late to do anything about it; by 1986 a number of early ISDN implementations were already under way. But Q.932 took an entirely different approach, basing its syntax upon the OSI Application layer.

What OSI layer does DSS1 belong to? That's a trick question! The OSI Reference Model was developed for data communications and doesn't really take voice telephony into account. ISDN's Layer 3 sets up connections, which is generally a function of the Network or a higher layer. But it provides the OSI Network Service only in a narrow case, in conjunction with packet-mode data communications.

A telephone call is not the same thing, nor is a circuit-mode data connection. The latter is a bit pipe operating at Layer 1 of the OSI reference model, providing a Physical layer service. But the former is actually a complete end-to-end application, commanding a complex entity (a telephone network) to establish an end-to-end path between two end users, so it fits better into Layer 7! Yet to ISDN the two are almost the same thing.

In OSI terms, DSS1 basic call control has this paradoxical nature, dancing from top to bottom of the reference model. Supplementary services are often more clearly oriented toward the Application layer. That gives protocol developers a large degree of freedom, which is reflected in DSS1's supplementary service protocol. The OSI Application layer has more flexibility than the lower layers, being structured as a group of miniprotocols called *Application Service Elements* (ASEs). One ASE in particular, the Remote Operations Service Element (ROSE), has found widespread acceptance for many applications. It began as part of the CCITT Message Handling System (X.400) and entered Signaling System No. 7 as part of its Transaction Capabilities Applications Part (TCAP). From there it was adopted as a key feature of Q.932.

Since Q.932 had to fit into the message structure already established by Q.931, its ROSE-based messages are encapsulated within Q.931 information elements. In effect, Q.932 operates at a higher layer than Q.931. Does that make Q.931 into a Transport or Session layer protocol too? Let's not go that far!

Stimulus versus Functional Signaling

Essentially all pre-ISDN telephones, ranging from rotary dial to multiline electronic featurephones, have little processing capability of their own. When they engage in call control signaling, they are really only sending simple minded messages to a far more intelligent switch. As far as the telephone set is concerned, they are only sending messages like "Button 3 has been pressed," "Feature button 17 has been pressed," and "The handset has gone off-hook." The switch then recognizes the meaning of each button according to its own programming. Signaling from the switch to the set is equally simple-minded, with messages like "Ring with pattern 1" and "Turn on feature indicator 3."

DSS1 is normally far more symmetric. The TE, be it a mainframe computer or simple telephone set, is expected to maintain a state machine for all of its active calls and to understand the syntax and semantics of the signaling protocol. That's not a big burden for a computer. But it does make telephone sets more complex.

In ISDN terminology, TE-network Layer 3 signaling that does *not* require the terminal endpoint to maintain knowledge of call state is classified as *stimulus* signaling. Pre-ISDN telephones are all thus stimulus devices. The full peer-oriented protocol found in DSS1, which requires the TE to maintain knowledge of the state of every call, is called *functional* signaling. Packet-switched data network protocols like X.25 are examples of pre-ISDN functional signaling.

Since DSS1 supports both telephony and packet switching in one protocol, should it use stimulus or functional procedures? In the 1984 Red Book, both were supported. But by 1988, consensus had moved away from supporting stimulus for basic call control. Only functional signaling is now supported. Some field trial versions of ISDN (notably Northern Telecom's) used stimulus call control, but by now functional is the norm.

For supplementary services, however, functional signaling is often impractical. Functional signaling requires a detailed protocol to be implemented at both sides of the UNI. If TE vendors had to wait until Q.932-derived functional protocols were ready before any supplementary services could be implemented, ISDN wouldn't be competitive for years to come! Q.932 thus supports both stimulus and functional signaling. Stimulus (which can be as simple as "star codes") is more common today, but functional will gain in popularity as more services are completed.

Q.931: DSS1 Basic Call Control Protocol

The portion of DSS1 that is defined in CCITT Recommendation Q.931 provides basic call control functions. Both circuit and packet mode calls are supported. This Recommendation includes a syntax of its own: All messages are structured in a certain manner, each formed from specified information elements. Figure 7.1 shows the DSS1 message structure.

Message Structure

Every Q.931 message begins the same way. The first octet is the *protocol discriminator,* a constant that identifies the protocol. Q.931 messages are always given a value of 8; this allows call control messages to distinguish themselves from other protocols that may share the same link.

This is also a function of the lower-layer addressing. Modern protocol design makes limited use of self-identification. What if two protocols written by different groups independently chose to identify themselves in the same way? But a protocol discriminator is useful if one organization (e.g., the CCITT) is producing more than one protocol that may share the same service access point of the lower layer. Thus LAPD uses SAPI 0 to carry DSS1 messages, and other SAPIs may be used for other future purposes. The protocol discriminator today is more of a sanity check on the link than anything else.

The second field in every message is the *call reference value.* This identifies, in general, the call to which the message pertains and begins with a

Figure 7.1 *DSS1 message structure. All messages begin this way; the actual message length is variable. The call reference value is generally two octets for Primary Rate interfaces.*

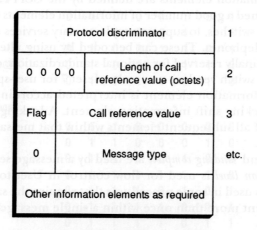

Protocol discriminator		1
0 0 0 0	Length of call reference value (octets)	2
Flag	Call reference value	3
0	Message type	etc.
Other information elements as required		

Note: Flag in cell reference value is 0 if sent from the side that originated the call reference value, 1 if sent to the side that originated it ("mine/yours").

8	7	6	5	4	3	2	1	Information element identifier
1	:	:	:	-	-	-	-	*Single-octet information elements:*
	0	0	0	-	-	-	-	Reserved
	0	0	1	-	-	-	-	Shift
	0	1	0	0	0	0	0	More data
	0	1	0	0	0	0	1	Sending complete
	0	1	1	-	-	-	-	Congestion level
	1	0	1	-	-	-	-	Repeat indicator
0	:	:	:	:	:	:	:	*Variable-length information elements:*
	0	0	0	0	0	0	0	Segmented message
	0	0	0	0	1	0	0	Bearer capability
	0	0	0	1	0	0	0	Cause
	0	0	1	0	0	0	0	Call identity
	0	0	1	0	1	0	0	Call state
	0	0	1	1	0	0	0	Channel identification
	0	0	1	1	1	0	0	Facility
	0	0	1	1	1	1	0	Progress indicator
	0	1	0	0	0	0	0	Network-specific facilities
	0	1	0	0	1	1	1	Notification indicator
	0	1	0	1	0	0	0	Display
	0	1	0	1	0	0	1	Date/time
	0	1	0	1	1	0	0	Keypad facility
	0	1	1	0	1	0	0	Signal
	0	1	1	0	1	1	0	Switchhook
	0	1	1	1	0	0	0	Feature activation

Figure 7.3 *Information element identifiers used in DSS1.*

8	7	6	5	4	3	2	1	Information element identifier
	0	1	1	1	0	0	1	Feature indication
	1	0	0	0	0	0	0	Information rate
	1	0	0	0	0	1	0	End-to-end transit delay
	1	0	0	0	0	1	1	Transit delay selection and indication
	1	0	0	0	1	0	0	Packet layer binary parameters
	1	0	0	0	1	0	1	Packet layer window size
	1	0	0	0	1	1	0	Packet size
	1	1	0	1	1	0	0	Calling party number
	1	1	0	1	1	0	1	Calling party subaddress
	1	1	1	0	0	0	0	Called party number
	1	1	1	0	0	0	1	Called party subaddress
	1	1	1	0	1	0	0	Redirecting number
	1	1	1	1	0	0	0	Transit network selection
	1	1	1	1	0	0	1	Restart indicator
	1	1	1	1	1	0	0	Low layer compatibility
	1	1	1	1	1	0	1	High layer compatibility
	1	1	1	1	1	1	0	User-user
	1	1	1	1	1	1	1	Escape for extension
			Other values					*Reserved*

Figure 7.3 *(continued)*

that indicates, in octets, how many octets follow it. The length may thus be as low as 0 if the information element has no other contents.

Within the information element, data is typically arranged into octet groups. An octet group is one or more octets long and generally ends when bit 8 is set to 1. Each octet group is composed of arbitrary fields. A field is generally assigned as many bits as are required to provide the required number of values. If there are 20 values, then a five-bit field is generally adequate, since that can provide up to 32 combinations. The remaining two bits in the octet group may be assigned to some other related function.

As an example, examine the *calling party number* information element in Fig. 7.4. This identifies the origin of a call. Octet 1 is the IE identifier, with a binary value of 01101100 (decimal 108). Octet 2 is its length, which varies depending upon the number of digits in the number that it's carrying. Octet 3 begins an octet group. Three bits indicate the type of number (international, network specific, unknown, etc.), and four bits identify the numbering plan to apply if the type of number is "international," "national," or "subscriber number." Most often this will be coded 0011, indicating the ISDN numbering plan (CCITT Recommendation E.164), but it can also indicate an unknown plan, a national plan, or the data network numbering plan in Recommendation X.121.

If bit 8 of octet 3 is 0, then octet 3a is present. In octet 3a, bits 6 and 7 are a *presentation indicator*, indicating whether or not the calling party intends its number to be transmitted to the called party. Bits 1 and 2 are the *screening indicator*, indicating whether or not, and how, that number is verified. Bits 3, 4, and 5 are spare.

The rest of the calling party number information element, beginning with octet 4, contains the number digits themselves in International Alphabet No. 5 (equivalent to ASCII) format. These are seven bits long, with the high-order bit always 0.

As one can see, the coding of information elements doesn't follow a single, simple rule. Each information element has its own specific coding, generally based upon the common syntax but requiring knowledge of the specific element in order to decode.

Message Semantics—Basic Call

The way in which DSS1 models circuit-mode calls is not entirely novel, although it might look that way at first. DSS1 defines a list of call *states* that a call may be in. These in turn are divided into *network* states and *user* states, since in functional signaling, both sides of a call must be aware of its state, but may take complementary roles. Each message, in turn, may drive a state transition. For example, a CONNECT message moves a call from state 4 (call delivered), or any of several other states, into state 10 (active). A RELEASE

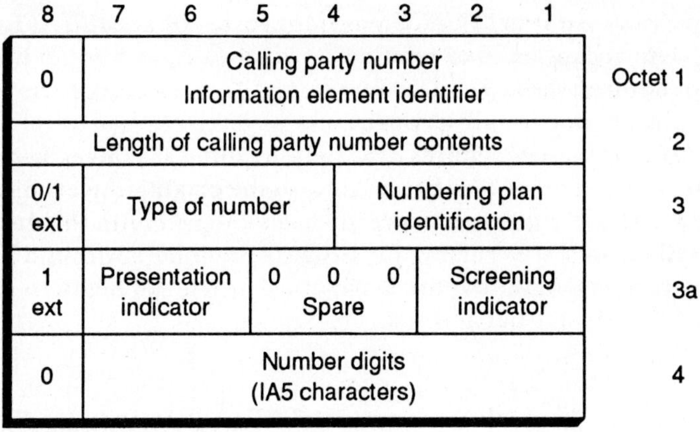

8	7	6	5	4	3	2	1	
0	Calling party number Information element identifier							Octet 1
Length of calling party number contents								2
0/1 ext	Type of number			Numbering plan identification				3
1 ext	Presentation indicator	0	0 Spare	0	Screening indicator			3a
0	Number digits (IA5 characters)							4

Figure 7.4 *Calling party number information element.* *Reprinted with permission by ITU/CCITT (International Telecommunications Union/International Telegraph and Telephone Consultative Committee), CCITT Blue Book, vol. VI.11, © 1988. The full text may be obtained from the ITU Sales Section, Place des Nations, CH-1211 Geneva 20, Switzerland.*

message moves an active call into state 19 (release request), a step toward state 0 (null).

Upon closer examination, though, the message set becomes rather familiar. With a few differences it essentially models the states of a call as established through a step-by-step telephone exchange! An ISDN call is initiated with a SETUP message. This must indicate the *bearer capability* desired and may have a number of other optional information elements attached to it. If sent with no *called party number*, then it's roughly equivalent to picking up the telephone, and the network responds with a SETUP ACKNOWLEDGE message. Figure 7.5 illustrates the DSS1 call establishment procedures.

En-bloc versus Overlap Sending. Note two very divergent options for sending the destination address. It may be included in the SETUP message, in which case it is called *en-bloc* sending. That's the way X.25 and most other data networks work: The data terminal equipment (DTE) that initiates the call already knows the destination number, so it can be sent at once.

The other option, *overlap sending*, leaves all or part of the number for INFORMATION messages, sent after the initial SETUP message. These INFORMATION messages contain the dialed digits in the keypad facility IE (North America) or the called party number IE (Europe). That's more like the way telephones are dialed. (Analog networks drop the dial tone after receiving the first digit. There's no exact DSS1 equivalent of that, though a signal IE sent in response to SETUP may come close.) Q.931 accommodates both data and voice services, so it accommodates both forms of sending. (Some networks may only accept en-bloc sending for data calls, and some have been observed to require overlap sending for voice calls, even though the standard clearly permits en-bloc for all services.)

Overlap sending procedures also help in some instances because the length of an ISDN number may be variable, so the originating exchange isn't aware that the entire number has already been entered until the destination exchange tells it so. In Germany, for instance, numbers within a given exchange may vary in length, but the originating switch can begin to route the call on the basis of a partial address.

Offering the Call. When the network is satisfied that enough digits have been received, it may send a CALL PROCEEDING message to the originating TE. That's the ISDN equivalent of the click that many analog switches generate when they receive enough digits. When the destination TE is notified of the incoming call by a SETUP message, the network then sends an ALERTING message to the caller; that equates to the ringback tone that analog networks send back to callers to indicate that the call is ringing.

SETUP thus corresponds to two very different analog functions. It is both "go off hook" (outgoing) and "line seizure" (incoming; frequently, this is the same as "commence ringing"). Both functions can use the same message because SETUP really tells its recipient that a new call is being initiated. Analog networks are asymmetrical and thus require two different methods of indicating the same function. Thus the offering party tells the network to initiate an outgoing call, while the network tells the destination to initiate an incoming call. The various optional information elements included with the outgoing SETUP message may be passed along in the incoming message as well, although under some circumstances the network may not pass along certain of them, such as the calling party number, to the recipient.

Call offering is one instance in which the passive bus feature of the Basic Rate interface affects other protocols. An incoming SETUP message is typically sent to the LAPD broadcast Terminal Endpoint Identifier (TEI), so that all TEs are aware of the incoming call. The TEs may then compare their own capabilities with those specified in the incoming call to determine whether or not they should even consider taking the call.

Several IEs are useful for this purpose. *Bearer capabilities* establishes parameters for a call between TEs and the network. *Low-layer compatibility* sends information protocols up to Layer 3, while *high-layer compatibility* (not recommended in the United States) describes higher layer protocols (i.e. teleservices). *Called party number* and *subaddress* allow TEs that share an interface to determine whether they are the desired destination. A data device that sees a call for itself may choose to answer immediately by sending a CONNECT message to the network using its own TEI. A voice device is more likely to

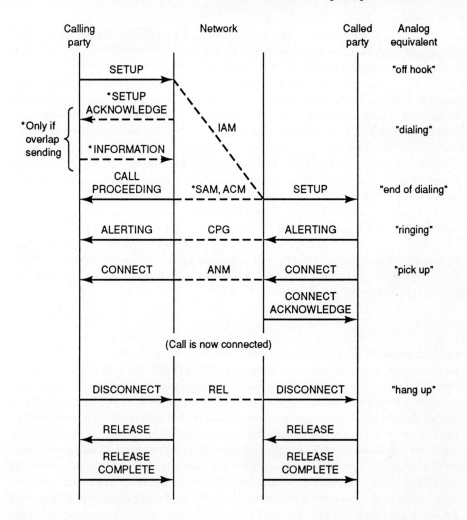

Figure 7.5 *In DSS1 call establishment procedure some messages have only local significance. Others correspond to Signaling System No. 7 ISUP messages operating across the network.*

just ring, waiting for a human to answer the call. If there are multiple telephones on the bus, then the first one to answer owns that call. The network then sends a CONNECT ACKNOWLEDGE message to inform the TE that its TEI is the chosen one and sends RELEASE COMPLETE to any others that attempted to answer it.

During the call offering stage, several timers are required. Some can be set; others will follow values defined in the protocol standards. Procedures are defined for the various timer expiry cases.

As might be noted at this point, the ability to attach more than one device to the same user-network interface (especially the passive bus) makes the call-offering process considerably more complex than it need be. Not only is basic call offering made more complex, but supplementary services and error handling are also affected. This may be beneficial in a few instances but adds considerable complexity to DSS1 in general. Further impact of the bus will be noted below.

At this point, with one recipient of the call selected, a CONNECT message is sent from the network to the originator of the call, who optionally responds with CONNECT ACKNOWLEDGE, and the bearer service may then be used. So to the initiating party, CONNECT is the equivalent of hearing the ringing stop and the line get answered. But it's better, since it provides positive supervision. While analog networks provide call supervision to the calling central office, ISDN provides it back to the originating subscriber. That allows PBX-based call rating systems to know the difference between a completed call and an unanswered one.

Call Clearing. Once a call is active, it continues until either side chooses to terminate it. DSS1 provides a three-way handshake for call clearing. First, one party sends a DISCONNECT message to the network. This causes the bearer service to be discontinued; a DISCONNECT message is also sent by the network to the distant party. The party who sent the initial DISCONNECT message then receives a RELEASE message from the network to acknowledge that the bearer channel has been disconnected and the call reference value has been freed by the network. That message is in turn acknowledged by a RELEASE COMPLETE message, which releases the bearer channel and call reference value for reuse and really ends the call! The party who received the DISCONNECT from the network acknowledges it with RELEASE, which in turn is acknowledged by the network, which sends RELEASE COMPLETE.

What if the call doesn't go through? Analog networks have busy signals, sent by the distant exchange, and congestion signals (fast busy), sent by the network. Various other recorded announcements may also be sent inband. Just as ISDN replaces inband ring tone with the ALERTING message (which doesn't necessarily tie up a bearer channel in the trunk network), ISDN replaces busy signals with DISCONNECT, RELEASE, or RELEASE COMPLETE messages, depending upon the call state. The Cause information element has dozens of codepoints assigned to it. These range from "Unallocated number" to "User busy" to "Number changed" to "Network out of order" to "Bearer capability not presently available."

In some cases, inband voice announcements may still be appropriate. For example, when the called number has been changed, DSS1 allows the Cause IE to carry the new number in a diagnostic field, but this might be a bit much for a simple telephone set to handle (unless it has a display). An even more common occurrence will be interworking between ISDN and analog networks. If you make a call on an ISDN phone and it terminates on an analog exchange that is unequipped for ISDN signaling, the terminating exchange won't be able to send you RELEASE COMPLETE messages with the Cause information element. It will just send back a busy tone inband!

 This interworking scenario is accommodated by the PROGRESS message, which informs the initiating caller to listen for inband signaling, if it isn't already, as the call has left the ISDN. Actually, since it implies interworking with analog networks, a better name might be the "lack of progress" message!

Packet-Mode Variations

DSS1 is really optimized for circuit-mode bearer services, since it models telephony so well. But it provides the full call establishment phase for Frame Relay calls and sometimes plays a role in the establishment of other packet calls. Enough information elements have been defined to allow DSS1-based networks to provide the complete OSI Connection-oriented Network Service.

But for packet mode calls, the virtual call is still made by using the X.25 call establishment protocol. DSS1 might first be needed to create the B-channel path between the packet handlers and the TEs. That is typically done for the first virtual call on a B channel. But once that path is established, no DSS1 activity takes place. Once the last virtual call on a bearer channel is cleared, then DSS1 call clearing procedures may be invoked to free the channel. Specific procedures vary between the Case A and Case B service arrangements, Case B providing closer connection between the circuit and packet phases.

Supplementary Services Protocol

By the time work was ready to begin in earnest on the supplementary services portion of DSS1 that became CCITT Recommendation Q.932, it was widely felt that Q.931 should not simply be extended by the addition of new messages. To be sure, some proprietary ISDN implementations did just that, shifting to alternate codesets as required. But Q.931 is not a model protocol for the complicated applications that can be formed from supplementary services.

That's not to say that the Q.931 syntax is totally absent for supplementary services, just that it requires a lot of supplementation of its own. Q.932 actually defines *four* different syntactic models for the invocation of supplementary services! The first two are *stimulus* signaling, while the latter two are *functional* signaling:

1. *keypad facility,*
2. *feature key management,*
3. *separate messages,* and
4. *facility information element.*

Each of these schemes exists for a different reason. ISDN represents the output of a consensus process, and that process sometimes accommodates different views by allowing multiple options. Different vendors and different types of users have different preferences, and all sides had their say in writing Q.932! (Well, not that users had much say.)

Keypad Facility

Any ISDN telephone (or other TE) can, in theory, have access to any relevant supplementary service, present or future, by making use of stimulus service invocation. The TE need have no knowledge of the service; only the user has to know how to invoke it. The network simply defines a digit string by which the service can be selected. For example, a network may choose to implement the *dial call pickup* service, a form of call redirection that answers another ringing phone, for which no functional protocol had yet been written at the time the user's ISDN telephone set was built. The network can then make the service available by having the user dial *97 followed by the desired number. The specific code assignments are typically uniform across a customer's group of lines or even across a carrier's network.

The Q.932 coding for this makes use of the *keypad facility* information element, carried within the Q.931 SETUP or INFORMATION messages. Q.931 here provides lower-layer support for Q.932 by providing messages and an information element structure that can encapsulate what is in effect a higher-layer protocol. From a hardware designer's perspective this is ideal. Even a rotary dial set can invoke a feature by dialing, say, 1197. ISDN simply continues this tradition.

But from the human user's perspective this is the method of a last resort. It's generally hard to use, and most ordinary telephone users don't like to dial feature codes. In most existing PBX systems in which features are accessed this way, the majority of users never make use of most features. PBX systems have been using this extensively since the 1970s, but customers are migrating toward more ergonomic techniques. And that brings up the second stimulus alternative.

Feature Key Management

Some telephone sets, particularly proprietary electronic featurephones associated with PBX systems, are equipped with dedicated feature buttons. A set
may have only a few (say, *hold* and *transfer*), or it may have dozens. Generally,
the larger sets have both feature and line appearance buttons, but to ISDN
a multiline key telephone instrument is just another supplementary service
that requires a large number of buttons.

Feature key management uses a Q.932 information element, *feature ac-
tivation*, that corresponds to a button's being pushed on a featurephone.
Each such *feature activator* has no intrinsic meaning, and each telephone set
typically has its own button assignments, up to the number of feature buttons
that are physically present on that set.

A feature button may invoke call transfer, call hold, call forwarding,
conference calling, or any other available service, and it may also be used to
select a call appearance from one of many on the set. On ISDN it doesn't
take multiple "lines" to have multiple active calls per set, just the ability to
use the call hold feature and have multiple call reference values.

Just as multiline key telephone sets have buttons that light up, ISDN's
feature key management allows lights as well. Q.932 provides the *feature indication* information element for this purpose. Each feature indication
(lamp) is typically associated with a feature activator (button) and may be
switched into one of several patterns: steady, fluttering, winking, blinking,
and (nodded) off.

Functional Signaling with Separate Messages

The first supplementary service to have its own functional protocol written
for it was Call Hold. This service is unique in that its functional protocol
makes use of separate Q.931-formatted messages. It is doubtful that much
more use will be made of this technique, since the facility information element is more in vogue. Both of these are often viewed as a single generic
protocol, the functional protocol, but they are quite different in operation.

Some other supplementary services, to be sure, are also accommodated
within Q.931, but they are supplementary in name more than in operation.
(In other words, you pay extra.) These include calling line identification and
restriction, subaddressing, direct dialing in, and multiple subscriber number, features that naturally fit into Q.931's call control protocol. No supplementary service other than Hold has its own messages.

The Call Hold service makes use of six messages. HOLD is sent by the TE
to the network to request the service, and the network accepts it with HOLD
ACKNOWLEDGE or rejects it with HOLD REJECT. The call can be retrieved with
RETRIEVE, and the network responds with RETRIEVE ACKNOWLEDGE or RE-
TRIEVE REJECT.

Vectored Call States

The Hold service introduces another feature of Q.932. Basic call control (Q.931) has a call state machine in which every call is at any given time in one or another network state and one or another user state. "Hold" is not included in that state machine. Instead, a separate state machine governs the operation of the supplementary service. The call itself can then be described by a vector of the relevant basic and supplementary states, such as [Active, Held]. Other services besides Hold may also make use of supplementary service states as functional protocols for them are defined.

Functional Signaling with the Facility Information Element

This protocol, the principal method for defining functional signaling in Q.932, is based upon building blocks found in the OSI Application layer (see Fig. 7.6). Procedures are based upon the OSI Remote Operations Service Element (ROSE), while syntax is based upon OSI's Abstract Syntax Notation No. 1 (ASN.1). The entire upper-layer message is encapsulated within a Q.931 facility information element, which may be sent in a Q.931 FACILITY message or piggybacked into other Q.931 messages. Note that this does not

Figure 7.6 *In the facility information element in Q.932, based upon Remote Operations and tag-length-value coding, parameters may be as long as required.*

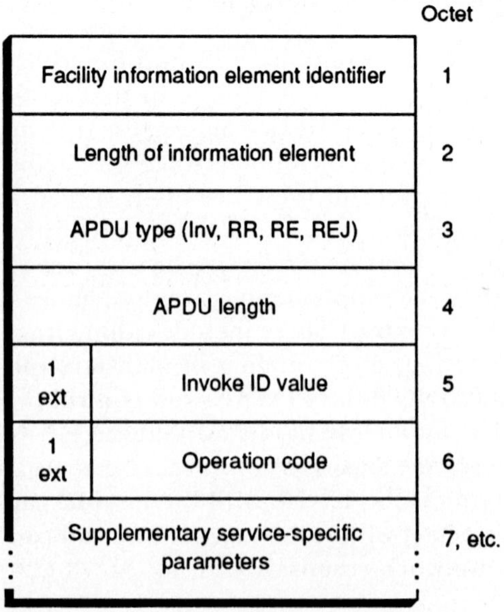

make Q.932 an OSI protocol, since it omits the layer 4–6 protocols required by OSI, as well as the OSI Layer 7 Association Control Service Element (ACSE).

Before going into more detail, one can first examine Q.931 to see how the network and the TE relate to each other when services are requested. The basic call control protocol does not explicitly acknowledge most requests. Instead, a given message causes its recipient to transition from one state to another, which may in turn lead to another message. Certainly the receipt of a SETUP ACKNOWLEDGE or CALL PROCEEDING message serves to acknowledge a SETUP message, but most such acknowledgments are really more implicit than explicit.

Remote Operations. The facility information element is, compared to the rest of DSS1, different. Services are requested along the lines suggested by ROSE, an OSI Applications Service Element that began life in CCITT Recommendation X.400 (Message Handling Systems) and was subsequently accepted as part of OSI. The protocol features four types of *component. Invoke* begins a transaction, specifies the requested service, and assigns an Invoke ID. If the recipient of the Invoke (typically, but not necessarily, the network) accepts it for processing, a *Return Response* component is sent. This is keyed to the Invoke ID and may include feature-specific parameters of its own. Thus there is a request-response sequence required for all invocations.

If the recipient of an Invoke component is unable to accept it, then it may send a *Return Error* component to the invoking party. This too uses the Invoke ID and may provide parameters, such as the reason for failure. Examples of Return Error could be that a requested service is not subscribed to or a required resource is not available. The *Reject* component is sent when the Invoke component contains an error, such as an unrecognized parameter or unknown facility identifier.

By following this syntactic model the facility information element moves ISDN another step into the modern world. While its use is limited to supplementary services, one might even envision the potential for using such a straightforward approach for a future call origination protocol. But subsequent developments might choose instead to go all the way to using the OSI Applications layer, rather than just toying with it the way Q.932 does.

Abstract Syntax Notation No. 1. While Q.931 syntax features a terse bit-bashing style, most OSI upper-layer protocols take a very different approach. Practically all data is encoded in three-part strings, consisting of a *tag*, a *length*, and a *value* (or *TLV* coded). Some hint of this is found in Q.931, in which each variable-length information element begins with a tag and length, followed by an octet sequence. But Q.931 encodes many different fields in each information element.

A stricter form of TLV coding is found in the OSI Application layer. *Abstract Syntax Notation No. 1* (ASN.1) is an established OSI standard for TLV-coded data. Like ROSE, ASN.1 started life as part of the X.400 series (X.409, to be specific, a name that still sticks), and it too was promoted into OSI. ASN.1 provides a recursive method of defining codepoints: The value of one TLV element may be a construct that includes additional TLV elements.

The disadvantage of TLV coding is obvious: It is considerably more verbose than simple bit bashing. While it's a good way of expressing complex data structures, it is less well proven for service request functions. And it's an additional burden upon simple TEs. Its elegance and deterministic parsing have made it popular among computer scientists and the OSI community. To be sure, adding this to the inside of a DSS1 information element actually makes parsing more difficult, since the receiver has to deal with *both* Q.931 *and* Q.932's TLV coding, but it does offer potential advantages for the development of complex new services.

To be formal about it, ASN.1 really describes the way a syntax is expressed on paper (i.e., in the abstract), not the way it is rendered on the wire. But the rules for converting abstract syntax into transfer (or *concrete*) syntax are strictly defined by its *Basic Encoding Rules*, so the protocol writer need merely write the ASN.1 code in text format, and a compiler can convert it into binary form.

Functional Protocol Definitions. The development of functional signaling for supplementary services is an ongoing process. A few of the first to be completed include *Call Waiting, Hold,* and *Calling Line Identification Presentation and Restriction.* Many others are being defined, with the specifics compiled by the CCITT in series Q.950–Q.957. Each individual Recommendation will provide the protocol for several related services.

Service Profiles

Annex A of Recommendation Q.932 discusses another "feature" that results from the passive bus option, the service profile. If several different terminals share a single BRI, and they do not support the exact same array of feature keys or service capabilities, a service profile allows the network to identify the capabilities of the terminals.

A service profile describes the characteristics of the TE. More than one TE on a given passive bus may share a service profile, identified by the *user service identifier* if they have identical capabilities. Each such terminal then has a unique *terminal identifier.* These values are associated with a given LAPD terminal endpoint identifier during datalink initialization.

Service profile information is sent along with DSS1 messages when the interface supports this feature. This enables individual terminals or groups of terminals to be properly addressed. But the procedure adds considerable complexity to the protocol and is really of interest only when several TEs are attached to a passive bus. It may even be viewed as a work-around for problems introduced by the passive bus. That's a rare enough arrangement as is; the service profile could end up being one of those marginal ideas that got standardized because one particular vendor (in this case AT&T) thought it was a good idea at the time.

ISDN Network Management

A protocol suite as complex as DSS1 would not be complete if it were not accompanied by a set of management and maintenance functions. In creating a framework for ISDN maintenance, in particular at the user-network interface, the CCITT started with the OSI maintenance model. But that's not to say that ISDN simply uses OSI maintenance protocols for its own management (or that "simply uses OSI" is not an oxymoron!).

All ISDN protocol layers have management functions associated with them. This follows the OSI model: While a given layer communicates with adjacent layers by means of functions described by primitives, every layer also has layer management primitives by which it communicates with a layer management entity (LME), whose management data is organized in a Management Information Base (MIB). The LME is thus logically adjacent to all layers! A system management application process (SMAP) in turn provides access to the MIB, allowing management data to be queried, parameters to be set, and so on.

The model of ISDN management found in Recommendation Q.940 was inspired by the OSI model. But the actual management protocols that were proposed for inclusion in the 1988 Blue Book (as Q.941 and Q.942) failed to achieve consensus: They were based upon early draft versions of OSI's Common Management Information Protocol (CMIP) and did not conform to the actual ISO-approved versions.

To some extent this may stem from hostility between the computer (OSI) and telecom (ISDN) worlds: OSI protocols are generally quite complex; CMIP requires the full seven-layer stack, including Transport, Session, and Presentation layers, which are often missing from ISDN equipment. But some of the differences may also have been gratuitous; once a telephone company accepts a protocol, it is not likely to want to change it. Since CMIP was still evolving at the same time that Q.941 and Q.942 were being developed, the two were easy candidates for divergence. Some agreement on ISDN management should be arrived at soon, a study period later.

Just what do you do with these protocols? If a device implements them, then it becomes possible for a management station anywhere on the network to remotely manage the device. And that management station may also support non-ISDN devices using their protocols.[1] For example, an NT2 (say, a PBX) could be queried about the error rate on its D channel, which might be a useful indication of line quality. But this might not be so easy with smaller devices, such as an NT1 or a telephone set, for which these management protocols are too complex. But even then it's possible, at least in theory, for one device that implements the Q.940 series protocols to use a simpler means to communicate with another device and in turn report on its behalf to the management station.

ISDN management is still not a well-developed art. But as networks grow, it will gain in popularity. The ability to participate in a managed network will be another added value for ISDN, compared with predecessor telephone networks.

Signaling System No. 7

Both DSS1 and SS7 are the brainchildren of CCITT Study Group XI, and both were designed to handle part of the ISDN signaling requirements. But while DSS1 has essentially no life of its own outside of ISDN, SS7 is intended to be used with other types of networks as well, including analog telephony.

SS7 provides signaling between central offices and between offices and adjunct processors or servers (e.g., in the context of Intelligent Networks). In the early days of telephony, interoffice signaling was handled by operators. The first dial networks were limited to a single exchange. The earliest interexchange dialing arrangements were based upon sending dial pulses between electromechanical switches. For very short hauls, DC voltages could be interrupted, but for longer distances, "on-hook" and "off-hook" were represented by the presence or absence of a tone. In the United States a 2600 Hz tone occupied idle trunk circuits, and dial pulses could be sent by turning that tone on and off.

By the 1960s, multifrequency (MF) tone signaling systems had become common. These resembled the Touch-Tone signaling used by modern subscriber instruments but of course used different tones (for security and other reasons). This sped up signaling considerably, as a telephone number could be sent by using tones in about one second. Billing information could also be send that way; many central offices use inband tones to send Automatic

---

[1] The Simple Network Management Protocol (SNMP), developed for use in TCP/IP networks, has achieved considerable acceptance recently, even though it is not part of OSI. A management station could conceivably use SNMP to manage some devices while using ISDN and OSI protocols to manage others.

Number Identification to the toll switching center, where the billing details are collected.

Multifrequency signaling remains in widespread use, but it has some clear disadvantages. One problem is security: Larcenous end users can sometimes fool the system by sending certain tone sequences, enabling toll calls to be made for free.[2] Another is flexibility: Inband tone signaling is not amenable to sophisticated routing techniques, such as looking ahead to see that all required trunks are available before beginning to route the call. Finally, tone signaling, based upon analog technology, doesn't fit well into an all-digital environment.

During the 1970s, AT&T updated most of its toll network to use *Common Channel Interoffice Signaling* (CCIS) instead of MF. The CCITT defined a related CCIS protocol, Signaling System No. 6. The CCIS protocol was optimized for the slow (2400 bps) modem links of the day and provided little in the way of additional features but improved call routing and security. At the CCITT the world's telephone administrations were conceiving the interoffice signaling system to end all interoffice signaling systems, the protocol suite that became known as Signaling System No. 7 (SS7).

SS7 Architecture

In the architecture of an SS7 network an end node is called a *signaling point* (SP), while the specialized packet switch is called a *signaling transfer point* (STP). SPs include *switch SPs*, which include central offices; *service switching points* (SSPs), which provide access to external processors; and *service control points* (SCPs), which are processors that provide various network functions (see Fig. 7.7). SCPs and SSPs are part of the evolving Intelligent Network architecture, which seeks to move some of the network's intelligence out of the switching systems themselves. SCPs are already used for some functions, such as 800 number translation and calling card validation.

A Layered Model of Its Own

Signaling System No. 7 is a complete protocol suite, occupying, as it were, all seven layers of the OSI Reference Model (though not all OSI layers are included). Indeed the CCITT standards themselves (found in the Q.700 series of CCITT Recommendations) allude to SS7's relationship to OSI, although the layers do not precisely line up (although SCCP was designed to provide a true OSI Network Service in conjunction with MTP). Nor do all of the SS7 protocols follow careful layering rules. The SS7 protocols themselves are organized into *parts*, and a given part may have the functions of more than one layer within it (see Fig. 7.8).

---

[2] During the 1970s the so-called "Blue Box" tone generator was popular among American "phone phreaks."

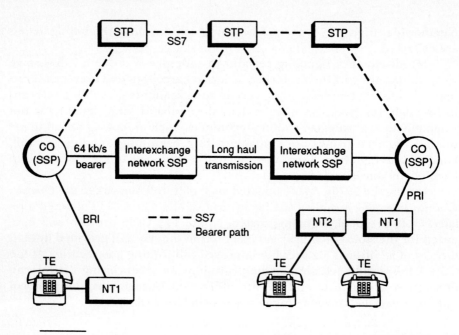

Figure 7.7 *In Simplified Signaling System No. 7 network architecture the path followed by a call after it is set up may differ from the path followed by the messages used to set up the call.*

SS7 is designed to run over 64 kbps digital circuits, although other speeds, including operation over modems at 4.8 kbps, are possible. That physical layer is a considerable improvement over the 2400 bps channels that CCIS originally used and a quantum leap from ten pulses per second!

Message Transfer Part. Both the Data Link layer and part of the Network layer are provided in the *Message Transfer Part (MTP)*, which is actually two related protocols. The *Signaling Link Level*, described in Recommendation Q.703, uses HDLC framing: Each frame is delineated by the standard flag, and transparency is provided via bit stuffing. Frames also end with a 16-bit CRC-CCITT.

But the semblance between MTP and HDLC ends there. MTP frames, called *signal units*, do not use HDLC addressing or elements of procedure. Three types of signal unit are provided. A *message signal unit* (MSU) has a three-octet (not counting the flag) Level 2 header, followed by a payload of higher-layer information and the CRC. A *link status signal unit* (LSU) has exactly six octets between flags. A *fill-in signal unit* (FISU) has exactly five octets between flags.

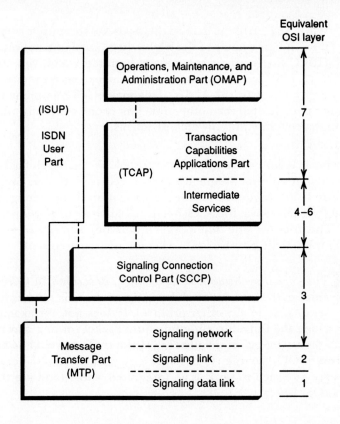

Figure 7.8 *Signaling System No. 7 protocol architecture. Note that its parts do not line up precisely upon OSI layer boundaries. ISUP makes optional use of SCCP.*

All signal units include a backward sequence number (BSN), acknowledging a received signal unit, and a forward sequence number (FSN), numbering the frame. These are seven bits long (modulo-128). The third octet contains a six-bit length indicator, allowing the longest MSU payload to be 63 octets long. The LSU differs from the FISU by the presence of a status field. Note that the three types of signal units are distinguished by length.

The FISU mechanism is unique to SS7 and, in practice, one of the more difficult to implement. While HDLC allows flags to be sent in between frames when a line is idle, SS7 requires idle time to be filled with FISUs. While the FSN is not incremented by FISUs or LSUs, both types of service units must have the FSN of the last MSU and carry in the BSN the sequence number of the last successfully received MSU. At 64 kbps, one FISU is sent every 750 microseconds.

While SS7 partisans defend this as useful for minimizing down-time, it contributes to the high cost of implementation. While HDLC flag stuffing is normally handled exclusively in hard-ware, FISUs require processor assistance to keep their sequence numbers in alignment with the MSUs. This makes MTP implementation somewhat more complicated than other data link protocols. Many other networks have high reliability without such problems.

Two forms of error correction are supported. Normally, go-back-N procedures are used; if an out-of-sequence MSU is received, the receiver sends back a retransmission request. But when propagation delay is long, as with satellites and long terrestrial links, a scheme called *preventive cyclic retransmission* is used. This uses the idle time between new MSUs to retransmit unacknowledged MSUs. Only positive acknowledgments are then sent.

The *Signaling Network Level* of MTP, described in Q.704, provides part of the Network layer function. This too has little resemblance to any other protocol. It does not, for example, include the full addressing function: Packet routing may require "peeking into the envelope" of the next higher layer. That would be an egregious violation of OSI layering rules, but it is acceptable in SS7 because all of the layers are designed to work as an integrated whole (and are thus not as versatile as OSI layers).

Two different types of address are used for SS7 packet routing. A *point code* refers to a specific SP, while a *global title* refers to a destination address such as a telephone number. MTP itself is concerned only with point codes, but sometimes global titles need to be translated to provide the appropriate point code needed to route a message. (A global title is thus more of an Application entity, like a name, rather than a Network layer address.) A point code is 14 bits long, with a CCITT-assigned and a nationally assigned portion. This limits the number of possible point codes, thus limiting the scope of SS7 networks at this level.

Other functions of MTP include congestion control (with congestion avoidance signaling accommodated via LSUs), signaling link management, and *changeover and changeback,* a procedure by which traffic over a link can be rerouted to an alternative facility in case the first fails and rerouted back when the circuit is restored. While MTP is not simple and is probably more exceptional than it has to be, given the state of modern data communications, it serves its main purpose well: Signaling System No. 7 networks must provide extremely high levels of reliability, with consistent levels of performance, even under adverse conditions, except when there are software errors, in which case MTP networks have been known to collapse.

Signaling Connection Control Part. The Signaling Connection Control Part (SCCP) was not part of the original SS7 architecture but is used for most modern ISDN applications. It provides the final part of the OSI Network layer service. SCCP Class 0 was defined first and provides a connectionless network service, routing datagrams between upper-layer protocols. Connection-oriented SCCP classes have since been defined, although existing SS7 upper-layer protocols do not require it.

MTP and SCCP together may be collectively called the *Network Service Part* (NSP). Like the OSI Network layer, NSP is processed by intermediate nodes (STPs) that have no interest in the upper-layer protocols that form its payload. These higher-layer protocols operate end to end between relevant SPs.

Telephone and Data User Parts. Upper-layer protocols in SS7 are called *user parts*. The oldest user part, whose development began in the 1970s, is the Telephone User Part (TUP). It is concerned with circuit-switched telephone circuits only, effectively similar in scope to CCIS. TUP was never widely implemented in North America, but has seen some application in several countries. Indeed, it is nominally not part of ISDN at all, as the newer ISDN User Part (ISUP) was supposed to replace it. But some early ISDN implementations in Europe are based on TUP; at some point in the future they are expected to be transitioned to ISUP.

The *Data User Part* (DUP) is even rarer than TUP, and it too becomes redundant with ISUP. DUP was designed to support circuit-switched data networks (i.e., those based upon Recommendation X.21).

ISDN User Part. The ISDN User Part (ISUP) provides the intranetwork support for the call control functions supported by DSS1. The interworking between ISUP and DSS1 is indeed a critical part of making ISDN possible; it is thus understandable that both protocols are defined within CCITT Study Group XI. But they are defined by different Working Parties within Study Group XI, with different goals and priorities. And because SS7 is something normally used only by the carriers themselves, there may be some interest in keeping the protocols different, as a primitive form of security and as a way to establish "turf."

The structure of ISUP is reminiscent of DSS1 but is by no means based upon the same rules. Each ISUP *message* is carried by SCCP or directly within an MTP message signaling unit. (The former is preferred.) Messages are made up of *parameters*, which roughly correspond in function to DSS1 information elements but are coded differently.

Each message begins with a *mandatory fixed part*, a group of fixed-length parameters required for that message type. One side effect of fixed-length parameters is that lower-layer protocols, such as MTP, can look ahead into the payload and extract information such as global titles. This may be an egregious violation of layering, but SS7's authors accept it as a way of saving a few bytes.

This is followed by the *mandatory variable part* of the message. Here the coding is again rather unique: The beginning of the mandatory variable part of the message consists of pointers to the various variable-length parameters themselves, which begin following the pointers. As with the mandatory fixed part, the type of each parameter does not have to be tagged because each is mandatory and the order of parameters thus implies their type. The pointers indicate the location of the length field for each mandatory variable-length parameter; the length field is followed by the parameter data itself. Each message ends with the *optional part*, which consists of self-contained parameters in tag-length-value order.

ISUP messages are concerned with various functions, including call setup, supervision, routing, disconnection, and the transfer of certain end to end information. Other ISUP messages are concerned with supplementary services. Another group of messages is used to inform SPs of the condition of groups of trunk circuits, which is useful for modifying network call routing tables. Almost 40 ISUP messages are defined, and more may be added in the future as additional services are defined. From the perspective of the ISDN user, ISUP is by far the most critical part of Signaling System No. 7.

Transaction Capabilities Application Part. The newest of the established ISDN upper-layer protocols is the Transaction Capabilities Application Part (TCAP). This is perhaps the most OSI-like part of SS7, being derived from the OSI Remote Operations Service Element and using ASN.1-based syntax. But its OSI heritage is countered by the way in which it combines OSI layers 4, 5, 6, and part of 7 into one. TCAP requires the services of SCCP.

TCAP is used for most functions that do not map directly into ISUP, including activities that are not directly related to call setup. Most Intelligent Network functions make use of TCAP. For example, if a user dials an 800 number, TCAP may be used to query an SCP to determine the actual telephone number to which the call should be routed. It may also be useful for developing flexible roaming arrangements for mobile telephone services. TCAP is also likely to be specified for the development of new ISDN supplementary services. Indeed, it was TCAP's adoption of the remote operations model that inspired DSS1's developers to adopt a similar protocol for Q.932 supplementary service signaling.

Operations, Maintenance and Administration Part. Signaling System No. 7 networks themselves need to be tended and cared for. To support this function, the *Operations, Maintenance, and Administration Part* (OMAP) has been defined. This part is not a general-purpose maintenance entity but a specialized set of functions for determining and maintaining the health of the SS7 network itself. OMAP is widely used, since these networks are both complex and mission-critical, two characteristics that lead to giving maintenance a high priority. Indeed, SS7 networks in general tend to need "7 by 24" staffing: If a problem is detected in a public network, letting it wait until regular business hours resume can be disastrous.

Future Expansion of Signaling System No. 7. The existing user parts are sufficient to support all of the ISDN bearer and supplementary services that have already been defined, but the collection is by no means complete. The development of Broadband ISDN has already led to the beginning of work on a new user part that provides a superset of ISUP services. Broadband ISDN will provide a distinction between a "call," which is a relationship between two TEs, and a "connection," which is the provision of a bearer service to the parties making up a call. A single call may have multiple connections, such as a narrowband voice channel and a wideband video channel. ISUP is not designed to support this, so a new user part will probably be adopted during the 1990s. This *Integrated Services Control Part* (ISCP) will most likely be based upon the OSI Application layer structure. Before it is complete, an interim expansion of ISUP may support Broadband ISDN. Another possible extension of SS7 is the proposed *Mobile Application Part* (MAP), which some European administrations are interested in developing.

Chapter
Eight

Broadband ISDN

The Glass Network

Narrowband ISDN, in both its Basic Rate and Primary Rate arrangements, is an evolutionary development that combines a set of well-established services and technologies with a fairly modest, albeit terribly well-studied, set of new protocols. But there is another dimension to ISDN, one that promises a far greater range of new potential services while breaking with the baggage of a century of analog telephony.

Broadband ISDN (B-ISDN) is more revolutionary than evolutionary in scope. While it promises to provide access to the same services as Narrowband ISDN (N-ISDN), it also appears to have a few new tricks up its sleeve. B-ISDN, though, doesn't begin by taking existing telephone and packet-switching technology. Instead, it is built almost entirely out of newer ideas and components.

The key principle behind B-ISDN is the development of a network in which optical fiber, not wire, is the predominant means of transmission. This transition, from copper to glass, is already well under way in the interexchange transmission network. Optical carrier systems have replaced radio and coaxial cable as the medium of choice for most new telephone company bandwidth. Only in the local loop, that last mile, is copper still dominant.

And it is the local loop that represents a disproportionate share of the cost of the entire network. Telephone companies rarely charge the full cost of their loop plant as part of the subscribers' bills; instead, basic rates are held down by an elaborate scheme of cross-subsidies. Toll calls in particular pay for the cost of the embedded copper network. And because copper wire has a long lifespan, this network is depreciated very slowly to reduce the apparent cost that rate payers have to bear.

Narrowband ISDN is designed to run over existing copper local loop facilities. As a corollary, it provides little incentive for the telephone industry to upgrade its loop plant to new fiber optic systems. Fiber may be used for digital loop carrier systems and is commonplace even today, but the customer interface remains a copper loop. The trend, however, is toward more use of optical fiber. The cost of copper facilities is dominated by the cost of the labor required to install it, which continues to rise, while the cost of optical fiber facilities, still dominated by materials, which are more expensive but getting less so, is falling. Glass is already cheaper than copper for some large customers, and the break-even point continues to fall.

That economic trend provides much of the incentive for the development of B-ISDN. A second cause of the telephone companies' interest in high-bandwidth optical networks is the potential "turf battle" with the cable TV industry. Especially in the United States, CATV (cable TV) companies provide an alternative source of bandwidth to the home. This threat has hung over the telephone companies for many years and has to date proven to be rather an idle one, since most of the CATV industry views its business as entertainment, not common carriage. But rather than take chances, telephone companies have positioned B-ISDN as a counterthreat against the cable companies. B-ISDN is not only capable of providing voice, data, and the other N-ISDN services, but can also provide the high digital bandwidth needed to distribute High-Definition Television (HDTV). Another view, of course, is that the telephone industry is really the aggressor here, seeking to expand into markets that are now served by separate CATV companies. There's probably an element of truth in both views; the two industries are eyeing each other cautiously.

It is against this backdrop that one can observe the development of B-ISDN: Lagging N-ISDN development by at least five years, B-ISDN features a combination of adopted and purpose-built technologies.

Evolution from the Metropolitan Area Network

A Local Area Network (LAN) is a high-speed shared medium that provides packetized data transfer within a tightly constrained distance. The popular Ethernet LAN requires bridges (specialized switching devices) to connect any two points that are no more than a couple of kilometers apart. Token Ring LANs tend to allow somewhat larger radii but are still usually limited to a building or campus in scope. The Fiber Distributed Data Interface (FDDI), a 100 Mbps token ring, can theoretically go for hundreds of kilometers (50 km between stations) using single-mode optics. But like other LANs, it requires dedicated optics and is therefore not very amenable to merging into the public telecommunications infrastructure. FDDI runs at *exactly* 100 Mbps, which is simply not part of the 64 kbps-based telecommunications hierarchy!

Telephone companies are aware of this problem and are aware that Narrowband ISDN does not, by itself, provide the bandwidth that many customers need. And with Broadband ISDN taking years to develop, they have sought an interim step, something to offer in the early 1990s.

To be sure, the telephone companies didn't really see it this way at first. Many promoted ISDN as a LAN substitute and failed to see the need for something faster. But by the late 1980s, most had embraced a new technology that provides LAN-like speeds over ISDN-like distances, or at least over the radius of a large city, using standard telecommunication transmission gear. The Metropolitan Area Network (MAN) is a hybrid of LANs and telephony, providing LAN-like services over telephone company facilities.

The MAN is one step in the evolution of public networks, a step along the path from N-ISDN to B-ISDN. In a sense the telephone carriers have made a major theological accomplishment by combining the theories of creationism and evolution: They have created their own evolution! It begins with N-ISDN and the MAN, evolves into a new high-speed data service called SMDS, and, if all goes according to plan, ends with B-ISDN.

The Distributed Queue Dual Bus (DQDB)

The Australian PTT and its affiliated firm QPSX Communications are responsible for promoting a MAN technology that is now called the Distributed Queue Dual Bus (DQDB). It was originally called the Queued Packet and Switched Exchange (QPSX), but when it was submitted to the IEEE for standardization, in Project IEEE 802.6, the name was changed to be different from the corporate name of its sponsor.

DQDB is functionally a superset of a LAN. It provides the same type of packetized data service as other IEEE 802 LANs but also provides an isochronous (circuit-mode) service. Bandwidth may be *pre-arbitrated* for isochronous use or *queue-arbitrated* for packet-mode asynchronous (data or other variable-bit-rate) transfer. Unlike most LANs, it is not wedded to any particular transmission speeds. Any given DQDB *subnetwork* may operate at any chosen speed, from 1.5 Mbps on up. The design center appears to be the 34/44-Mbps range (E3/T3), but it can also run over SONET STS-3 (155 Mbps).

All information is sent over DQDB in the form of fixed-length *segments*. In the initial DQDB design, segments carried 64 bytes of payload with a four-octet header, preceded by a one-octet *access control field* (ACF) used by the queue arbitration process. Variable-length data packets were framed and addressed by means of information carried within the segment payload. This resulted in a total *cell* size of 69 octets.

By the nature of the DQDB arbitration algorithm, cell delivery is very reliable; only transmission noise or equipment error will result in a lost cell. Thus variable-length data packets can be fit into a succession of segment payloads using a simple *Segmentation and Reassembly* protocol, with a *Convergence* protocol used to provide per-frame information such as source and destination addressing.

Congestion loss does not occur within a DQDB subnetwork; each device simply slows down as the load increases. Congestion losses may occur in intersubnetwork bridges, but these can simply throw away complete packets, not cells. End systems can retransmit these packets as required. In this sense, DQDB is no different from a LAN or a packet network. The cell-switched nature of DQDB is thus transparent to both data and voice users. This will come back to haunt us later; B-ISDN has adapted much from DQDB, but by its nature, B-ISDN has to run in a tougher environment than DQDB, so we cannot trust that these optimistic assumptions will carry over.

Switched Multi-Megabit Data Service (SMDS)

The basic data service offered by a LAN, and the most important service offered by the DQDB MAN, is connectionless data transfer. This fits nicely into the subnetwork role of the OSI Network layer. (Note that IEEE 802.6 terminology is not in alignment with other standards; what is called a "subnetwork" in the DQDB standard corresponds to a "segment" in other 802 standards and not the "subnetwork" in the OSI reference model.[1])

While DQDB was designed as a telephone company offering, telephone companies in the United States cannot legally offer DQDB service! That's because DQDB combines transmission with customer site gear. Telephone companies may provide, usually under tariff, the high-speed transmission facilities needed to build a private DQDB MAN. And they may provide, on an unregulated basis, the customer premise equipment needed to build the

---

[1] See ISO8648 for a useful discussion of the internal organization of the Network layer.

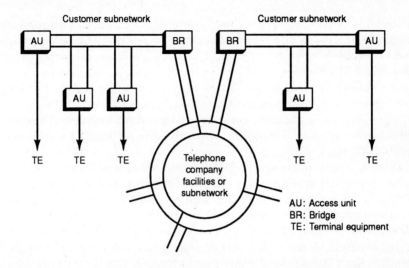

Figure 8.1 *This Metropolitan Area Network is based on DQDB (IEEE 802.6) model. In the United States, telephone companies provide only raw bandwidth to MAN users. However, SMDS is a telephone company service equivalent to a shared data-only MAN.*

MAN. But they cannot require the customer to use these private line transmission facilities for MAN purposes: U.S. law[2] states that like services (such as private lines of a given bandwidth) must carry like tariff charges, regardless of use. Discriminatory tariffs are illegal. Thus customers can order the high-speed facility and use it to, say, carry telephone calls, replacing costlier alternatives.

Another consequence of this regulatory environment is that these MANs may belong to only a single customer at a time. Since the customer orders raw bandwidth, the telephone company cannot provide a shared backbone network. Telecom Australia, on the other hand, has built a shared DQDB backbone network (*Fastpac*) that provides high-speed data service across that country. The company owns the access devices, so it takes responsibility for what goes on or off of the shared medium.

Switched Multi-Megabit Data Service (SMDS) is one possible solution to this problem. Developed by Bellcore, it is a connectionless packet-switched data service that uses DQDB as the basis of its protocol. See Fig. 8.1. The SMDS Interface Protocol (SIP) has three levels, like X.25, but both its Level 2 and Level 3 come from DQDB. It differs from the private MAN principally

---

[2] Telecommunications regulation in the United States is governed by the Communications Act of 1934, which allows the Federal Communications Commission to write regulations to enforce its provisions.

in addressing. SMDS requires the use of telephone company–assigned ISDN addresses (15 digits, in binary coded decimal, and thus 60 bits long, assigned per CCITT E.164) in each packet. Other MANs may choose that option or use the 48-bit IEEE-assigned addresses that are more common in a LAN or private network environment. SMDS also defines the use of the DQDB header option field as a means of specifying transit carriers: Customers in the United States must be able to specify an inter-LATA carrier of choice, on either a subscription or per-packet (since there is no "call" in a connection-less service) basis.

From a service perspective, SMDS is in a sense a modern complement to X.25. Both are models for public packet-switched networks. SMDS, though, is orders of magnitude faster and provides a connectionless service (with no assured delivery of packets and no connection setup). From an implementation perspective a typical SMDS network may be built from DQDB equipment with a *multiport bridge* acting as an intersubnetwork packet switch. In effect, it's a shared MAN that customers can access only through a bridge that's located on the phone company's premises.

From an evolutionary perspective, SMDS is one more step along the path to B-ISDN, which adopts SMDS as the model for its own connectionless bearer service.

Asynchronous Transfer Mode

Perhaps the single most novel feature of B-ISDN is neither its optical fiber delivery medium nor its speed but the nature of the bearer services themselves that B-ISDN will provide. While some early concepts for Broadband ISDN resembled speeded-up versions of N-ISDN, with more and bigger bearer (B and H) channels, that vision was abandoned in favor of a more radical approach.

The Physical layer of N-ISDN separates the B, D, and H channels from one another using synchronous time division multiplexing (TDM). The primary and basic rate protocols at all reference points provide some frame of reference (a framing pattern of some sort) from which to separate out the channels. In TDM, channels are thus distinguished by their context, or their place in the multiplex structure. This is highly amenable to circuit switching.

In B-ISDN a different multiplexing technique is used. Originally called asynchronous time division multiplexing (ATDM), it has since come to be known as the Asynchronous Transfer Mode (ATM), though the more mar-keting-oriented term "Fast Packet" refers to the same general technology. In ATM the various bearer and control channels are transferred in fixed-length blocks, called *cells*, each of which has a short header followed by its payload. (Hence the term "cell switching," another name for this technology.) Like the header in a packet network, the ATM header identifies the *virtual channel* to which each cell belongs.

But ATM, while not quite the same as circuit switching, is also not packet. ATM operates within the Physical layer, providing transfer of bits, not error-checked frames or packets. (It also scratches the surface of the Data Link layer, since statistical multiplexing is generally not considered a Physical layer function. But it doesn't even come close to offering the Data Link service.) The bits are delivered in larger blocks than the octets that are typical of N-ISDN bearer services, but the block size is fixed by the network, unlike Layer 3 packets, whose sizes are set, within limits, by the user. ATM is thus a hybrid of circuit and packet modes.

The key principle behind ATM is a simple, if slightly risky, one: If an ATM network is fast enough, it can emulate both packet- and circuit-mode bearer services. It is the bearer service for all seasons, one size fits all. Making this work, of course, poses quite a challenge!

The ATM Cell

Broadband ISDN transfers all information by means of cells. While cells behave somewhat as packets do, their fixed size has several advantages for the implementor. The cell delineation technique requires no overhead akin to an HDLC flag. Instead, if the underlying layer indicates the beginning of one cell or cell alignment is gained by other means, then all subsequent cells begin a predictable number of bits later. (ATM actually provides two means for this.) Cell switches can also use buffer allocation techniques that are simplified in comparison to packet switches.

Long or Short Cells? But what is the right size for a cell? This was one of the major questions that had to be answered before B-ISDN could be standardized. The answer was not easy to come up with.

At one extreme is voice telephony. This is very sensitive to transmission delay owing to the echo caused by analog telephone instruments and local loops. Delays of even a few milliseconds can lead to audible degradation of a call if typical echo is present. And analog telephones will persist for many years. Longer cells lead to longer *packetization delay*, as a larger voice sample has to be collected before the cell can be transmitted.

At the other extreme is bulk data transfer. This is not sensitive to delay. Longer cells are thus preferable, since the cell header then takes up a smaller percentage of the total bandwidth.

An early experimental ATM network, called *Prelude*, was built in 1982 by the French PTT. It used an 18-octet cell, with a two-octet header and 16-octet payload. The packetization delay for PCM voice, two milliseconds, was quite acceptable. This experience led France to be a big ATM booster at the CCITT, and the French, deciding that 16 octets was really too short, favored a 32-octet cell payload.

DQDB, on the other hand, was designed around a 64-octet cell payload. The United States and Australia strongly supported this as the B-ISDN cell size. From the North American perspective the 8-millisecond speech packetization delay was not a problem that could be solved by shorter cells: Transmission delays caused by the speed of light already force the use of echo cancellation hardware on transcontinental telephone calls. Shaving a few milliseconds from the total end-to-end delay wouldn't do much good. Only in a smaller country (say, France) would the shorter packetization delay be of any real benefit.

In classic CCITT fashion a compromise was reached at Study Group XVIII in 1989. The B-ISDN cell will have a five-octet header and a 48-octet payload. It's not clear that this payload is small enough to allow voice packetization without echo cancellation, and it's smaller than one would like for an efficient data service, but it's in the true spirit of the standards process, a "mutually unacceptable compromise."

The ATM Cell Header

The five-octet ATM cell is derived, with some major changes, from the DQDB cell header (see Fig. 8.2). That may simplify interworking between private MANs and public B-ISDN, but it has other consequences that aren't so fortunate.

Normal CCITT procedures call for service definition to precede protocol development. And protocol development generally begins with semantics (what functions are to be performed) and ends with syntax (how the bits are arranged). In this case, though, the DQDB syntax was adopted first, leaving the semantics and service to follow! This has proven (not surprisingly) to be somewhat of a constraint upon subsequent B-ISDN development. There just aren't enough bits available to take care of all of the proposed and desirable functions (such as more congestion control options and cell priority classes than are actually available).

Generic Flow Control. The easiest place to find a difference between the ATM and DQDB headers is in the first octet. DQDB begins each of its cells with an eight-bit access control field, which does not actually belong to the segment but is needed for the contention algorithm.

Some delegations to Study Group XVIII, notably the United States and Australia, wanted to carry this forward into B-ISDN to facilitate interworking with DQDB. (It's not clear, though, what function these bits could serve across a user-network interface, and that's the most important point at which the B-ISDN cell is standardized.) Others saw no reason to use B-ISDN to promote DQDB and did not want to prejudice the market. The United Kingdom, for instance, wanted to leave room for its home-grown (by British Telecom) protocol.

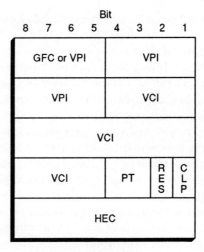

GFC: Generic flow control
(only at user-network interface)
VPI: Virtual path indicator
VCI: Virtual channel indicator
PT: Payload type
RES: Reserved
CLP: Cell loss priority
HEC: Header error control

Figure 8.2 *In the Asynchronous Transfer Mode cell the boundary between Virtual Path Indicator and Virtual Channel Indicator may vary with application. Generic Flow Control is provided only at the user-network interface; its four bits are used for additional address bits at the network node interface.*

The compromise that was reached by the CCITT in 1989 was to allow four bits, half of the first octet, for a function called *generic flow control* (GFC). The specific usage of these bits will be determined at some future point and in any case may be reserved to customers for their own use. One GFC option supported by many Americans is basically a simplified version of DQDB. British Telecom has developed MSFC (Multi-Service Flow Control), which it adapted from its own MAN, the Orwell Ring.

Addressing: VPI and VCI. DQDB has a 20-bit address field. This is not used at all for its connectionless service but is reserved for a future asynchronous connection-oriented service. B-ISDN's ATM bearer service happens to map rather closely to that concept, but it has 24 address bits in its header (four bits having been taken from the first octet). The B-ISDN connection-oriented bearer services use these bits to identify the virtual channel to which the cell belongs.

A further refinement of this concept resulted in a two-level address. The first eight or 12 bits of the address (by local agreement) constitute the *Virtual Path Identifier* (VPI), while the rest form the *Virtual Channel Identifier* (VCI). A virtual path connection is a bundle of virtual channel connections sharing the same source and destination. A group of trunk circuits between two switches, for example, might make use of a virtual path. It might also be useful for a private network, which could subscribe to a virtual path service to carry many virtual channels. When the network is providing a virtual path service, only these bits are used for cell routing. The remaining bits, the VCI, belong to the subscriber.

Other subscribers will receive a virtual channel service in which the entire address field is used for cell routing. This corresponds more closely to traditional packet practice. Like other connection-oriented services, addresses are local: The channel ID (VPI or VCI) at one end of the connection need not be the same as the channel number at the other.

Header Checksum. The last eight bits of the cell header contain a cyclic redundancy checksum (CRC). This serves as a check on the accuracy of the rest of the header to prevent cells from being misrouted (which could occur from a bit error in the address field). Here, the recommended procedure for using the CRC is somewhat more complex than usual. Instead of simply discarding a cell if the CRC tests bad, the CRC may be used to correct the error.

But while the CRC is capable of detecting a two-bit error and is also capable of correcting a single-bit error, a multibit error is likely to be mistaken for a correctable one-bit error.[3] To reduce the likelihood of this occurring, the CRC-8 will not be used to correct errors in successive cells. If one cell has an apparently correctable error, the next cell will be discarded, not corrected, if the CRC shows any error. Error correction will be attempted only on cells that follow error-free cells.

This appears to be workable because the error rates on optical fiber are very low and usually Gaussian in nature (and thus uncorrelated), and the errors usually take the form of single or double bits, not multibit bursts. Lengthy burst errors (actually dropouts of about 30 milliseconds) sometimes occur as a result of switchovers in backbone transmission media. During these switchovers, no data is received, so in effect half of the apparently received bits are in error.

[3] This code has a *Hamming distance* of 3. The Hamming distance indicates how many bits must be in error before an error can go undetected. The number of bits that may be corrected by a checksum is equal to half the Hamming distance, rounded downward.

Priority Bits. After generic flow control and channel identification, only four bits are left in the cell header. One of these bits may be used as a priority indicator. Services that do not tolerate cell loss (for example, circuit emulation) may use a higher priority than those that do tolerate loss. A second application of priority is enforcement of rate-based congestion controls: If a subscriber exceeds its negotiated rate, excessive cells may be marked down to a lower-priority class. This procedure is called usage parameter control (UPC). Note that the same bit serves both purposes; both user-defined priority and UPC are indications to network switches that a given cell should be discarded before others are. Note also the semblance to Frame Relay's DE bit.

While priority is certainly an effective way to allow some traffic to get through congestion at the expense of others, it is far from a complete solution. The reason is fairly obvious: Who is going to want a low-priority service? As will be noted below, the "adaptation layer" protocols being designed for B-ISDN do not tolerate high amounts of cell loss, nor do most existing video digitization schemes. While voice telephony (using standard means of digitization) can tolerate 1–2% dropout, many other audio applications, such as facsimile, cannot. The suitability of priority-based schemes thus depends upon the overall mix of traffic that the network will carry, which is not known yet.

Another bit is likely to be used for networkwide congestion control, though its use has not been agreed upon yet. A likely model is the forward explicit congestion notification (FECN) bit used in Frame Relay, which indicates that congestion has been encountered somewhere in transit. The two remaining bits in the header indicate cell type and are used for special functions, such as indicating whether the cell is carrying customer data or network management information. More bits would have been useful here, of course, but the premature decision on header format left little room for growth.

Continuous and Variable Bit Rate Services

The ATM bearer service has two major variations. The *continuous bit rate* (CBR) service is essentially a circuit-mode emulation service and should theoretically be able to carry whatever bandwidth the user negotiates, with negligible probability of cell loss. CBR makes use of high-priority cells.

The *variable bit rate* (VBR) service is more useful for bursty traffic, such as packet-mode data. Each VBR virtual channel (or virtual path) is characterized by both an average and a peak information rate. (These two rates are, of course, identical for a CBR service.) The priority treatment of VBR cells may be based upon the congestion management strategy that is finally adopted for B-ISDN.

All existing N-ISDN bearer services are expected to be mapped into either CBR or VBR services. Packet modes can be supported by VBR, circuit modes by CBR. Telephony can be packetized, but packetized voice does not necessarily sound as good as circuit-mode voice. And transmission quality is especially critical in nonvoice uses of the telephone network, such as facsimile. The adoption of packet voice (VBR) for B-ISDN, while desirable from the network's point of view, might thus be hard to sell to a public that is just getting accustomed to the higher-quality sound of N-ISDN. So B-ISDN retains the CBR format for voice, at least at present.

New applications of B-ISDN, such as broadcast video, will need one or the other, depending upon the protocols adopted for them. Existing video digitization protocols tend to be CBR-oriented, but some can be adapted to VBR. Most of those, however, are not tolerant of cell loss; a single lost cell will result in a 384-bit dropout. Thus VBR video may still require high-priority treatment. Newer protocols are likely to be developed that allow low-priority video cells to be identified and tagged.

Architecture and Reference Configuration

The ISDN architecture and reference configuration described in Chapter 5 has required some modifications for Broadband use. While the CCITT and ANSI positions are (again) not identical here, a practical perspective on the reference model finds much of the narrowband version left intact but with some new elements added.

Telephone Company Facilities

Much of the added complexity in the B-ISDN reference model occurs just within the boundaries of the network cloud. Bringing dedicated optical fiber transmission media from the central office to each customer would be relatively costly and would have higher potential bandwidth than any single B-ISDN user-network interface will require. Thus the concept of a single local loop, going back from UNI to the central office switching fabric, is inappropriate.

The ATM switching system that takes the place of the N-ISDN exchange terminator is called the *local exchange node* (LEN). Subscriber-side interfaces here are typically multiplexed among many geographically-close UNIs. If necessary, a smaller ATM switch, the *access node* (AN), sits somewhere between the UNI and the LEN. Again if necessary, a time division multiplexor, the *remote multiplexor node* (RMN), allows one physical facility to be shared among multiple UNIs. This latter node resembles the digital line carrier that is used to derive analog and narrowband services from a shared fiber, but in this case its subscriber side bandwidth is higher. Figure 8.3 shows the B-ISDN carrier-side reference configuration.

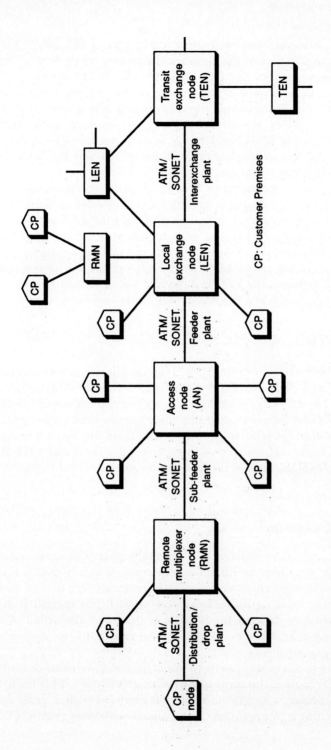

Figure 8.3 In the broadband ISDN carrier-side reference configuration the central office function (local exchange node) may be supplemented by optional access nodes and remote multiplexor nodes. Reprinted courtesy of the Exchange Carriers Standards Association (ECSA), T1S1.5/90-001. Note that this is derived from a working document and may be subject to change.

197

Note the distinction between these three classes of node. The LEN provides access to the rest of the network, including other exchanges and the *transit exchange node* (TEN). The AN is an ATM switch, but the RMN is not; the RMN takes advantage of the nature of the physical layer to simply bundle multiple UNIs onto a single fiber. Every cell, idle or occupied, is sent through an RMN; an AN, on the other hand, discards idle cells. Thus the bandwidth between the RMN and the AN is an exact multiple of the bandwidth of a UNI, while the bandwidth between an AN and the LEN may be provisioned statistically.

Broadcast video is expected to be one of the major applications of B-ISDN. The most likely place for it to be injected into the network is at the AN. A subscriber can thus "dial up" a channel, and the LEN need not even be involved. This is efficient because a single link between an AN and a LEN may have many different subscribers watching the same program at the same time; were video added at the LEN, then each one would be redundantly using bandwidth between the LEN and the AN. Video cannot be added at an RMN, though, because that node has no switching capability at all.

Subscriber Side

The B-ISDN subscriber reference model begins with the same basic components as found in N-ISDN (see Fig. 8.4). An NT1 terminates the optical span, providing only physical layer functions. An NT2 and a TA are optional. Reference points T_B and S_B exist much like their narrowband counterparts.

A new addition, at least to the ANSI model, is the *network terminator–shared* (NTS). This is the device that interconnects a customer's Local Area Network to the B-ISDN. LAN access points are given a new designation, reference point Z.

Multiple Virtual D Channels

Because of the high bandwidth of B-ISDN, many potential combinations of components are possible. Another consequence of this is that a single D channel is no longer provided across a UNI; instead, there may be multiple virtual D channels, each identified by a different VCI. The specific D channel arbitration technique defined for N-ISDN is (happily) discarded. A single virtual D channel may still serve multiple TEs, but that is an option under the subscriber's control.

The network, of course, needs to know how many virtual channels are providing the D channel function and what their VCIs are. This leads to the *meta-signaling channel*, a single ATM virtual channel with a reserved VCI whose sole function is to negotiate the parameters of other (virtual) D chan-

(a) Conventional NT2

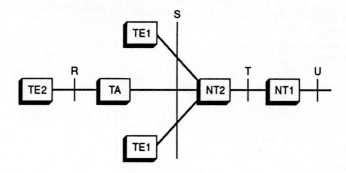

(b) Distributed NT2

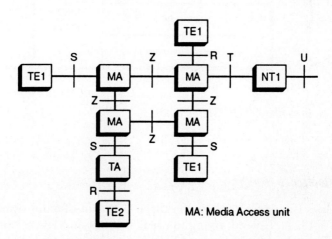

MA: Media Access unit

Figure 8.4 *An instance of Broadband ISDN reference configuration. The customer side has numerous options, not all of which can be illustrated here.*

nels. A meta-signaling protocol will have to be developed for this function; it is under development. Naturally, this will require some kind of arbitration protocol of its own, but it need not operate rapidly, since D channel creation will not need to occur frequently. And like the narrowband passive bus, it has led to various complications (like the service profile). A subscriber need not use meta-signaling in a two-point arrangement, since a default VCI for the D channel can then apply.

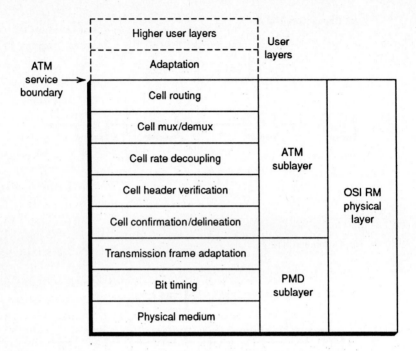

Figure 8.5 *Broadband ISDN layered model.*

Protocol Reference Model

B-ISDN does not exactly follow the three-layer out-of-band signaling model found in N-ISDN. Indeed, trying to break B-ISDN into layers can be a daunting task. Even the Physical layer ATM service alone can be broken into nine separate sublayers! Then there are the higher layers used for signaling, including the meta-signaling and virtual D channels. Figure 8.5 is a breakdown of the identified layers defined for Broadband ISDN, not counting the higher layers that users might run end to end.

The ATM bearer service itself has a service boundary, above which the protocols belong to the user. This is often referred to as the B-ISDN connection-oriented service. While it is theoretically possible to use ATM to access an X.25 or Frame Relay switching system, B-ISDN's features a packet-mode bearer service that is connectionless, based upon SMDS.

The ATM Adaptation layer (AAL) is, essentially by definition, the layer that provides the glue between ATM and higher layers that need not be bothered by the fact that the network is ATM. This layer is defined within the B-ISDN standards. B-ISDN's developers expect essentially all applications to include it, but since it often will only run end to end (in customer equipment, not seen by the network), its use will often be optional. AAL protocols are discussed below.

B-ISDN Physical Layer

Much of the nature of the Broadband ISDN physical nature is determined by the fact that one of the major reasons behind the interest in B-ISDN is the move toward optical fiber transmission. But just as N-ISDN's physical layer goes well beyond defining copper media, B-ISDN's physical layer has required considerable design of its own. It is thus somewhat surprising that the basic definitions of this layer have been agreed upon with relative ease—and with only two irreconcilable schools of thought as to what the UNI should look like!

Among the earliest agreements was that on the raw bandwidth of a UNI. Just as N-ISDN has both a Basic Rate and a Primary Rate, B-ISDN has two speeds of its own, 155 Mbps and 622 Mbps. Both of these are standard speeds for SONET (and the CCITT Synchronous Digital Hierarchy), in which they are known as STS-3 (STM-1) and STS-12 (STM-4), respectively.

In the United States it has been agreed that the B-ISDN UNI will use SONET, at least at bottom. SONET is already being deployed in the networks of all major long-distance carriers and in some local exchange carrier regional networks. So it makes sense to use similar technology in the B-ISDN UNI, providing economy of scale and simplifying maintenance. In this scenario, SONET becomes the one optical fiber protocol of choice.

Naturally, the CCITT could not simply accept this, however logical it might seem. After all, not only is SONET an American invention, but it was invented for intranetwork use. While the CCITT did accept much of it for its own use, some PTTs were simply uncomfortable allowing the same technology to appear both at the subscriber interface and within the backbone network. Just as DSS1 and Signaling System No. 7 are used in different domains, SONET and the B-ISDN UNI should, in this scenario, be kept separate. And some PTTs don't want to use SONET at all for B-ISDN, preferring a pure ATM approach without SONET's synchronization. The French Telecom is particularly vociferous in its opposition to SONET.

Thus the CCITT has begun to define a non-SONET UNI for B-ISDN at the 155 Mbps speed. This need not even be optical, though in practice it probably will be.

SONET Physical Layer

The Synchronous Optical Network (SONET) was initially promoted by Bellcore as a technique for trunk transmission. It is called *synchronous* because it begins with the assumption that the underlying transmission media are all running in synchronization with a network master clock. The earliest digital transmission systems (T carrier systems) were introduced into an analog network and thus could not be assured of digital connectivity to any given master clocking source (although it was always desirable). Thus the accuracy of the bit rate of any given digital carrier system depended upon its own local clock and could be as inaccurate as 75 parts per million. But nowadays, with digital transmission predominant, digital carrier systems can be accurate in the short term to within a few parts per billion or better, by being synchronized to the master clock.

This assumption actually makes transmission systems a lot simpler than they used to be. A T3 carrier system carries seven separate DS2 streams, each of which could theoretically be synchronized to a different clock (though this would be most unusual), each running at a slightly different speed. Each DS2 in turn carries four separate DS1 streams, each again clocked independently. The multiplexing protocol has to have enough flexibility to take into account the worst-case inaccuracy in clocking. This required many *justification* bits, basically content-free bit stuffing, and a complex framing procedure as well.

SONET, on the other hand, can be multiplexed directly from its own speed (as high as 2048 Mbps and possibly even higher in the future) down to individual 64-kbps channels. Because of its simple row/column arrangement (see Fig. 3.4), bandwidth can be flexibly allocated, in multiples of 64 kbps, by using simple synchronous TDM techniques.

Figure 8.6 *SONET layered model.*

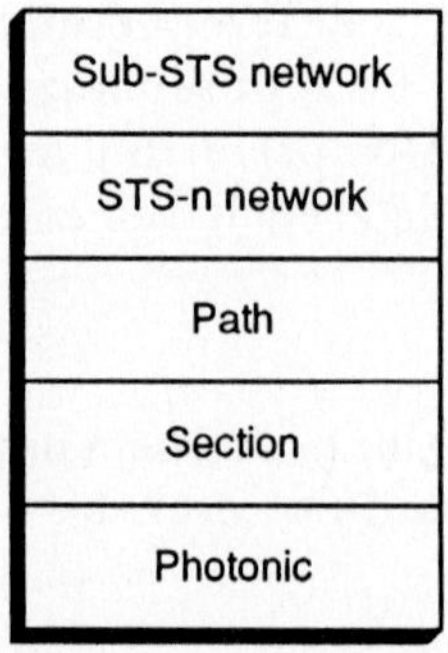

SONET Reference Model. SONET has a layered reference model of its own (Fig. 8.6). At the bottom of the model is the *photonic* layer. This defines bit transmission and lightwave multiplexing, specifying details like wavelength (color), optical power (brightness), and type of fiber. The next layer up, the *section* layer, operates between adjacent regenerators. Its functions include framing (identifying the 8000 frames per second), scrambling (a simple seven-bit fixed scrambling pattern is exclusive-OR'd with the contents of the frame to increase the randomness and frequency of on/off transitions, which helps performance), and optical regeneration.

The *path* layer, above that, operates on the SONET frame and STS-sized portions of the frame, between terminals and cross-connect switches. This is where protection switching is applied in the long-haul transmission network. The next higher layer, *STS-n network*, maps DS-3 (44.7 Mbps) and faster user services into SONET payloads, while the highest layer, *sub-STS network*, maps narrowband services as small as 64 kbps into the payload.

While SONET is presumed to be synchronized to a network master clock, some timing variations are inevitable. Thus a virtual container, or for that matter any path within a section, may "float" in relation to the frame. A few justification octets are thus found in the frame header. Other header functions include maintenance channels (which generally use an OSI-based maintenance protocol), alarm channels, and an "order wire" channel providing reserved bandwidth for use by network personnel. Some of these functions will be useful for B-ISDN UNI, while others may not be, but the availability of the bandwidth should help SONET technology to remain viable for many years.

SONET Mapping of ATM Cells. SONET was developed independently of B-ISDN. The decision to use ATM as the technological basis of B-ISDN was separate from the decision to use SONET as a physical medium. Some of SONET's services are ignored in the mapping of ATM into SONET.

B-ISDN essentially makes use of the SONET span layer services, ignoring its "network" (not to be confused with OSI Network) layers. The row and column mapping are generally ignored, except as required for the section and path (span layer) overhead. The STS-3 span delivers a total payload of 149.76 Mbps. (The rest of its 155.52 Mbps rate is section and path overhead.) This payload is known in ANSI as the STS-3c *consolidated* payload and in CCITT as a *Virtual Container* at rate VC-4.

ATM cells are mapped into this consolidated payload, one octet after the other, wrapping across rows and frames as required. Since there must be a way to identify which octet is the first one in a 53-octet cell, a pointer in the path overhead indicates the offset from itself to the beginning of a cell. Subsequent cells follow at 53-octet multiples. Framing may thus be accomplished deterministically within a single 125-microsecond SONET frame. But this isn't the only way to maintain framing: Non-SONET ATM access facilities locate cell boundaries by seeking a sequence of cells with valid header checksums. With ATM over SONET, both techniques are viable, and the choice is left to the implementor.

Scrambling. In the usual SONET network layers, user channels are multiplexed by column: A given DS-1 facility occupies three adjacent columns, forming a virtual tributary (in this case, VT-1.5). As a consequence of this, the actual optical layer never carries more than 24 bits at a time from any given VT-1.5. In B-ISDN, user cells are transmitted en bloc without regard to columns, so all 384 bits of a cell payload may be transmitted uninterrupted. This has an interesting consequence: If the user were to transmit a data pattern that matched the seven-bit SONET scrambling sequence, then there would be no on/off transitions for the duration of the cell. Since SONET is self-timing, a marginal path might lose synchronization were that to occur.

To prevent this from happening, B-ISDN specifies a second level of scrambling. Unlike the SONET scrambler, which puts the data through a fixed pattern, the B-ISDN scrambler is *self-synchronous*: The data is scrambled with itself. In this case, each bit is exclusive-OR'd with the bit that was transmitted 43 bits earlier. This does not provide the degree of randomness that the SONET scrambler does, but it produces a scrambling pattern that is almost impossible to spoof: The likelihood of creating a cell that causes the scrambled data to have a long string of 1's or 0's is roughly 1 in 2^{43}.

On the other hand, this scrambling also multiplies errors: If a single-bit error occurs in transmission, then that bit *and* the bit that is scrambled by it, 43 bits later, is also in error. This has had to be taken into account in B-ISDN error control strategies; some potential payload error detection checksums may be compromised by this error multiplier. This also makes forward error correction somewhat more difficult.

The 43-bit distance was selected because it did not conflict with the existing checksums, and it also was longer than the header. Thus the one-octet header CRC would not encounter a two-bit error caused by error multiplication. After this decision was made, it was agreed that the header itself would not be covered by the self-synchronous scrambler; it would operate only over cell payloads. But the 43-bit distance remains.

622 Mbps SONET Interface. The SONET STS-3 (155.52 Mbps) interface has a structure of 270 columns, including nine of section overhead and one of path overhead, leaving 260 columns for payload. SONET was designed to facilitate simple multiplexing of higher rates. Thus four STS-3 streams can be easily combined, via octet interleaving, into an STS-12 (622.08 Mbps) stream.

That was one option discussed for the 622 Mbps B-ISDN interface; it would have allowed individual ATM virtual channels to be no faster than on a 155 Mbps interface, but there could be four times as many of them. However, a more flexible arrangement was selected: The virtual container incorporates the entire payload, and individual virtual channels may be flexibly assigned within the nearly 600 Mbps of payload bandwidth.

Of course, this is all even farther out into the future than the 155 Mbps interface! Most likely, the STS-12 format will be found first within networks and for intercarrier connections before being widely deployed for the user-network interface.

Non-SONET Physical Layer

The non-SONET physical layer that is preferred by some PTTs lacks the overhead of SONET frames. But it then needs a way to locate the start of each cell, something that is otherwise handled by a pointer in the SONET path header. This is solved by taking advantage of the cell header checksum.

There is one chance in 256 that a given cell header eight-bit CRC will be correct when applied to random data. Thus a receiver that is fed white noise will falsely see a correct cell one out of every 256 times. Cell framing thus requires the receiver to detect a succession of cells (probably about five or six) with an apparently correct CRC before locking up. Once this occurs, a new cell boundary is imputed after receipt of 53 octets. However, if a sequence of cells with bad CRCs is received, the receiver will assume that it has lost lock and will attempt again to retrain on received cell CRCs.

An interesting consequence of having this option and the SONET option is that cell framing may occur in either of two different "layers"! If SONET is used, then framing may be provided by the Physical layer (SONET). But the cell header technique takes place within the ATM layer itself. This reflects a lack of agreement about B-ISDN architecture on the part of different participants in the standardization process.

ATM Adaptation Layer

The ATM bearer service is provided by Broadband ISDN at the user-network interface. The entire 48-octet payload of the ATM cell is thus user information. But there are times when higher protocol layers are defined by the B-ISDN network and its associated standards. One such instance is signaling: The signaling channels require a standardized protocol. Another is the *Connectionless Bearer Service*, in effect the provision of an SMDS-like service (compatible with SMDS) via ATM access facilities. A third is *interworking* with other networks, in which the network provider must convert ATM into something else.

These are examples of applications for the *ATM Adaptation layer* (AAL), which, in the B-ISDN reference model, sits directly atop the ATM service itself. Indeed the AAL generally refers to whatever protocol occupies that role and is not one single protocol.

Why an AAL?

The ATM Adaptation layer owes its existence, at least in part, to the difficulty in mapping B-ISDN, as defined, into the OSI Reference Model. It is quite simple to view ATM as a Physical layer switched service, like the circuit-mode bearer service of N-ISDN. But some ATM proponents do not accept that view, since the ATM cell has some of the characteristics of a packet and a packet-switched network operates (by definition) at a higher layer.

If the ATM service is treated as Layer 1, then the layer atop it is generally the Data Link layer (2). Indeed some data-oriented AAL protocols include the functions of OSI Layer 2. But they also include some functions that may belong in higher layers. AT&T has even claimed, without much concurrence, that the AAL can offer the OSI Transport service. By using new terminology like "adaptation layer" that does not draw upon the OSI vocabulary these taxonomic issues have been sidestepped. B-ISDN is a world of its own.

Classes and Types

In developing the AAL the CCITT identified four *classes* of ATM user. Class 1 is a continuous-bit-rate application such as PCM telephony. Class 2 is a variable bit rate non-data application such as video. Class 3 is connection-oriented data; Class 4 is connectionless data (in which the network provides its connectionless bearer service). Originally, each of these had its own AAL. Later, the AAL was broken into four independent *types*, which are intended to generally correspond with the like-numbered classes. But by separating class and type it is possible for one AAL protocol type to serve more than one class of user. In particular, this met an American desire to use similar AAL protocols for both connection-oriented and connectionless data applications.

AAL Type 1: CBR. The Type 1 AAL is designed for continuous bit-rate (Class 1) services. The protocol defined in the CCITT's preliminary Recommendations (I.363) makes use of one octet in each cell, which carries a four-bit sequence number protected by a four-bit checksum. This is presumably helpful in establishing the timing relationship between sender and receiver. The sequence number may actually operate modulo-15, rather than modulo-16, by reserving a sequence number value for carrying control information instead of user information in the cell payload.

Actually maintaining a synchronous timing relationship across an ATM connection is somewhat harder than simply keeping track of sequence numbers in order to detect lost cells. One possible technique for this, with some support in North America (especially Bellcore and GTE), is called the *Synchronous Frequency Encoding Technique* (SFET). It makes use of a single bit in each cell that indicates the relationship between the carried signal's own clock and the SONET network's clock. This works because the SONET physical layer is presumed to be locked to a network master clock.

AAL Type 2: Video? A Type 2 AAL protocol was initially defined for variable-bit-rate digital video applications. It has not been accepted yet, however, because the video coding protocols that it is supposed to support don't exist yet. And they may never exist: It is possible that if an ATM-oriented video coding technique is developed, it will incorporate its own error detection functions and not require the services of an active AAL. (But it's also conceivable that new video coding schemes will be developed to support the Type 2 AAL.)

The proposed protocol incorporates a four-bit sequence number and four-bit cell type field at the beginning of the payload, and a six-bit length field and a ten-bit CRC at the end of the payload. This leaves an AAL payload of 45 octets per cell. The CRC may be used for both error detection and correction: Since a single-bit error can be corrected by a CRC with a Hamming distance of 4 (which the ten-bit CRC has when applied to a 48-bit cell), one-bit errors can be corrected rather than have cells discarded.

AAL Types 3 and 4. The need for separate Type 3 and Type 4 AAL protocols is by no means universally agreed upon. The U.S. position is that the Type 4 protocol can support both Class 3 and Class 4 services, perhaps requiring different options. Some administrations, however, have supported the development of a separate Type 3 protocol for connection-oriented applications.

The Type 4 AAL protocol is closely based upon DQDB. Its operation is divided into two sublayers (see Fig. 8.7). The lower one, *Segmentation and Recovery* (SAR), makes use of a two-octet AAL header and two-octet AAL trailer in each cell. The cell header includes a two-bit *type* field, identifying the cell as the first, last, middle, or only cell in a segmented packet. This is followed by a four-bit sequence number, intended to detect cell delivery sequence errors, and a ten-bit *multiplex identification* (MID) field designed to allow multiple packets to be interleaved at the same time over the same channel. This also corresponds to the DQDB *message ID* (not coincidentally, also abbreviated MID) field. The SAR sublayer also provides a cell trailer, with a six-bit length indicator (useful for partially filled cells, mainly useful in streaming mode) and a ten-bit CRC covering the cell payload.

The upper sublayer, *Convergence*, provides a set of services that includes those needed to complete a Data Link service. It provides several optional services, including a *streaming mode*, in which fragments of upper-layer packets are passed through transparently, and *message mode*, corresponding to a more normal Layer 2 service. Message mode may be assured or nonassured, corresponding roughly to the connection-oriented and connectionless forms of Data Link layer protocol or to the Class 3 and Class 4 AAL services. Assured service features a selective recovery mode of operation, with a large enough

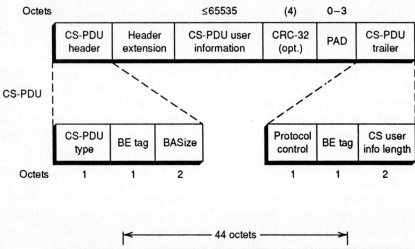

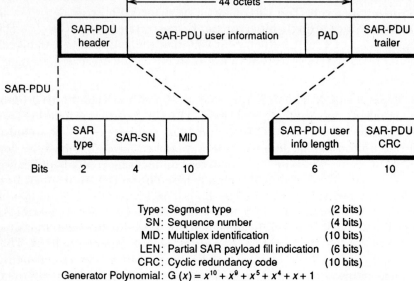

Type: Segment type (2 bits)
SN: Sequence number (4 bits)
MID: Multiplex identification (10 bits)
LEN: Partial SAR payload fill indication (6 bits)
CRC: Cyclic redundancy code (10 bits)
Generator Polynomial: $G(x) = x^{10} + x^9 + x^5 + x^4 + x + 1$

Figure 8.7 *ATM Adaptation layer for variable bit rate data (Type 4).* Reprinted
*courtesy of the Exchange Carriers Standards Association (ECSA). Note that this is derived from a working
document and may be subject to change.*

window size to accommodate thousands of packets in transit at a time. But a
go-back-N recovery option is also likely to be provided, for simplicity at low
speeds. (The impact of a go-back-N recovery protocol upon a high-speed
connection with significant transmission delays is left as a trivial exercise to
the reader.)

The Convergence protocol appends both a header and trailer to its variable-length payload. The header has two parts. The *common header*, exactly four octets long, includes an eight-bit *begin-end tag* (BEtag), which appears again in the *common trailer*. The BEtag exists to detect errors that occur when the last cell of one packet (CS_PDU) and the first cell of the next packet are both dropped, and by coincidence the length field is still correct. The common header has a 16-bit *buffer allocation size* (BAsize), and the common trailer has a 16-bit *length* field. These two are normally the same, though the BAsize may in some cases be longer than the actual CS_PDU, while the length field must be precise, since it allows the receiving entity to determine how much of the final cell was padding. If a receiving entity receives a header BAsize that is longer than the amount of buffer space that it has available, it can ignore the rest of the CS_PDU. This helps prevent buffer lockup. The remaining eight bits in the common header are used for service-specific protocol control information.

A variable-length *header extension* may follow the common header. This provides room for *service-specific* optional information, such as the sequence numbers needed for the assured mode selective recovery protocol. This, in effect, is yet a third sublayer. The SMDS-based connectionless service header is also located here.

Key to the nature of the AAL Type 4 protocol is the order of layering, as illustrated in Fig. 8.8. The frames are assembled at a lower sublayer, and error recovery takes place at a higher one. Thus if a single cell in a multicell packet is lost, the entire packet, or at least the entire convergence sublayer protocol data unit (CS_PDU), must be retransmitted. If the network has a significant cell loss rate, then this loss is in effect multiplied by up to the number of cells in the CS_PDU. In practice, it might not be quite this bad, since losses might be clustered among the various cells within a single frame or a small group of frames. But it poses a risk under some circumstances. One proposed work-around is to break user frames into multiple CS_PDUs, but then the AAL has two separate levels of segmentation within itself.

If the ATM network has significant congestion problems, then widespread use of the AAL may make matters worse! A few lost cells will result in retransmission of entire CS_PDUs, thus increasing the load on an already congested network. This will not be a problem if the network has a strong congestion control policy, but this area of B-ISDN is still quite undeveloped.

Another potential weakness of the AAL is its reliance upon a CRC-10 in each cell, plus the BEtag mechanism, in lieu of any higher-layer (CS_PDU) checksum. While the CRC-10 has a Hamming distance of 4 (and thus will note any random three bits in error), it will not necessarily detect a noise burst that is greater than ten bits in length. And if it does fail to detect the error, the odds of its randomly giving a false "valid" reading are only 1 in 1024. The CRC-32 used in LAN protocols also has a Hamming distance of 4, but that's almost secondary: Even beyond that, the odds of a random value resulting in an undetected error are about one in four billion.

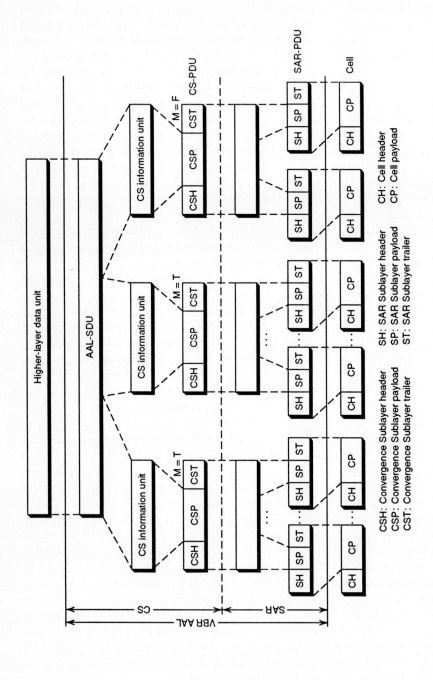

Figure 8.8 *Segmentation of CS_PDU frames into SAR_PDU cells.* *Reprinted courtesy of the Exchange Carriers Standards Association (ECSA), T1S1.5/91-003. Note that this is derived from a working document and may be subject to change.*

CSH: Convergence Sublayer header
CSP: Convergence Sublayer payload
CST: Convergence Sublayer trailer

SH: SAR Sublayer header
SP: SAR Sublayer payload
ST: SAR Sublayer trailer

CH: Cell header
CP: Cell payload

While the telephone company fiber optic backbones have an extremely low probability of multibit errors within a cell payload, B-ISDN will occasionally use microwave radio transmission, whose error characteristics can deteriorate with the weather. And when customers start installing their own single-mode fiber optic connectors on the user side of the CPE, with a 10-micron diameter in the actual conductive strand, the raw error rate might be much higher than the telephone companies had planned on. Thus the key *undetected error rate* of the AAL is still open to question. Users might need an additional end-to-end CRC added to the Convergence sublayer if data integrity is to be sufficient for the most critical applications. This is at best optional.

From the perspective of the telephone companies the Type 3 or 4 AAL should be used on an end-to-end basis by essentially all data users of the ATM connection-mode service. But there is nothing to require it: Since the AAL lives within the cell payload, the network has absolutely no business looking at it. Thus users are free to use other protocols that may be better suited to their circumstances. For example, it is quite possible to design a protocol that uses cell sequence numbers, bulk acknowledgments, and selective retransmission to first provide an assured cell delivery service and perform frame segmentation at a higher sublayer.[4] Since it does not multiply losses, this type of protocol will not be particularly sensitive to loss and can thus be carried at a lower priority than Type 4 AAL traffic. Whether or not such a protocol will be required is not likely to be known until ATM services are widely deployed.

The Type 4 AAL will, however, be required for users of the B-ISDN connectionless bearer service. The full 60-bit (E.164) address of the source and destination, along with other information, will be carried in the header of the CS_PDU, found in the first cell of a multicell packet. The network will then provide best-effort delivery of the entire packet. Standard interworking between Frame Relay and the AAL is also being developed.

As a reaction to the complexity of AAL Type 4, some computer companies have proposed a newer "Type 5" AAL. This is extremely simple, with little or no SAR overhead and just a checksum for its CS_PDU.

An issue that is still to be resolved is how to apply the AAL for call control signaling. Its assured message mode provides the same type of data link layer service that Q.921 (LAPD) provides for narrowband ISDN. But since the overall bandwidth of the virtual D channels will be low, some administrations favor adoption of LAPD procedures or use of go-back-N operation for the signaling Convergence protocol.

---

[4] An example of such a protocol is Broadband Link-Layer Block Transfer (BLINKBLT), proposed by the author in ANSI T1S1.5/90-009. While its syntax is generally compatible with the Segmentation and Reassembly sublayer, it replaces the multiplex ID with a 14-bit cell sequence number.

Signaling

The DSS1 and ISUP protocols defined for N-ISDN require enhancement for B-ISDN use. While they can be modified easily enough to take into account the higher bandwidths and novel channelization of B-ISDN, the anticipated nature of some key applications provides an impetus for additional changes. In the short term, B-ISDN signaling will make use of modified DSS1 and ISUP, carried over the AAL.

Separation of Connection and Call Control

The key feature that is expected to be added for long-term B-ISDN signaling is the *separation of connection and call control*. A *connection* is a single instance of a bearer service being provided between endpoints. A *call* is a collection of one or more connections.

As an example, consider a videoconference using high-definition television signals transmitted over B-ISDN. The video itself might require a variable bit rate connection with an average rate of 100 Mbps. The stereophonic high-fidelity audio might itself require two continuous bit rate connections of 0.5 Mbps apiece, and a separate computer graphics display might require a variable bit rate connection of 2 Mbps. Each of these connections forms part of a single call.

A new Signaling System No. 7 user part is being considered for B-ISDN. This *ISDN Signaling Control Part* (ISCP) could replace ISUP for B-ISDN calls and could in turn use B-ISDN's ATM service in place of the existing SS7 Message Transfer Part. ISCP is being modeled by using the OSI Applications layer.

Support of Multiple Terminals

While DSS1 already provides some support for multiple terminals sharing a single user-network interface (the passive bus), B-ISDN will allow far larger numbers of terminals to share a single UNI. While the final signaling arrangements have yet to be completed, a likely scenario has been described.

The meta-signaling channel is used to assign VCIs that will serve as virtual D channels. Each terminal will have one VCI of its own. In addition, terminals may also respond to shared VCIs, one of which will exist for each "terminal profile" present at the UNI. A terminal profile identifies a class of terminal. For example, all telephone sets might share one terminal profile, so an incoming telephone call would be presented to that profile's VCI. This provides a more granular multicast service than the simple multicast found in N-ISDN signaling.

When Will B-ISDN Be Real?

Broadband ISDN is a far more ambitious project than N-ISDN. Since the narrowband service has itself taken over a decade to come to market, is there any reason to expect the broadband service to be delivered before the end of the century?

Opinions about that question vary widely. Skeptical observers see no reason to expect B-ISDN to leave the realm of vaporware for years to come. But the climate in which B-ISDN is being developed differs markedly from the one in which N-ISDN was first proposed. Not only has the technology advanced quite far, but the majority of the world's telephone administrations have begun to get some notion of the term "competition"! Measuredly slow, overcautious development is no longer their near-universal goal.

But several hurdles need to be overcome before B-ISDN can become reality. One is switching technology. At 155 Mbps an ATM interface has to be able to process about a third of a million cells per second, a considerably faster rate than current-generation packet switches can handle. A few switching architectures have been proposed, and some early prototype ATM switches have been built, but more research is required before ATM switches at B-ISDN rates will be cost-effective on a large scale.

Another hurdle is economics: How much will an all-optical network cost? The price of optical fiber has been falling continuously for years, but it still requires considerable effort to install. Activities that are simple for copper, such as splicing and connectorization, can be far tougher for glass. And then how should B-ISDN be tariffed? With ATM providing flexible bandwidth, how can the telephone companies set a price that is low enough to encourage widespread use without appearing to discriminate against users of other services or discouraging use of the recently installed N-ISDN?

Given these problems, it appears most likely that the earliest field deployments of B-ISDN will occur during the mid-1990s, with more widespread deployment occurring toward the end of the decade. Until then, one can only speculate about the future of B-ISDN, whether it will be a commercial success, and for that matter whether it will really work at all.

Chapter
Nine

ISDN in Practice

ISDN Is Getting Started Slowly

So now that Integrated Services Digital Networks are becoming available, what are we going to do with them? ISDN has been a buzzword for so many years that the applications that once seemed so promising appear today to be old hat. But has the forward march of technology left ISDN behind? Hardly! There are many practical ways to make use of ISDN, at least once it becomes more widely available.

That has been much of the problem with ISDN. Many telephone companies are reticent to spend too much money on upgrading their networks to support ISDN, since demand has been slow. Many customers are reluctant to invest in ISDN, especially given the high price of today's ISDN terminal gear. And terminal manufacturers are unable to lower prices on terminal gear, since ISDN, at least in its early days, has been a low-volume marketplace. In other words, chickens and eggs are both in short supply.

But newly deployed technologies like ISDN become more inexpensive as volume and competition build up. Most of the cost of ISDN terminal gear is in two areas: semiconductors and software. Both of these are characterized by very high up-front costs and relatively low marginal costs. Being an early player in such an industry requires deep pockets. Being the fiftieth requires much less.

Thus the price of ISDN terminal gear, which is set by a competitive marketplace, is likely to follow the downward trend followed by prices of personal computers, modems, disk drives, and similar products. The price of ISDN network services, which is set by the telecommunications industry and its regulators, is likely to remain far more stable.

ISDN in Retrospective?

Given the amount of ink devoted to ISDN since its inception, the rate at which ISDN has become a reality has been awfully slow. Some of the original visions that went into ISDN, such as integrated voice-data terminals and PBXs, have not been well accepted by the marketplace. And newer services, like Metropolitan Area Networks, are beginning to steal some of ISDN's thunder. This has already led to an "ISDN is dead" movement. Reminiscent of a theological debate of the 1960s that suggested the mortality of a certain well-placed deity, reports of ISDN's demise are probably exaggerated. But they are also not a total surprise.

ISDN has had a slow start for many reasons. The technology is complex and has taken a long time to develop, and the proactive development standards has been a tedious process. Now that ISDN is reality, though, it's possible to seek reasons for the slow pace of its acceptance.

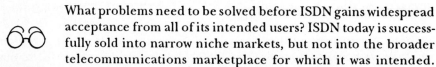 What problems need to be solved before ISDN gains widespread acceptance from all of its intended users? ISDN today is successfully sold into narrow niche markets, but not into the broader telecommunications marketplace for which it was intended. One approach to solving this puzzle was found in a question posed by a marketing consultant working for the telephone industry. He asked for opinions about the five most important reasons why ISDN was not succeeding in the marketplace. Here is one possible list:

- *Ubiquity:* ISDN simply isn't available in enough places yet. Customers won't order it if they can't get it! This concept sometimes seems to evade telephone company marketeers.

- *Connectivity:* The benefits of ISDN are often best realized when both ends of a connection are on ISDN. Why subscribe to the 64 kbps service if there's nothing to call? This is the flip side of ubiquity.

- *Equipment compatibility:* Not much ISDN equipment is available yet, nor is this ISDN gear all compatible. There are, after all, so many standards to choose from, with vendor and national variations on the protocols.

- *Price:* There are often alternatives to ISDN, so ISDN will only be selected when the price is right.

- *The (fill in this space) phone company:* Many customers have a natural skepticism toward a powerful and entrenched monopoly. And the telephone carriers don't always show a clear customer orientation. This is a serious marketing and perception problem, especially in the data arena.

These are all serious concerns of customers. Indeed, the rest of this chapter addresses these issues. They are of different relative importance in different markets. Not all telephone companies are alike, and certainly not all customers are alike. It will take a few years for all of these problems to be sorted out, but eventually they will be. ISDN, in some form or other, is inevitable. The analog telephone network is obsolete; ISDN can and will be cost-effective. It will just take a little time.

ISDN Deployment

There are almost as many different ISDN deployment scenarios in the world today as there are telephone administrations. Each PTT and operating company has its own strategy and time frame. Some are aggressively promoting ISDN and striving to make it universally available; others are grudgingly planning to deploy it some time during the 1990s. Most are somewhere in between those extremes. Both availability and ubiquity of ISDN depend upon this.

Scenarios for ISDN Deployment

Since ISDN is more of an enabling technology than a product per se, a telephone company's ISDN deployment will often focus on certain services for which ISDN appears to represent a comparatively advantageous technology. This might or might not be what the customers have in mind, as telephone companies and especially PTTs are famous for forcing their own agendas upon their subscribers.

ISDN Centrex. In the United States the *Centrex* scenario has been a popular one for the Bell Companies to play out. Centrex service was nearly dead and buried in 1981. AT&T was still in control of the Bell Operating Companies and used them as its exclusive channel for distributing PBX systems and other terminal equipment. Centrex was out of fashion, thanks to AT&T's "Installed Base Migration"[1] strategy, by which Centrex tariffs were pushed upward to encourage customers to acquire newer electronic (analog) PBX systems. But in 1984 the Bell companies were newly independent, while AT&T kept the installed PBX base. Suddenly Centrex was the Bells' best hope for retaining large business customers.

But Centrex was dowdy and gray, weakened by years of neglect. A revival of Centrex required some new flash. What could be better than ISDN? Two major benefits were foreseen. For one, ISDN Centrex would be digital, allowing integrated voice and data transmission to the desk. (It seemed like a good idea at the time.) For another, ISDN promised to provide a standard for multibutton electronic telephone sets, just like the fancy proprietary ones that were included with the new PBXs. That was especially important given AT&T's continued ownership of the installed base of Centrex station instruments, an uneasy relationship characterized by rapidly rising rental rates. A third possible benefit was derived from the passive bus option, allowing two telephones (and several other terminals) to share a single line, which seemed to be a significant savings in comparison to needing two lines.

Almost all of the ISDN installed in the United States before 1991 was in the form of Centrex. For the telephone companies an ISDN Centrex sale was ideal: Only a single central office had to be upgraded at a time. Centrex contracts were typically several years long, ensuring sufficient revenue to pay off the investment. Customers too could also be more sure of compatibility among prestandardized terminals.

Yet this scenario almost proved to be too good to be true. It wasn't a big success. While a few important customers did buy ISDN Centrex, its market share was still quite small in comparison to customer-owned PBX systems. Large customers generally found that PBXs were cheaper, while small ones who were more likely to want Centrex were not large enough to merit the ISDN upgrade. And the growth of Local Area Networks made ISDN's data capabilities seem quite unimpressive for most Centrex customers. Why spend the high prices for early ISDN TEs and TAs when LANs were faster? Only in certain niche markets, such as multisite customers, was sending data through ISDN Centrex economical.

Interexchange Carrier Access. Another avenue by which ISDN was first deployed in the United States was followed by the long-distance companies, especially AT&T Communications. Much of the retail price of long-distance telephone calls was going to the local telephone companies, in the form of "access charges." If a customer could connect directly to the long-distance

---

[1] The initials by which this strategy was known were not coincidental; a certain well-known computer company was said to have earlier employed similar tactics to encourage its lease customers to acquire new equipment.

carrier (as some might say, "bypass" it) without going through a local exchange, then the local company could be dealt out, and the customer could get a lower rate. This led to another round of early ISDN deployment.

One avenue for this is the Primary Rate Interface. Since it makes use of standard T1 carrier, available on a private line basis from the Bell Companies, customers simply connected their PBX systems directly (via T1) to the long-distance carriers' own switches, like the AT&T No. 4ESS. These switches, in turn, can use ISDN protocols on a D channel for call control, allowing advanced features like "call-by-call service selection" (in which a channel on the T1 pipe is not assigned to a single service but can instead be accessed by different bearer services or tariffed services) and calling number identification. In addition, they provide circuit-switched 64 kbps and 384 kbps data services. Other available services include virtual private networks (with a discounted rate for some calls, often using a private number plan), 800 Service, and even 900 Service (in which the recipient sets any price for the call in exchange for "information").

For the most part, though, the interexchange carriers don't even emphasize the ISDN nature of their services and often provide conventional analog (bit-robbed) signaling. ISDN is simply an enabling technology, a better way to provide access, and a standard to which the industry can build. While taking a low-key pragmatic approach, the interexchange carriers have made Primary Rate ISDN available essentially everywhere in the United States.

But interexchange carriers can't replace local telephone companies. While they do provide special telephone numbers (800 Service and 900 Service), they don't provide local telephone numbers—at least not yet. And they don't provide cheap local calling. So Primary Rate ISDN is most widely available for long-distance services only, and only to customers with enough traffic to warrant the cost of the connection. It's a big step toward adequate connectivity, but more needs to be done.

The Public Data Network. While many European PTTs have embraced ISDN as a blueprint for an upgraded public telephone network, they have also focused on ISDN as a means of providing a circuit-switched data service. In this sense, ISDN complements the X.25-based packet networks that most PTTs deployed in the late 1970s. Since these packet networks are widely available and fairly inexpensive, ISDN's packet modes are viewed as being of secondary importance.

Some circuit-switched public data networks have existed in advance of ISDN. CCITT Recommendation X.21 addresses this area, and X.21-based networks have found some use in the Scandinavian region, Germany, and France. But X.21 had the misfortune of coming into being at the same time that ISDN was being developed, and it didn't take too great a crystal ball to realize that ISDN would make a far better long-term investment.

Some early European ISDN services have been limited to circuit-switched data. Swissnet, for one, went on line without even offering voice. The PTT, after all, had an existing voice network and an existing packet network, so the ISDN began by filling in a vacant niche. Eventually, of course, it should evolve into full ISDN.

Happily for the European public at large, the initial dream/nightmare scenario of some PTT visionaries has not come to pass: ISDN has not extended the scope of the PTT monopoly into the computer arena. Instead, governmental pressures (especially from the European Community) to open up markets to freer trade have made competitive provisioning of terminal equipment, such as NT2s, more the norm than the exception. While technical barriers and minor national incompatibilities have slowed down vendors, who still must go through arduous approval cycles, the trend is clearly in favor of more competition, not less.

Time Frames for Further Availability

So when will ISDN reach out and touch the masses? Before that can be answered, one first has to decide just what level of availability one is referring to. If one seeks to demonstrate that ISDN is a pie-in-the-sky technology with little acceptance for the foreseeable future, one can simply evaluate the percentage of total telephone company access lines that will be ISDN. Given the typical 20- to 30-year depreciation cycle of central office switching equipment, it's highly unlikely that the total count of analog lines will decline too precipitously. ISDN instead will represent much of the telecommunications industry's growth.

A more realistic measurement, then, is to estimate ISDN's *availability:* What percentage of a telephone company's subscribers will be within an ISDN service area? Here, the major determining factor will be the digital central office switch. If the local switch is digital, then it can probably be upgraded to ISDN for a fraction of the price of a new switch. If the local switch uses analog electromechanical technology (i.e., step-by-step or cross-bar), then it is likely to be upgraded to digital within a few years anyway. Last on the list are customers served by analog electronic switches. Most of these have several good years left.

Even then, ISDN can be made available if there is sufficient demand. Digital adjuncts have been designed that allow analog switches, such as the AT&T No. 1AESS, to provide ISDN. (That this particular arrangement was developed by NEC Corp., not AT&T, is somewhat curious but provided a niche market for NEC, with little presence among most Bell Companies, to exploit.) Digital central offices are essentially all capable of providing service to remote switching modules, which are cheaper than full-scale switches. And both Basic Rate and Primary Rate can be offered on a foreign exchange (served via leased channel from a remote central office) basis. So telephone companies can deploy a single ISDN-compatible base switch in one office and put remotes in other offices, where the central office is otherwise incapable of providing ISDN.

Once ISDN has that degree of ubiquity, then connectivity will follow, and large organizations will adopt ISDN for more applications. Before that occurs, ISDN will require additional interworking, with non-ISDN networks, which will make it costlier and harder to use.

United States. All of the Bell companies and most of the major independent telephone companies already provide limited ISDN service. It is likely that by 1992, 10–20% of access lines will be in ISDN-equipped areas. By 1995, most should be. The Bell companies have emphasized Basic Rate but will also make Primary Rate available, which will be especially attractive for PBX trunks.

Initial services focus on telephony, with Centrex features and support for multiline instruments. Circuit-switched 64 kbps data and packet-switched X.25 data are also included in most ISDN offerings, with Frame Relay expected to follow shortly. Higher-bandwidth services (H channels) will become available somewhat (possibly several years) later.

Europe. The rate of ISDN deployment in Europe varies widely by country. Perhaps the most advanced is France, where the PTT decided to deploy its ISDN, called *Numeris*, quickly. By the end of 1991, ISDN Basic Rate will be available almost everywhere in that country. Ironically, this stems in large part from France's long period of telephone neglect. Since the French network was so underdeveloped in 1975, the bulk of the switching and transmission systems are much newer. Digital exchanges were already the norm before ISDN.

Germany, on the other hand, has long had a reliable, if expensive, telephone network. And while the Bundespost has been very active in ISDN development, its well-maintained but aging electromechanical switching plant has not left as much room for rapid ISDN deployment. Several exchanges were on line in 1990, but widespread national coverage isn't expected until around 1993.

ISDN in the United Kingdom was sidetracked by a home-grown pseudo-ISDN called IDA. This was made available in the mid-1980s but was not very successful. True CCITT-standard ISDN is now being deployed, however, with availability in many major cities by 1992.

While Italy and Sweden had some ISDN services by 1991, most other countries were somewhat behind. By 1993 a widespread European ISDN market should appear. The telecommunications infrastructure in Eastern Europe is far more backward, though, so the ISDN picture is not clear there.

The European Community has undertaken an initiative to modernize its telecommunications infrastructure. Features of this are a common European (ETSI) standard for ISDN, encouragement of rapid ISDN deployment, and deregulation of key telecommunications markets such as terminal equipment and value-added services. Thus the typical European attitude toward ISDN is more positive than its North American counterpart.

Asia and the Pacific Rim. ISDN is already widely available in Japan. Nippon Telephone and Telegraph (NTT) began offering it in 1988, and it is becoming available in many areas. Japan's telecommunications industry has features of both the North American and European models, including Centrex, and the recently privatized NTT faces competition. ISDN is even more ubiquitous in the tiny city-state of Singapore. An impetus for ISDN development in these countries is the widespread use of facsimile; their ideographic languages are harder to represent in using common data techniques like ASCII files.

Australia is rather unusual in that its PTT deployed Primary Rate before Basic Rate. This strategy is based on the assumption that ISDN will be sold largely to large organizations that use PBX systems, so the PBX is left to distribute the service to the desktop. Australia is also taking the lead in developing Metropolitan Area Networks, so ISDN is less critical for its data market.

Most other developing countries are expected to deploy some ISDN during the early to mid 1990s, but the decision to use ISDN is likely to be made on economic grounds. If ISDN turns out to be cheaper than analog telephony (which is quite possible), then ISDN is likely to be deployed quickly.

ISDN Terminal Equipment

So what type of equipment is being deployed into the ISDN terminal endpoint role? A number of vendors were showing off ISDN wares as early as 1987. It would be pleasant to say that their number, and the variety of equipment provided, has since grown at a steady rate, but the reality is that TE vendors have had to face a rocky road. The rate of ISDN deployment just hasn't been adequate to keep all sectors of the TE market booming. More accurately, it can be said that a few vendors have managed to keep a moderate presence, while the 1990s are likely to finally see the market take off.

Telephone Sets

ISDN telephone sets (TE1) generally come from two types of suppliers. Switching equipment vendors like Siemens, Ericsson, and AT&T produce ISDN-compatible versions of their proprietary PBX telephone sets as well as more generic ISDN sets. Given the pace of standardization, though, essentially all have required some proprietary features. Northern Telecom's earliest version of ISDN used stimulus signaling for basic call control as well as supplementary services. This option was present in the 1984 CCITT Red Book and deleted by the 1988 Blue Book, but NT found it an expedient way to produce a modest-priced ISDN telephone set.

In the Blue Book, essentially no supplementary services (besides Hold) have functional signaling defined, so stimulus is the norm. Yet AT&T produced its own line of ISDN instruments using home-grown functional signaling (using the separate-message coding technique) for the most popular features, including multiline key telephone service.

Over time, of course, AT&T and Northern Telecom are moving toward compatibility. But it won't happen overnight. Still, some compatibility between AT&T and Northern Telecom central offices has already been noted; some third-party manufacturers, mostly Asian, produce instruments that can be set up to work with either vendors' protocols.

Terminal Adapters

The most expedient way to use ISDN for data is to place a terminal adapter between the non-ISDN device (TE2) and the ISDN interface. As with telephone sets, incompatibilities have been the order of the day for early models, standards compliance becoming the norm over time.

Data-only TAs are produced by several vendors. These must deal with both the ISDN signaling protocols and the inband rate adaptation required for most data TE2s. With both V.110 and V.120 as competing CCITT standards, many early TAs use neither. V.110 has seen more popularity in Europe, where it has been supported by several PBX vendors. V.120 was largely the work of AT&T and IBM and is likely to become more popular in the United States, yet AT&T did not even produce a V.120-compatible TA until 1991. Earlier models relied upon the AT&T-defined Digital Multiplexed Interface (DMI) protocols. Some also provided the full X.25 PAD function.

Voice-data TAs are less common, although Harris and Motorola-Codex demonstrated models in 1987 that took Touch-Tone digits from a standard analog telephone line and connected it to ISDN. This type of device could prove popular in residential markets.

Computer Adapters

While ISDN is a long way from becoming a ubiquitous communications option on computers, several vendors have produced ISDN adapters that plug into computer backplanes. At least a dozen companies have built ISDN cards for the popular "Industry Standard Architecture" based on the IBM Personal Computer bus. Several of these have already been withdrawn owing to lagging sales, but others have taken their place.

Many of these PC adapters reduce ISDN data communications to a fairly low common denominator, emulating asynchronous modems. They use one or another rate adaptation protocol and look, to the computer, like a 19.2-kbps modem. Other cards are capable of running the full 64 kbps synchronously, supporting protocol suites such as TCP/IP and SNA. In 1988 the University of Michigan demonstrated TCP/IP over ISDN, using a PC adapter built by Teleos. This provided 64 kbps connectivity.

Many high-performance workstations (most of which use the Unix operating system) also have on-board ISDN capabilities. In part this is due to a desire to be prepared for ISDN, but in part it's a happy side effect: Since these systems already need an audio codec for its digitized sound capabilities, they have been able to use an ISDN S-interface chip, such as the AMD 79C30A, to provide both capabilities at once. But these accidents have a way of defining future markets, so it's quite likely that ISDN will become popular among the Unix community.

ISDN Applications

So what do users think ISDN is for? Sometimes they don't see things in quite the same way as the telephone companies and PTTs do. As we noted in Chapter 1, there are three basic types of ISDN application: telephony, wide area data, and local area data.

Telephony

Two common applications should dominate ISDN telephony. One is the use of the Basic Rate interface to provide service to telephone instruments, either Centrex or otherwise. The other is the use of the Primary Rate interface to provide PBX trunks.

ISDN telephone sets are widely used in applications that would otherwise make use of multiline key telephone sets or multibutton featurephones. But they are too expensive for most organizations to deploy on a widespread basis. An ISDN telephone line might still cost a bit more than an analog line, but that difference pales in comparing the price of a telephone set, so customers are naturally sparing.

For Centrex customers, ISDN telephone sets are often the best choice for secretarial coverage positions. Even at prices approaching $1000 for some of the fancier models, they're less costly, especially considering maintenance and installation charges, than the electromechanical type 1A2 key telephone sets that dominated most early Centrex installations. ISDN allows multiline coverage and multiple call appearances on a single set. (This requires only one B channel, since the single handset can only be on one call *at a time;* the other calls are on hold in the switch.)

But for PBX customers, ISDN sets have been slower to catch on. In part the reason is economic: ISDN requires functional signaling for basic call control, and that requires significantly more processing power and memory than a simple stimulus instrument. Proprietary (vendor-specific) sets, which almost always use stimulus signaling, are thus cheaper to build. Some digital featurephones are (as of 1991) in the $100–200 range and provide essentially the same service as ISDN.

But part of the reason that proprietary PBX phones cost less than ISDN is that PBX vendors price them that way for strategic reasons. If a customer has a PBX system and many proprietary instruments, then when that customer is ready to replace the PBX, it will be less likely to buy another vendor's switch; that would cause the sets to be made obsolete. Proprietary telephones are a lock-in; ISDN sets, on the other hand, would be more likely to be usable on another vendor's switch.

Some European PBX vendors are more amenable to ISDN. They work with PTTs that discourage or prohibit proprietary telephone sets, and may still harbor dreams of using ISDN to promote voice-data integration to the desktop. However, most European markets are less accustomed to multiline telephone sets than are U.S. markets. The traditional keyset was never very popular in Europe, where even small businesses (another keyset market in which ISDN may catch on) typically used small PBXs.

For PBX vendors, ISDN trunks are a different story. One Primary Rate interface (PRI) can provide an inexpensive route for 23 or 30 trunks. Since essentially all new PBXs are digital anyway, the ISDN trunk interface doesn't need the analog circuitry and codecs found on analog trunk interfaces. Performance is also improved by the use of D channel signaling. So the PRI is a common feature of PBX systems even today. Local telephone companies in some areas have been slow to offer PRI tariffs, but the PRI is likely to become the bread and butter of PBX attachments and, by inference, of most business telephony. In the United States the PRI is becoming a mainstay for bulk long-distance carrier offerings like 800 Service and virtual private networks. The PRI is therefore popular for automatic call distributors, specialized PBXs that accommodate large volumes of incoming calls, often via 800 Service.

Private ISDNs

Many large organizations with operations spread across multiple locations have private telephone networks. Most of these are dominated by carrier-provided tie lines, typically using T1 carrier. Private voice networks provide superior connectivity within the organization but are usually justified on cost savings. Tariff rates for leased lines in the United States and the United

Kingdom are quite reasonable, though some PTTs charge too much for this to be a viable option, and a few, as in Germany, either ban the practice outright or use non-cost-based tariffs to make it uneconomical.

ISDN protocols were designed for public network use. DSS1, while fairly simple to implement, is designed only to request services across the boundaries of a network. Inside the public network, Signaling System No. 7 is the norm. But very few PBX systems implement SS7; it is far too costly and complex. (Some models of central office switch are used as large PBXs, including the Northern Telecom SL-100 and AT&T 5ESS; these have SS7 options.) This gave rise to the question of whether DSS1 can be extended to provide interswitch signaling for private ISDNs.

Not surprisingly, the CCITT has shown relatively little interest in this. Direct connections between adjacent PBXs are accommodated by an annex to Recommendation Q.931, but that doesn't begin to address multihop calls. The European Computer Manufacturers' Association (ECMA) released a fairly lengthy Technical Report on private ISDN, but it never developed into a complete network protocol. A similar fate was met by a project at ANSI T1S1, which produced a technical report giving little detail. Both did produce enhancements to the ISDN reference model. ECMA defines the link between PBXs as reference point Q, while ANSI notes that direct trunks can use reference point T, and intertandem trunks are defined as a new reference point B. Neither Q nor B has a complete protocol, though. The task of developing this standard has moved under the umbrella of the ISO/IEC Joint Technical Committee 1 (JTC1/SC6), the same body that defines OSI protocols.

British Telecom didn't even wait for Q.931 to be written to develop its own private network protocol. Its Digital Private Network Signalling System (DPNSS) was in use by the early 1980s. While it isn't particularly close to any CCITT protocol (and may be more akin to a simplified SS7 than to DSS1), it provides a degree of feature transparency between PBXs linked via a PRI or equivalent arrangement. DPNSS has seen a small amount of use outside of the United Kingdom as well, mainly because Canadian PBX vendor Mitel, a British Telecom affiliate, has added DPNSS to its switches. Siemens, Ericsson, and Alcatel have more recently agreed upon a Q.931-based protocol for PBX linkage. Both this and DPNSS will provide a reasonable degree of ISDN services on a private network, as should the future ISO standard.

Local Area Data Communications

Since ISDN was conceived during the integrated voice-data PBX fad that preceded the widespread acceptance of LANs, much of ISDN reflects an attempt to make it the standard for wiring the integrated office. Many ISDN telephone sets include an option for attaching a data terminal. And many of the early ISDN customers did use it for intrafacility data communications.

But this has turned out to be one of ISDN's weak points. Local Area Networks are superior to ISDN for most short-haul data applications. While ISDN's speech services are an enhancement to the ever-popular telephone network, ISDN's local area data services are an alternative to the IVD PBX and the "CO LAN." That oxymoronic service tends to be strongest in niche markets that go beyond the geographic radius of the LAN itself, such as organizations with multiple buildings in a city.

Coax Elimination. For ISDN to even appear to be competitive for local area data communications, the alternatives must be fairly unattractive. One such example of an ISDN data application is "coax elimination." The standard means of wiring an IBM 3270-family synchronous terminal to a cluster controller is via RG-62/U coaxial cable. This is not only fairly costly, but it is thick enough to clog conduits and weigh down ceilings. Many companies have found themselves drowning in coax. ISDN, by promising universal twisted pair wiring, seems like a good alternative.

Coax was used because it could run at a high enough speed to refresh the terminal screen in an instant. The 64 kbps speed of ISDN isn't quite equivalent, but it's not easy to see the difference. Still, a costly terminal adapter is needed. ISDN sometimes pays off, but a more common approach is to use a LAN and personal computers that can emulate the 3270 or a LAN with synchronous terminal servers near the terminals.

Asynchronous Terminals. Millions of "dumb" asynchronous computer terminals are in use, and millions of PCs emulate them. Most of the common "telecommunications" and "modem" software for PCs falls into this category. ISDN's 64 kbps synchronous bearer channel requires rate adaptation to be able to carry this type of data traffic. Terminal adapters to do this should become quite common.

But within a facility this is again a very expensive alternative. A LAN can connect dumb terminals by means of a terminal server, a device that usually costs under about $300 per port. ISDN TAs cost much more than this, especially with today's low volumes, and also require switching capacity. With ISDN as with any similar circuit-switched approach, connections are also required from the ISDN to the host computers, so every connection is going through two lines. LAN-based servers typically connect to the host computer through the LAN directly, so no host-side server hardware is required.

Thus ISDN is most useful for terminal traffic in out-of-the-way locations that a LAN simply doesn't reach. Remote corners of large buildings and small buildings on large campuses are examples of places where existing telephone wiring can provide ISDN data access at lower cost than a LAN connection.

However, widespread use of ISDN for data connectivity in the office is rarely cost-justifiable.

Wide Area Data Communications

This may be ISDN's greatest area for long-term growth. The data communications market is expanding far more rapidly than voice, and ISDN promises to play a major role, becoming a dominant technology for the switched services. The 64 kbps and faster circuit-mode services will gradually lead to the obsolescence of modems when and if ISDN becomes ubiquitous in the residential and small business market. And for casual users, such as consumers, the D channel packet service might be a very popular way to access bulletin boards, databases, electronic mail, and other computing services.

ISDN won't make private lines obsolete; economics and the nature of data networks dictates that full-time circuits will still be desirable for many applications. Private line services will also be available at higher speeds (i.e., 45 Mbps) than ISDN. Related technologies like the Metropolitan Area Network and SMDS will complement ISDN. Eventually, these high-speed services might be subsumed into Broadband ISDN, should that latter service approach the universal appeal that its proponents expect.

Backbone Links and Time Cutting. While private lines will remain the mainstay of many corporations' backbone data networks, ISDN's circuit-mode service already provides its users with new options for network optimization. Backbone networks typically carry many users' data at once, often using connectionless protocols so that they can't simply turn the channel on and off when the end user initiates an upper-layer connection. Even connection-oriented backbones might not operate efficiently that way. Instead, the ISDN circuit is operated in a *time-cutting* mode, in which a call is initiated as soon as a packet needs to be transmitted and the call is ended after a particular time has gone by without any packets.

The duration of this time-out is generally based upon local tariffs. If the call is billed in integral minutes (as most often occurs in North America), then there is no point in using a short timer that could conceivably cause multiple calls to take place during the same minute—especially if the first minute carries an extra charge. If the call is billed in the more common European "meter pulse" mode, in which the duration for a given charge unit varies with distance, then long-distance calls might have a time-out not much longer than one or two meter pulse intervals.

Simple time cutting uses dedicated router ports (or their equivalent); the hardware resources are dedicated full time, even though the circuit is switching on and off. A variation on time cutting is to dynamically allocate channels between different points, allowing the same computer port to route traffic to different destinations, as demand requires. The software needed to support this type of function isn't trivial, but it might develop.

Time cutting of circuit-mode connections might also operate in tandem with packet. A packet-mode connection is more suitable for low levels of usage, while circuit mode is better for more fully utilized bearer channels. Some paths on a computer network may be left up continually in packet mode with circuit-mode connections made when traffic warrants, on either a demand or a time of day basis.

Access to Public Data Services. A large and growing fraction of modem use is associated with public data services, in effect time-sharing computer systems that are made available to the general public. Probably the most popular of these has been the service provided by the French PTT to its millions of Minitel customers. Originally justified as an electronic telephone directory, it provides a gateway to thousands of providers' services. In the United States, Sears and IBM have invested hundreds of millions of dollars in their Prodigy service, which emphasizes ease of use and consumer-oriented services. Other public services such as CompUServe and GEnie tend to attract more of a computer hobbyist crowd. Then there are the electronic mail services, such as MCI Mail, AT&T Mail, Bell Canada's Envoy, and the various European X.400 services.

This is a fertile ground for ISDN. The D channel packet mode might substantially reduce the net cost of moderate-speed access, providing somewhat better performance than 2400 bps modems without tying up a telephone line for the duration of the call. The B channel 64 kbps circuit service mode opens up the door to greatly enhanced interactive performance, especially with graphics-intensive services.

Acceptance of ISDN in these markets is likely to be gated mostly by the rate at which ISDN is made available to residential customers, who make up the largest potential block of consumers. ISDN is well positioned as a gateway to an *information utility*. For this scenario to be successful, ISDN must be made available in residential areas as well as in business centers, and the price of both the telephone company's service and the required customer premise gear must be competitive with modems. The latter simply requires a volume marketplace; the former requires telephone companies to not misuse their monopolies.

Telecommuting. In the combined aftermath of the 1973, 1979, and 1990 oil shocks, the concept of *telecommuting*—high-tech working from home—has continued to gain acceptance. Many types of worker do not need daily physical interaction with others in their own office and can instead do at least some of their work at home computers networked to their employers.

ISDN is an ideal medium for telecommuters. By providing ample data bandwidth (at least compared to a modem) it gives them ready access to corporate databases, data storage, and printer services. And the voice capability of ISDN also has application for telecommuters. Certain tasks, such as taking telephone orders or providing customer service, can be farmed out to telecommuters, using one B channel for data and the other for voice. Creative use of D channel signaling (such as the User Signaling Bearer Service or D channel packet) might even allow these remote workstations to appear to be part of the company's centralized Automatic Call Distribution system. Telecommuters can thus check "in" or "out" several times a day without ever having to leave home. This can be done via analog lines, but ISDN should improve its performance substantially.

Telecommuting is not without its downside. Working at home is frowned upon in some jurisdictions because of historic abuses of workers in "cottage sweatshops." Some types of workplace have already been dubbed "electronic sweatshops," and regulations are being imposed in many areas upon the use of video display terminals (including personal computers). ISDN is simply one tool in support of telecommuting. It doesn't change the fundamental nature of work; it just allows more flexibility in its location.

Price: Will the Rates Be Reasonable?

Early ISDN tariffs vary widely. British Telecom (to name one example) charges the same rate for a 64 kbps circuit-mode data connection as for a voice channel, which is certainly as much as an ISDN customer can hope for. France Telecom set its initial rate at 1.7 times the voice *long-distance* rate, which is not unreasonable for long distance, but the tariff lacks low-priced local calling. This appears to be a deliberate attempt to slow down the traffic growth rate and to preserve the existing short-haul private line data market.

NYNEX,[2] on the other hand, introduced its first ISDN tariffs based upon an older, little-used circuit-switched data network. At 8 cents per minute for an intraoffice call (which, pretty much by definition, costs the phone company nearly nothing to carry) and higher-than-toll rates for interoffice data it was not likely to gather many customers! NYNEX continued to view ISDN primarily as an option for Centrex (which has no intrasystem usage charges), only grudgingly making ISDN available to other users. This situation is likely to be temporary.

Other ISDN rates vary widely, some adhering to the principle of voice-data parity and others applying separate rate schedules to the different bearer services. Local access line rates likewise vary. Some BRI charges are little more than for a single analog line, while others are closer to twice that level. Additional charges often apply for access to the different data bearer services.

[2] NYNEX is the Regional Bell holding company for New York Telephone and New England Telephone.

Consumer and regulatory pressures are likely to force ISDN to be reasonably priced in most areas. But where it is viewed as a premium service for a small cadre of computer aficionados, the price is likely to remain high.

Efforts to Ensure Compatibility

The CCITT Blue Book provided the first real worldwide standard for ISDN. Since its release in 1989, incompatibilities between different ISDN dialects have been reduced but not eliminated. As of 1991, ISDN TE vendors still needed to adapt their products for specific markets and network switches. Compatibility with France's Numeris does not necessarily equate to compatibility with Swissnet, and compatibility with AT&T does not equate to compatibility with Northern Telecom. Most major TE vendors have taken this as a cost of doing business and provide either separate models or separate options for each of their target markets. But it's not true terminal portability. Nor will the 1992 White Books solve the problem, since DSS1 Basic Call Control is essentially stable at the CCITT.

Additional agreements are necessary to reduce these differences, and progress is being made. Most European Community suppliers are moving toward ETSI standards, which are compatible with CCITT but fill in some of the gaps. And in the United States the Corporation for Open Systems, a consortium dedicated to compatibility for OSI and ISDN, has gotten the major CO and TE vendors to agree to a new specification, National ISDN 1. When both AT&T and Northern Telecom have implemented National ISDN 1 (due by late 1992), then TE vendors will not have to maintain separate options in order to sell into the North American market.

Broadband ISDN Applications

This is one of the most speculative parts of ISDN. What will people do with wide-area bandwidths in the 100-Mbps+ range? In large part this will depend upon economics: How much will B-ISDN cost?

If the price of B-ISDN access is held down to consumer levels, then mass-appeal services such as High Definition Television and dial-up movies could become market drivers. B-ISDN doesn't offer much new in the way of voice services. Its data services are potentially a useful means of LAN interconnection, but again the issue of pricing becomes critical. Will a 120 Mbps dial-up B-ISDN connection cost 100 times as much as a voice call or under 10 times as much?

Telephone companies will face the dilemma of trying to provide economical high-bandwidth services without taking away too much business from higher-volume low-bandwidth services, in particular telephony. With B-ISDN's ATM service nearly transparent to a wide variety of end user applications and capable of supporting both voice and data at the same time, the telephone company won't even be able to tell what the bandwidth is being used for.

But then that's essentially the same problem facing most technology-driven industries: How can a new product be introduced without ruining markets for profitable older ones? In the past, the slow-moving telephone industry hasn't often had to worry about that. But in the era of ISDN, telecommunications will finally be dragged away from its sheltered roots and into the real world. It's certainly a challenge. But for those who make the best use of this technology, it will be a rewarding one.

References

Angus, Ian. *ISDN, A Manager's Guide to Today's Revolution in Business Telecommunications,* Telemanagement Press, Ajax, Ontario, 1990.

Appenzeller, H.R. "Signaling System No. 7 User Part," *IEEE J. Select. Areas in Commun.,* vol. SAC-4, pp. 366–371, May 1986.

AT&T. "5ESS Switch ISDN Basic Rate Interface Specification," AT&T 5D5-900-301, Sept. 1985.

AT&T. "5ESS Switch ISDN Primary Rate Interface Specification," AT&T 5D5-900-302, Oct. 1985.

AT&T. "Integrated Services Digital Network Primary Rate Interface Specification," Technical Reference Pub. 41449, March 1986.

Cerni, D.M. "The United States Organization for the CCITT," *IEEE Commun. Mag.,* pp. 38–42, Jan. 1985.

Helgert, Hermann J. *Integrated Services Digital Networks,* Addison-Wesley, Reading, MA, 1991.

Jain, R. "A Timeout-Based Congestion Control Scheme for Window Flow-Controlled Networks," *IEEE J. Select. Areas in Commun.,* vol. SAC-4, No. 7, pp. 1162–1167, Oct. 1986.

Luetchford, J.C. "CCITT Recommendations-Network Aspects of the ISDN," *IEEE Select. Areas in Commun.,* vol. SAC-4, pp. 334–342, May 1986.

McNamara, John E. *Technical Aspects of Data Communication,* Third Edition, Digital Equipment Corp. Press, Bedford, MA, 1988.

Minzer, S.E. "Broadband ISDN and Asynchronous Transfer Mode (ATM)," *IEEE Commun. Mag.,* pp. 17–24, Sept. 1989.

Partridge, Craig (ed.). *Innovations in Internetworking,* Artech House, Norwood, MA, 1988.

Pynchon, Thomas. *The Crying of Lot 49,* J.B. Lippincott, Philadelphia, 1966.

Schlanger, G.G. "An Overview of Signaling System No. 7," *IEEE J. Select. Areas in Commun.,* vol. SAC-4, pp. 360–365, May 1986.

Swartz, Mischa. *Telecommunication Networks: Protocols, Modeling and Analysis,* Addison-Wesley, Reading, MA, 1988.

Spragins, John. *Telecommunications: Protocols and Design,* Addison-Wesley, Reading, MA, 1991.

Stallings, W. *ISDN: An Introduction,* Macmillan, New York, 1989.

Thomas, M.W. "PABX/ISDN Networks," *Commun. Internat.,* p. 51, Feb. 1991.

Tomasi, Wayne. *Electronic Communications Systems: Fundamentals through Advanced,* Prentice-Hall, Englewood Cliffs, NJ, 1988.

Wolfson, J.R. "Computer III: The Beginning or the Beginning of the End for Enhanced Services Competition," *IEEE Commun. Mag.,* pp. 35–40, Aug. 1987.

Glossary

AAL ATM Adaptation layer. In Broadband ISDN the layer directly above the ATM service layer, generally used end to end to provide a specific service.

Analog Represented electrically in a manner directly analogous to acoustical waveforms; electronic circuits that deal in a continuum of potential rather than in discrete quanta.

Application layer The highest layer in the OSI Reference Model, providing a set of application-oriented services to the application process.

Asynchronous Occurring at other than a fixed interval in time. Widely used in data communications to refer to the mode of operation in which each character is encapsulated by its own start and stop bits, dating back to the teletype.

ATM Asynchronous Transfer Mode. The method of providing services in B-ISDN, a form of *cell switching* or *fast packet switching*. Information is transferred in small, fixed-length blocks with labeled headers.

Basic Rate Interface (BRI) The smaller of the Narrowband ISDN electrical interfaces, providing two 64 kbps B channels and one 16 kbps D channel (hence "2B + D"). Also called *Basic Rate Access*.

B channel A 64 kbps bearer channel used to carry subscriber information (voice, data, image, etc.).

Bearer service A particular telecommunications capability, such as the ability to carry speech, audio, and circuit-mode or packet-mode data.

Bellcore Bell Communications Research Inc., the "central services organization" of the seven Regional Bell Operating Companies created in the United States by the breakup of AT&T.

Broadband ISDN A type of ISDN based upon cell-switched (ATM) delivery of bearer services with access rates over 150 Mbps.

Checksum A value calculated upon the contents of a block of data, used to ensure the block's inte rity upon receipt.

CBR Continuous bit rate. Delivery of information (bits) at a constant rate, equivalent to isochronous or synchronous transmission. A form of ATM service.

CCITT International Telephone and Telegraph Consultative Committee. An arm of the International Telecommunications Union (itself a United Nations agency) that promulgates international standards ("Recommendations") for telecommunications.

Circuit switching The information transfer mode characterized by the exclusive allocation of a specific channel for the duration of a call. The ordinary telephone network is an example.

Common channel signaling A method of sending call-related information between switching systems by means of a dedicated signaling channel that is separate from the bearer channels.

Connectionless A characteristic of a service and protocol that does not require a connection to be established; each block of data is handled independently.

Connection oriented A characteristic of a service and protocol, requiring a connection to be established before data can be transmitted.

Control plane In the ISDN reference model, the entity that contains call control signaling functions, separate from the User plane.

Core Aspects The subset of LAPF seen by the network providing the Frame Relay service.

CRC Cyclic redundancy check. A family of error-detecting checksums widely used in data communications. The *CRC-CCITT* widely used in ISDN is 16 bits long.

Datagram A self-contained packet as used in a connectionless network.

Data Link layer Layer 2 of the OSI Reference Model, providing framing, error detection, and optional services including local error recovery and multiplexing.

D channel The channel on an ISDN access arrangement used for signaling purposes.

Digital Pertaining to fingers and toes; also, the representation of information via discrete numerical quanta, typically binary digits (1 and 0).

DLCI Data Link Connection Identifier. The address field found in the Frame Relay protocol.

DQDB Distributed Queue Dual Bus. The Metropolitan Area Network (MAN) protocol adopted by the IEEE 802.6 committee.

DS-1 Digital signaling level 1 in the common North American transmission hierarchy, 1.544 Mbps. Note that DS-n is also the capacity of a corresponding T carrier transmission system Tn.

DSS1 Digital Subscriber Signaling System No. 1. The user network access signaling protocol for ISDN, found in CCITT Q.931, Q.932, and other related standards.

ETSI European Telecommunications Standards Institute. The telecommunications standards body of the European Community.

Fast packet switching Another name for cell switching, such as ATM (q.v.), which blocks of information are transferred by the network with minimal processing.

FDDI Fiber Distributed Data Interface. A Local Area Network operating at 100 Mbps using token ring technology, usually over optical fiber.

Frame (1) A block of data at the data link layer (layer 2). (2) In transmission systems the group of bits transmitted during a timing interval (usually 1/8000 of a second).

Frame Relay A packet-switched bearer service in which the network routes frames on the basis of the DLCI of an HDLC (LAPF) frame, disregarding any elements of procedure. More common than *Frame Switching* (q.v.).

Frame Switching A packet-switched bearer service based upon the LAPF layer 2 protocol, in which the network terminates LAPF elements of procedure while routing frames based upon the DLCI.

Functional group One of the standard combinations of functions used to describe ISDN components, such as the NT2 (frequently a PBX) and the TE (frequently a telephone instrument) in the abstract.

Functional signaling In DSS1 a signaling technique in which the terminal and network are both required to maintain the state of the call.

H channel A high-capacity ISDN bearer channel. This includes **H0** (384 kbps), **H10** (1.472 Mbps), **H11** (1.536 Mbps), **H12** (1.920 Mbps), and some less widely used higher rates.

HDLC High-Level Data Link Control. A family of Layer 2 protocols characterized by flag-based framing, bit stuffing, and CRC trailers. Defined in ISO3309 and ISO4335 and widely adapted.

kbps Transmission rate measured in thousands of bits per second.

Internet A data network that may be comprised of multiple subnetworks operating in tandem. Also, the widely used *Internet Protocol Suite* (commonly called "TCP/IP") developed for the ARPAnet and its successors; also, that network ("The Internet").

IP Internet Protocol. The (connectionless) network layer protocol of the TCP/IP protocol suite.

ISDN Integrated Services Digital Network. An extensive program by the worldwide telecommunications industry to create a digital model for network evolution, supporting both existing and new services with a minimum set of interfaces. *Narrowband ISDN* uses copper interfaces at speeds up to 2.048 Mbps; *Broadband ISDN* (q.v.) uses optical fiber interfaces at much higher speeds.

Isochronous Self-clocked. Similar to synchronous transfer but without benefit of a separate clock signal.

LAN Local Area Network. A shared private medium for high-speed packetized data transmission over a short distance.

LAPB Link Access Protocol–Balanced. The Data Link procedure used in CCITT Recommendation X.25 and ISO7776.

LAPD Link Access Protocol–D channel. The HDLC family data link layer protocol used on ISDN D channels, defined in CCITT Recommendation Q.921.

LAPF Link Access Protocol–Frame. The HDLC family protocol specified for use over frame-mode bearer services, defined in CCITT Recommendation Q.922.

MAN Metropolitan Area Network. A shared-medium network offering high-speed data (and possibly other) services over a greater range than a Local Area Network, generally using common carrier transmission facilities.

Mbps Transmission rate measured in millions of bits per second.

Network A combination of switching and transmission that provides telecommunications between two or more points.

Network layer Layer 3 of the OSI Reference Model, providing routing of packets and optional flow control and sequencing. This layer may be either connection-oriented or connection-less.

Octet Eight bits, grouped. This term is often used in preference to the more common *byte* in telecommunications.

OSI Open Systems Interconnection. A program of the International Organization for Standardization (ISO) for creating widely usable data communications standards. The OSI Reference Model defined seven layers.

Packet A block of data, generally at Layer 3, carried as a unit across a network.

Packet switching A bearer service in which data is carried across the network in variable-length packets using a connection-oriented store and forward protocol.

PAD Packet assembler-disassembler. A device for adapting data for transmission across a packet-switched network, frequently used to provide dial-in access to an X.25-based network.

PBX Private Branch Exchange. A telephone switching system, typically on customer premises, that provides interconnection among subscriber instruments and the public network. Historically, a "switchboard."

PCM Pulse code modulation. A technique for digitizing audio by sampling the amplitude at regular intervals and representing the sample as an integer. The common ISDN format is 8000 eight-bit samples per second.

Presentation layer Layer 6 of the OSI Reference Model, responsible for negotiating the means by which data is represented.

Primary Rate interface The larger electrical interface in Narrowband ISDN. Common formats include 23 B channels (North America and Japan)

and 30 B channels (Europe) with one D channel.

Rate adaptation The process of adapting a data stream of one rate and format into a channel of a higher rate and possibly different format; that is, fitting a 9600 bps asynchronous data stream into a 64,000-bps ISDN B channel.

SDH Synchronous Digital Hierarchy. The CCITT form of SONET (q.v.), as defined in Recommendations G.707–G.709.

Session layer Layer 5 of the OSI Reference Model, providing a set of functions for managing an end-to-end dialog between applications.

Signaling System No. 7 The common-channel signaling protocol suite designed for use between switching systems within the public telephone network and used within ISDN.

SMDS Switched Multi-Megabit Data Service. A high-speed connectionless packet-switched public network data service.

SONET Synchronous Optical Network. An optical fiber transmission system based upon multiples of 51.84 Mbps.

Stimulus signaling A stateless or semantic-free signaling protocol, such as a simplified subset of DSS1, and the use of "star codes" and other locally defined feature invocation messages.

Synchronous Transmission on a clocked basis, such that one bit is sent for every clock pulse and no byte framing information is required.

T1 carrier A standard North American digital transmission technique for sending 1.544 Mbps over copper wire. Note that T2 (6.312 Mbps) carries four T1 streams and T3 (44.768 Mbps) carries 28 T1 streams.

TA Terminal adapter. The ISDN equivalent (roughly) of a modem; that functional group which allows a non-ISDN device (audio, data, or otherwise) to communicate over an ISDN.

TE Terminal equipment. The functional group that is attached at the end of a network; the device to which the bearer service is ultimately provided. A generalization of the *Data Terminal Equipment* used with data networks.

Teleservice A telecommunications service incorporating both upper- and lower-layer functions.

Transport layer Layer 4 of the OSI Reference Model, providing for reliable transfer of information between end users, including flow control, segmentation, and other services as required.

User plane In the ISDN reference model, the entity that carries information between users, using the requested bearer service, separate from the Control plane.

VBR Variable bit rate. The delivery of blocks of information upon demand, typically providing a packet-like service over an ATM network.

Virtual channel A connection in an ATM network, providing the requested type of service.

Virtual circuit A connection in a connection-oriented packet-switched data network.

Virtual path A connection in an ATM network that supports a group of virtual channels between the same two points.

X.25 The established CCITT Recommendation for packet-switched data networks, providing a connection-oriented service.

8 kHz integrity The guarantee that all bits sent into the network within an interval of 1/8000 of a second will be delivered in order before any bits sent within next such interval.

Index